Agriculture and the State

Agriculture and the State
Market Processes and Bureaucracy

E. C. Pasour, Jr.

Foreword by Bruce L. Gardner

THE INDEPENDENT INSTITUTE

HM

HOLMES & MEIER
New York / London

Published in the United States of America 1990 by
Holmes & Meier Publishers, Inc.
30 Irving Place
New York, NY 10003

BOOK DESIGN BY DALE COTTON

The paper used in this publication meets the requirements of the
American National Standard for Permanence of Paper for Printed
Library Materials, Z39.48-1984.

Library of Congress Cataloging-in-Publication Data

Pasour, E. C.
  Agriculture and the State : market processes and
bureaucracy / E. C. Pasour, Jr.
    p. cm. — (Independent studies in political economy)
  Includes bibliographies and index.
    ISBN 0-8419-1272-6 (alk. paper). — ISBN 0-8419-1273-4 (pbk. : alk
paper)
    1. Agriculture and state—United States. 2. Agriculture—Economic
aspects—United States. 3. United States—Economic policy—
1981–
4. United States—Economic conditions—1981– I. Title. II. Title:
US economy and agriculture. III. Series.
HD1761.P37 1990
338.1'873—dc20   89-11067
                                                        CIP

MANUFACTURED IN THE UNITED STATES OF AMERICA

THE INDEPENDENT INSTITUTE is a tax-exempt, scholarly research and educational organization which sponsors comprehensive studies on the political economy of critical social and economic problems.

The politicization of decision-making in society has largely confined public debate to the narrow reconsideration of existing policies, the prevailing influence of partisan interests, and a stagnation of social innovation. In order to understand both the nature of and possible solutions to major public issues, the Independent Institute's studies adhere to the highest standards of independent inquiry and are pursued regardless of prevailing political or social biases and conventions. The resulting studies are widely distributed as books and other publications, and are publicly debated through numerous conference and media programs.

Through this uncommon independence, depth, and clarity, the Independent Institute pushes at the frontiers of our knowledge, redefines the debate over public issues, and fosters new and effective directions for government reform.

Contents

Foreword

A book on farm policy that owes more to Friedrich Hayek than to any agricultural economist may not shock the public, but it is definitely a new departure in published work on farm programs. *Agriculture and the State* broadens the subject not only by bringing in Austrian and public-choice economics and philosophical issues, but also in taking a wide view of the scope of agricultural policy. Pasour does not limit his discussion and analysis to traditional price supports and related forms of governmental intervention, but encompasses food distribution programs, conservation of natural resources, agricultural research, and income taxation.

As a result, this book is unique in tracing noncontroversial description, data, and textbook material to a critical assessment of the entirety of farm policy issues. Pasour states in his preface that farm programs "have failed to achieve their stated objectives." In principle, the remedy might be more or less intervention, but from the beginning it is clear that less is better.

What makes Pasour's approach particularly valuable is not so much his conclusion as the line of argument in which it is embedded. Economic analysis of the merits of agricultural policies has increasingly employed welfare economics, a tool which has generated many cost/benefit assessments of farm programs and found these programs wanting. But welfare economics is also well attuned to the market-failure aspect of economic problems, also endemic in agriculture. The agricultural and resource economics mainstream might sum up their policy toward, for instance, rural land-use planning: "The conclusion seems warranted that where it would work, the private market is to be preferred; but that in deciding a question of farm preservation, public action is required."[1]

For "farm preservation" others have substituted "price stability," "soil conservation," "milk marketing," and practically every other market outcome. Pasour is not having any of this: he insists on subjecting governmental activity to the kind of skeptical investigation that we typically address to market outcomes but from which we so often exempt public

---

[1] C. Lowell Harriss, "Free Market Allocation of Land Resources," in A. M. Woodruff, ed., *The Farm and the City*, Englewood Cliffs, N.J.: Prentice-Hall, 1980, p. 144.

action. Further, he shows what a problematical concept "public action" itself is. His discussions on collective choice, the economics of the political process, and biases in the process are all topics vital to agricultural economists.

This is not to say that everything that Pasour says will be convincing to all. Indeed he reaches some debatable conclusions. In chapter 10 he states that "large farms benefit most from farm programs"; but the arguments for this view, which is well within the mainstream, may be weaker than he suggests. Again, Pasour is to be commended for taking on the broader concept of economic justice (chapter 6), but he concludes that competitive markets are just, or at least not unjust, without seriously engaging opposing arguments.

Many land-grant agriculturalists will find the chapter on agricultural research and extension activities particularly problematic. Nonetheless, it is often when our hackles are raised highest that we learn the most. Even if Pasour does not ultimately carry the day against public research, the chapter contains many good points; almost any agricultural economist would benefit from reading it.

These remarks have been addressed to students of economics. *Agriculture and the State* will also be informative to the general public and journalists interested in agriculture, but this broader group will see the book from a quite different perspective. The press and the public, tending to distrust governmental officials, readily accept notions of "government failure," or worse; they have little respect for market forces and are ready to listen to conspiratorial theories of unfavorable market outcomes. Thus they view with suspicion payment of millions of dollars to large farm operations, the subsidization of wheat exports to the Soviet Union through payments to grain exporting companies, and foreign aid that fosters competitive agricultural development abroad. At the same time the majority of the nonfarm population believe that government should do more to help agriculture. Members of this group, too, can learn much from wrestling with *Agriculture and the State*.

In short, we can well use a dose of Dr. Pasour's medicine; and those of us who find it bitterest need it most.

Bruce L. Gardner

Preface

Despite record expenditures, government farm programs have not solved the farm problem. Financial stress on U.S. farms in the mid-1980s was at the highest level since the Great Depression of the 1930s. There is a growing awareness that U.S. domestic farm programs are more and more anachronistic in a world where agricultural production is highly competitive. Rationalized as measures to increase incomes of low-income "family farmers," farm programs provide most of the benefits to farmers whose incomes, on average, already exceed those of the nonfarm population.

Not only have farm programs failed to achieve their stated objectives, the programs themselves are frequently inconsistent. Some farm programs, such as price supports and food assistance programs, often serve to increase product prices. Other farm programs, including subsidized credit, conservation subsidies, subsidized crop insurance, and publicly financed research and educational activities, place downward pressure on product prices.

In late 1985, Congress enacted a farm bill, the Food Security Act of 1985. However, the 1985 farm act failed to resolve the many contradictions in U.S. farm policy. Indeed, the act so compounded the complexity of farm programs that it has been labelled "a full employment act for agricultural economists."[1]

The 1985 farm act represented a continuation of past farm policies rather than a major change in direction of U.S. farm policy. Moreover, it significantly increased the role of government in agriculture. It is ironic that agriculture has been largely unaffected by the deregulation movement of the past decade that has affected other industries, notably transportation and banking. Indeed after eight years of the "Reagan Revolution," U.S. farm policies remain firmly in the Great Depression mold.

There are two quite different explanations of U.S. farm programs: the "public interest" and income redistribution. The "public interest" approach, which holds that U.S. farm programs benefit the public at large, represents the conventional wisdom in agricultural policy texts. In this

---

[1] Vernon W. Ruttan, "Toward a Liberal Program for U.S. Agriculture," *Forum for Applied Research and Public Policy* 1 (Summer 1986): 81.

book, in contrast, it is assumed that current farm programs are better explained by income redistribution. That is, it is assumed here that the persistence of and increased expenditures on farm programs can be traced to the success of agricultural interests in using governmental power to transfer income from taxpayers and consumers to farmers, owners of land and other farm assets, government employees, and agribusiness firms that benefit from current farm policies.

The nature and persistence of farm programs is closely related to the operation of the political process. The purpose of this book is to present a description both of the policy-making process in agriculture and of the network of U.S. farm programs that have operated, with relatively little change, since the New Deal era of the 1930s.

Farm programs are incredibly complex, and it is easy to get engrossed in their details and to lose sight of their anticompetitive nature. In the following pages, a description of the effects of each general type of farm program is presented, with minimal discussion of the mechanics of program operation. The details of specific programs vary from year to year, but knowledge of these details is not required in understanding the economic effects of U.S. farm policies.

It is necessary to use some norm in assessing the effectiveness of agricultural markets and government policies. Current farm programs are often justified by measuring agricultural markets against the norm of perfect competition. Perfect competition, a highly abstract and idealized concept, assumes price-taking behavior by sellers and perfect markets, including perfect communication, instantaneous equilibrium, and costless transactions. It isn't surprising that economic analysts find "market failure" when real-world markets are contrasted with perfect competition since no real-world market meets these requirements. Moreover, when perfect competition is used as a benchmark, problems facing real-world decision makers who must operate in an environment of uncertainty and imperfect knowledge are assumed away.

Throughout these pages, in contrast, the competitive entrepreneurial market process is taken as the norm in the evaluation of agricultural markets and government programs. It is more accurate and realistic to view the market as a process over time where individuals are not fully informed and plans are not perfectly coordinated. In the market process approach, competition is assumed to inhere in the market of a modern economy unless constrained by non-market forces.

Farm programs have persisted in the United States since the 1930s despite dramatic changes in economic conditions. Although farm policies have changed relatively little, economic and political pressures now make changes more likely both in domestic farm programs and in the global agricultural production and trading system. The U.S. Food Security Act of 1985 expires in 1990 and new legislation will be enacted. In the international arena, negotiations to reduce agricultural trade barriers under the auspices of the General Agreement on Tariffs and Trade (GATT) have been underway since the "Uruguay Round" of trade talks was launched in 1986. An examination of the effects of U.S. farm programs is timely both because of the ongoing GATT negotiations and upcoming domestic farm legislation. Public policy should take into account the present and past record of government intervention in U.S. agriculture.

The author is indebted to Professor Bruce Gardner, University of Maryland, for the Foreword which sets the tone of the book. Thanks also are due to Gregory F. Rehmke of the Reason Foundation, Jo Ann Kwong of the Capital Research Center, G. W. Edwards of La Trobe University, Joan Kennedy Taylor, and an anonymous Independent Institute reviewer for their help at various stages in the development of this book. Jim Matson's help in locating and retrieving data on various government programs also is appreciated. Finally, the author appreciates the help of David Theroux, President of the Independent Institute, in the publication of this book.

E. C. Pasour, Jr.

Agriculture and the State

1

The Role of Economics in Agricultural Policy Analysis

There is a consensus that significant changes are on the horizon in U.S. agricultural policies. Record high outlays for farm programs, federal budget deficits, and current negotiations to reduce trade barriers are placing increasing pressures on our protectionist domestic farm policies. It is increasingly recognized that agriculture is closely linked both to other sectors of the domestic economy and to world markets for farm products. Indeed, during the early 1980s evidence mounted that the effects of international trade along with the monetary and fiscal policies of the federal government may be more important to agriculture than policies designed specifically for agriculture. Thus the agricultural economy cannot be considered in isolation.

In many respects the agricultural economy can be viewed as a microcosm of the entire economy. That is, economic activities in agriculture are similar to those in other sectors of the economy. Consequently, in evaluating the effects of various agricultural policies, it is necessary to understand how economic activity is coordinated in a market economy. First, consider the functions that must be performed in any type of economic system and the ways of performing these functions in a modern economy.

Functions of an Economic System

The functions of an economic system are quite general, regardless of political system and economic organization.[1] First, there is a problem of product mix, that is, the amounts to be produced of corn, wheat, milk, beef, textiles, autos, steel, and all other products must be determined. Second, and closely related, land, labor, and capital resources must be allocated to the production of the various products. In agriculture, the production of crop and livestock products is generally not restricted to a single technology. Grain producers, for example, can reduce the amount of tillage by using more herbicides and pesticides. Moreover, even with a given technology, the most profitable amount of any input generally hinges on relative prices of inputs.

Third, the economic pie must be divided or income must be distributed in some way. It should be emphasized, however, that wealth is not merely

1

given nor is there a fixed amount of income to be distributed. Instead, in free societies individuals *create* wealth through labor, cooperation, and ingenuity. Income distribution is not a separate activity but is an integral part of the production process.

Fourth, if economic progress is to occur, capital facilities must be maintained and expanded. If the expected receipts are less than the costs, productive facilities are likely to be depleted. And if new goods and services are to be made available, incentives must be sufficient to induce producers to assume the risks. Since productivity hinges on the amount of capital investment per worker, the maintenance and expansion of capital facilities is closely related to economic growth.

Finally, goods and services must be "rationed" in the sense of adjusting consumption, both at a particular moment and over time, to the available stock. Some goods such as agricultural crops are produced seasonally, and must be stored if the goods are to be available throughout the year. Regardless of whether production is seasonal or occurs throughout the year, however, the very nature of economic goods means that they are scarce and must be rationed at any point in time.

The Market System versus Central Direction

The economic functions just described must be performed in any type of economic system. However, there are basically only two methods of economic organization in a modern economy, the market system and central direction.[2] There is abundant evidence that the type of political and economic system used to achieve economic and social cooperation has the potential greatly to affect human welfare. Economic incentives and private property rights are fully as important in agriculture as in other areas. In Russia, for example, most of the state-owned land is organized as collective farms where the relationship between worker output and reward is tenuous at best. However, a highly disproportionate amount of food in the Soviet Union is produced on small plots of land leased to farmers by the state, on which workers are permitted to grow food and raise animals either for their own use or to sell. These private plots, which account for less than 1 percent of the agricultural land, are estimated to provide about a third of total farm output.[3]

This observed link between entrepreneurial incentives and productivity is not unique. Sven Rydenfelt analyzes the economic crises in fifteen socialist countries including Cuba, Tanzania, China and the Soviet Union. Rydenfelt shows how socialist policies, regardless of geography, population, or natural resources, undermine a nation's single most important economic resource, the entrepreneur.[4]

In a market or private property system, prices perform the economic coordination functions described above. Information about supply and demand conditions is coordinated and transmitted through market prices. When the expected price of soybeans increases relative to the price of corn, for example, farmers shift more land into soybean production. Similarly, changes in relative input prices bring about substitutions in input use. As the price of labor increases relative to prices of machinery and equipment, farmers substitute capital for labor. The substitution of capital for labor and land in U.S. agriculture has led to a significant increase in output per unit of labor used.

Individual incomes are determined both by one's control over productive resources and by the use made of the resources. The expectation of profits provides an inducement for individuals to engage in risky entrepreneurial activity and the individual decision maker must frequently make choices involving trade-offs between income and risk. Resource uses yielding higher incomes generally involve more risk.

The present value of expected income in any future time period is determined by the discount rate. The higher the discount rate, the lower the present value of income received in a future time period. Thus, an increase in the discount rate reduces the market value of the asset yielding the expected income. For example, if the rental value of a machine is $100 per year, the market price of the machine will be lower the higher the discount rate. Thus, the interest rate, the price of credit, is a crucial variable in investment decisions affecting durable resources, including land and capital facilities.

The rationing of goods and services both in the current period and over time is also performed by the price system. U.S. agricultural programs have long been plagued by economic surpluses. The existence of a persistent economic surplus (or shortage) is evidence that price is not free to perform the rationing function. Price is also important in rationing goods over time. The amount of corn stored at harvest, for example, hinges on the difference between harvest price and the expected price following storage. A farmer will store corn only if the expected increase in price is more than the storage cost.

One of the most interesting features of the market system is that it is automatic and unconscious. The market mechanism was not deliberately created and no one assigns market participants their roles or directs their functions. As Frank Knight put it, "No one ever worked out a plan for such a system, or willed its existence; there is no plan of it anywhere, either on paper or in anybody's mind, and no one directs its operation."[5] Stated differently, markets, being spontaneous in origin, are the product of "human action but not of human design."[6]

A key insight of Adam Smith's *Wealth of Nations* is that social cooperation is achieved by the price system in a decentralized market system as if by an "invisible hand." Economic cooperation occurs as individuals engage in mutually voluntary exchange. Without an order being issued, individuals are induced to use their knowledge and to cooperate with each other in ways that are broadly beneficial but which require individual market participants to have little information in order to make the "right" decision. The New York City housewife, for example, reduces consumption of orange juice when price increases. She need not know that production was decreased by a Florida frost in order to use the product more sparingly. Similarly, producers of oranges and individuals engaged in the production of inputs used in orange production and marketing are also induced to cooperate through mutually beneficial voluntary exchange.[7] The theory of the decentralized market economy shows how an overall order of economic activity is achieved which utilizes a large amount of information that is not concentrated in any one mind but exists only as the separate knowledge of millions of different persons.[8]

Market Prices and Market Socialism

The alternative to this decentralized market system is socialism (defined as government ownership of the means of production) or some other variant of central planning which does not rely on market price signals. If prices are not used as signals, some type of central direction involving coercion must be used to organize economic activity.

There has been a long-standing argument about the feasibility of "market socialism," a type of government ownership that allegedly preserves the advantages of the price system. In the 1930s, Oskar Lange, Abba Lerner, and other prominent economists argued that maximum social welfare could be attained by a central planning agency in a decentralized socialist economy.[9] In this approach, the central planner using information on consumer preferences, production possibilities, and available resources, for example, would set "shadow prices" for resources and products that would substitute for prices obtained through decentralized markets in a private property system.

This Lange-Lerner market-socialism approach was shown to yield results consistent with the marginal efficiency conditions of welfare economics that are stressed in microeconomic theory. Thus it was demonstrated that market socialism is possible, given knowledge of consumer preferences, production functions, and available resources. But of course, the necessary information to implement this type of central planning is not given. Moreover, as shown below, there is no known way that it can be obtained through central direction. Before further consideration of the problem of information gathering inherent in the market socialism (central economic planning) approach, let us first review the marginal efficiency conditions stressed in economic analysis.

Marginal Efficiency Conditions and Public Policy

The marginal efficiency conditions of welfare economics are derived under the assumption of perfect competition—which requires price-taking behavior on both sides of the market and the "perfect market" with

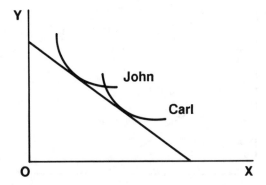

Figure 1.1. Efficiency among consumers in two-good case.

perfect communication, instantaneous equilibrium, and costless transactions.[10] Price takers are market participants who do not buy or sell enough of a good or service to influence the market price. This model assumes away various "market imperfections" including monopoly, imperfect information, and externalities. Under these highly idealized conditions, optimizing behavior by individuals and firms brings about the most productive pattern of resource use for the entire economy.[11]

Efficiency among consumers is achieved when the marginal rates of substitution are the same for all individuals. This is equivalent to the condition that indifference curves are tangent to the budget constraint (figure 1.1). Efficiency of input use among firms is achieved when the marginal rate of substitution between any pair of inputs is the same for all producers using the inputs (or in the production of all goods). This condition is satisfied at tangency points between the production isoquants and a given isocost line (figure 1.2). Finally, efficiency in the product mix occurs when the marginal cost of production is the same for all firms and is equal to product price (figure 1.3). As suggested above, these conditions are achieved when individuals and firms optimize under "perfect competition." That is, when a number of ideal conditions are met with product and input prices given to consumers and producers, maximization of utility by consumers and maximization of profits by producers yield the efficiency results depicted in figures 1.1, 1.2 and 1.3.

These efficiency conditions are useful to decision makers in agriculture and other areas as a "logic of choice." If a potential chooser is made aware of these principles, the decision maker is likely to weigh alternatives more carefully and to search more diligently for alternatives.[12] The principles, for example, are relevant in farm management problems such as finding the most profitable amount of nitrogen per acre to use in corn production or determining the least-cost combination of grain and silage to obtain (say) 100 pounds of milk from dairy cows. A great deal of applied work by

Agriculture and the State

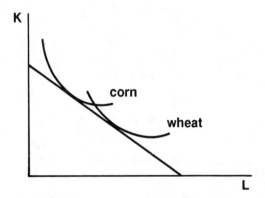

Figure 1.2. Efficiency of input use in two-input case.

agricultural economists deals with these marginal efficiency conditions and the usefulness of these optimizing principles has been demonstrated in many different production and marketing contexts. In a wide variety of economic situations, knowledge of marginal efficiency conditions may produce "better" choices as evaluated by the decision maker's own standards.

Marginal efficiency conditions, however, are of relatively little use in resolving public-policy problems. The data necessary to use the efficiency conditions for policy purposes are never "given" to a single person.[13] The economic problem of achieving a productive *pattern* of resource use is not a problem of how to allocate "given" resources among "given" ends. It is, instead, a problem of how to secure the best use of resources known to the various members of society for ends or purposes whose importance can only be known by them. When the planner is considered to have been given the necessary information about consumer preferences, production opportunities, and available resources, the economic problem is assumed away.

In attempting to achieve the most productive pattern of resource use, emphasis should be placed on the generation and utilization of widely dispersed knowledge.[14] F. A. Hayek stressed a generation ago that central planning poses insoluble problems. Market socialism implicitly assumes away these crucial information problems. Even today, however, the role of markets in discovering, coordinating, and transmitting information is seldom fully recognized.[15] No way has been found to overcome the information problems inherent in market socialism or other central planning approaches. Specifically, the central decision maker cannot obtain the information necessary to solve the problems inherent in central planning, whether the issue is wheat production, land-use planning, industrial policy, or socialism as such. In any type of central planning, information and incentive problems prevent the planner from achieving a pattern of resource use consistent with the marginal efficiency conditions outlined above. Incentive problems inherent in the collective-choice process are discussed in a later chapter.

Importance of Economics in Public Policy

Despite the limitations just discussed, economics has an important role to play in explaining the existence and effects of public policies. First, economic theory can help make individual decisions more intelligible as they affect public policies.[16] Why, for example, does Congress enact a sugar program or a dairy program which benefits a small number of producers at the expense of the public at large? As shown later, the fact that the benefits of such programs are concentrated on a small number of producers while the costs are dispersed over the entire population is important in explaining the actions of farmers, consumers, and legislators affecting these and many other government programs.

Second, economic theory can help trace out the direct as well as indirect effects and the unintended consequences of public policies including price supports, subsidized credit, and other agricultural programs.[17] What, for example, is the effect of agricultural price supports on output and land prices? Why does a price support program increase production costs? Why do government programs once initiated tend to grow, seemingly regardless of how economic conditions change? What are the effects of a price support program on imports and exports of the product? In answering these and similar questions, economic theory will be used in the following chapters in tracing out the direct and indirect effects of various agricultural programs and policies.

The Market Process: Competition and Entrepreneurship

In understanding the market effects of agricultural programs such as price supports, marketing orders, and so on, it is necessary to understand

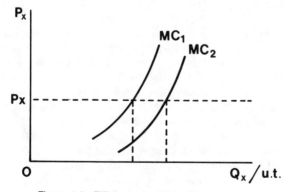

Figure 1.3. Efficiency in production.

how markets operate. Throughout this book, emphasis is placed on the market as a *process* in which prices provide signals to consumers and producers.[18] The market is a system in which *expected profits and losses* influence entrepreneurial decisions. If information on goals, costs, and returns is given or known with certainty, entrepreneurship is reduced to mechanical calculation.[19] It is important to stress that entrepreneurial decisions under real-world conditions are always made under conditions of uncertainty—completely accurate information on prices, yields, weather, and so on is never given to the decision maker. If these data were given, the entrepreneur with the most expertise in mathematics would be the most successful. Entrepreneurial success, however, is unlikely to hinge on proficiency in mechanical calculation. It is far more likely to hinge on the assessment of present and future conditions.

In the market process, entrepreneurship represents an attempt by alert decision makers to create or discover, and thereby take advantage of, profit opportunities not yet noticed by others. Where product prices reflect market forces and there are no government subsidies or "soft loans" to failing firms, only those firms survive that best anticipate market conditions. In this way, market forces cause resources to be deployed away from less productive firms. Government regulation of product and input markets, as shown throughout this book, often stifles and impedes the discovery process of the market.[20]

Perfect competition has little or nothing to do with real-world market activity since no real-world market can meet these conditions. However, this does not mean that agricultural markets in the absence of government restrictions are not competitive in a meaningful sense. In a market-process sense, competition inheres in markets since, in the absence of arbitrary restrictions, entrepreneurial activity follows the lure of expected profits. Consequently, freedom of entry is the key requirement in maintaining effective competition as a process in which competitors engage. Moreover, it is assumed in the following chapters that the major restrictions on the competitive market process in agriculture can be traced to government. It is shown that price support programs, marketing orders, and other farm programs are inconsistent with freedom of exchange both domestically and internationally.

What are the implications of the preceding discussion for the use of marginal analysis in the agricultural policy arena? Much economic analysis intended to guide or evaluate economic policy overlooks the functions and requirements of entrepreneurial decision making. A long-run view of what may appear to be excessive profits or losses is appropriate because every successful entrepreneurial venture gives the entrepreneur an edge that can be classified as a monopoly return.[21]

If perfect competition is taken to be the norm, as is often the case in policy analysis, then "market failure" in the form of monopolies, externalities, and information problems is inevitable, since no real-world market can match the conditions of perfect competition. Profits to innovators, for example, will appear to be socially harmful if real-world entrepreneurial activity is measured against the long-run competitive equilibrium benchmark where profits are zero.[22] Yet we know that expected profits under real-world conditions are the motivating force for entrepreneurial activity. The conclusion is that the use of perfect competition as a benchmark in analyzing the efficiency of real-world market activities ignores the functions and requirements of entrepreneurial decision making. Throughout this book, the competitive market process (rather than perfect competition) will be used as the norm in analyzing agricultural markets and the effects of government farm programs.

Summary

In any type of economic system five economic functions must be performed: (1) determine what goods and services to produce, (2) organize production, (3) determine how the economic pie is to be divided, (4) provide for economic progress, and (5) ration the available goods and services in the current period and over time.

There are basically only two methods of organizing economic activity in a modern economy—the private-property market system and central direction. There is no other known way to accommodate consumer preferences as fully as is done through decentralized competitive markets.

What is the role of economic theory in agricultural policy analysis? The marginal-efficiency conditions of conventional welfare economics are useful to the individual decision maker as a logic of choice but are of limited use in the evaluation of public policies. All real-world markets will appear to fail when measured against the norm of perfect competition. The alternative is to view competition as a process in which competitors engage and to use the competitive market process as a touchstone in explaining and evaluating the effects of government policies in agriculture. Throughout this book, this view of the entrepreneurial market process is taken, both in explaining individual decisions as they affect and are affected by public policies and in tracing out the direct and indirect effects of public policies in U.S. agriculture.

Notes

1. Frank H. Knight, The Economic Organization (Chicago: University of Chicago Press, 1933).

2. Don Lavoie, National Economic Planning: What is Left? (Cambridge, Mass.: Ballinger, 1985).

3. Milton and Rose Friedman, Free to Choose (New York: Avon Books, 1980), p. 2.

4. Sven Rydenfelt, A Pattern for Failure (New York: Harcourt Brace Jovanovich, 1984).

5. Knight, The Economic Organization, p. 31.

6. F. A. Hayek, Studies in Philosophy, Politics, and Economics (New York: Simon and Schuster, 1967), pp. 96–105.

7. For a vivid illustration of how voluntary exchange enables thousands of widely dispersed people to cooperate with each other see Leonard E. Read, "I, Pencil," The Freeman, December 1958.

8. Hayek, Studies in Philosophy, Politics, and Economics, pp. 91–92.

9. Oscar Lange and F. M. Taylor, On the Economic Theory of Socialism, ed. Benjamin E. Lippincott (Minneapolis: University of Minnesota Press, 1938).

10. Jack Hirshleifer, Price Theory and Applications, 3rd ed. (Englewood Cliffs, N.J.: Prentice-Hall, 1984), p. 418.

11. A brief summary of the efficiency conditions associated with perfect competition is presented in the following paragraph and in the accompanying figures. For a more detailed description and explanation of these conditions see Hirshleifer, Price Theory, pp. 479–481 (or other intermediate economics price theory texts). Readers not familiar with economics production and consumption theory at the intermediate level may skip the next paragraph which discusses the graphical analysis that depicts these efficiency conditions.

12. James M. Buchanan, What Should Economists Do? (Indianapolis: Liberty Press, 1979), chapter 2.

13. F. A. Hayek, Individualism and Economic Order (Chicago: University of Chicago Press, 1948), chapter 4.

14. Ibid, chapter 2.

15. See F. A. Hayek, "Competition as a Discovery Process," chapter 12 in New Studies in Philosophy, Politics, Economics and the History of Ideas (Chicago: University of Chicago Press, 1978); and Don Lavoie, Rivalry and Central Planning (New York: Cambridge University Press, 1985).

16. Israel M. Kirzner, "On the Method of Austrian Economics," in The Foundations of Modern Austrian Economics, ed. Edwin G. Dolan (Kansas City: Sheed and Ward, 1976), pp. 40–51.

17. Ibid.

18. Israel M. Kirzner, Competition and Entrepreneurship (Chicago: University of Chicago Press, 1973).

19. Ibid., p. 40.

20. Israel M. Kirzner, The Perils of Regulation: A Market Process Approach (Coral Gables, Fla.: Law and Economics Center, University of Miami School of Law, 1978).

21. Dean A. Worcester, Jr., "On the Validity of Marginal Analysis for Policy Making," Eastern Economic Journal 8 (1982): 83–88.

22. When markets are in equilibrium, decisions of all market participants dovetail perfectly, so that there is no scope for entrepreneurship.

2

Economic Efficiency and Equity in U.S. Agriculture

Agricultural policy in the United States has been heavily influenced by efficiency and equity considerations. However, prior to the New Deal era of the 1930s, government programs in agriculture were small and seldom affected the individual farmer. From 1862 to 1933, the U.S. Department of Agriculture (USDA) was mainly a scientific and statistical agency limited to research, extension programs, education, and some policing activities related to food safety. During this period, the major emphasis of government policy in agriculture was to increase productivity (sometimes described as economic efficiency).

Franklin Delano Roosevelt's New Deal was a watershed in government involvement in agriculture. At that time, a host of action programs were instituted with the goal of redistributing income to the agricultural sector.

As conventionally defined, economic efficiency is concerned with the size of economic pie produced while equity deals with how the economic pie is divided. The distinction between efficiency and equity is not as clear-cut as frequently implied, however, since the way the economic pie is divided affects the size of the pie. Stated differently, individual productivity is directly related to the expected reward.

Economic Efficiency: An Elusive Concept

It is often contended that economic efficiency is an objective concept in the sense that it can be empirically measured, but that equity is subjective. This distinction between efficiency and equity, however, cannot be sustained. Economic efficiency is sometimes contrasted with technical efficiency—the ratio of output to input in physical terms. Technical efficiency is of little interest, however, because by the laws of thermodynamics the ratio of physical output to physical input is always equal to unity.[1] Therefore, efficiency is meaningful only when both resources and products are measured in *value* terms.

Efficiency, if it is to be meaningful for decision making, is always a measure of *useful output* in relation to the *value of inputs used*. For instance, "The 'objective' efficiency of an automobile engine can be determined only after specifying the subjectively determined goal as the forward movement of the automobile. Otherwise, every engine is 100 percent efficient in the sense that all the energy input is used, either in the forward motion of the car, overcoming the internal friction of engine parts, or in random shaking of the automobile."[2] Consequently, the efficiency of any activity will change with changes in valuation of inputs or outputs. Consider the problem of whether it is more efficient for a homeowner to cut wood with a bow saw or with a chain saw. It depends, of course, not only upon the amount of wood to be cut and the cost of the saws but also on the subjective values associated with the use of each type saw, the value of time, and so on. One individual may rationally choose to use a chain saw while another individual in apparently similar circumstances may choose to saw wood by hand. The outside observer cannot legitimately conclude that either individual is inefficient.

Similarly, it is sometimes held in agriculture that the production of beef relative to corn is inefficient because more calories of food can be produced when a given amount of land, labor, and capital inputs are devoted to corn rather than beef production. The inefficiency conclusion does not follow, however, since consumers place a higher value per unit (calorie) of beef relative to corn. Again, the relative efficiency of corn versus beef production cannot be determined on the basis of physical measurements of inputs and products.

The subjective nature of economic efficiency limits the ability of the outside observer to identify real-world examples of economic inefficiency.[3] Efficiency measurements must be based on some norm or standard of comparison. The efficiency of real-world activities is typically measured against the economic model of "perfect competition." However, this is not a defensible approach in evaluating the performance of real-world activities since neither individuals, markets, nor economic systems will ever appear to be efficient when measured against the norm of perfect competition. That is, no real-world market will ever conform to the ideal concept of perfect competition which (as described in chapter 1) requires price-taking behavior on the part of individual traders and "perfect markets." Consequently, the fact that real-world markets do not conform to the competitive norm does not imply that these markets are inefficient in an economically meaningful sense. It is inappropriate to compare real-world markets with an unattainable ideal, since the relevant alternative to current markets is another possible institutional arrangement and not "perfectly competitive" markets. Moreover, a meaningful test of economic efficiency has not been devised for real-world conditions where some traders are not price takers and markets are never "perfect."[4]

The fact that economic efficiency cannot be measured by outside observers does not mean that the efficiency concept has no value. Economic efficiency is a useful concept as long as the inputs and outputs are defined in terms of the decision makers' own values. The data upon which individuals base choices, however, are inherently subjective and distinct

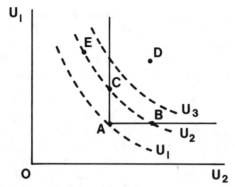

Figure 2.1. Criteria for making welfare judgments: the Pareto criterion, compensation principle, and "social welfare function."

from data that can be obtained by external observers. That is, the outside observer is not able to "read" individual preference functions.[5] Since utility is measurable only to the individual decision maker, the concept of economic efficiency is not useful as a touchstone of public policy.

Equity

How *should* the economic pie be divided? A number of criteria have been suggested for making welfare judgments but none of them provide a value-free approach to redistribution.

The Pareto Criterion

The most widely accepted criterion for making welfare judgments is the Pareto criterion, which holds that a change is beneficial if it benefits at least one person without reducing the welfare of anyone. This criterion for making welfare judgments is shown in figure 2.1. In figure 2.1. the utilities of individuals 1 and 2 are measured along the vertical and horizontal axes, respectively. If the initial situation is point *A*, points *B*, *C*, or *D* would represent "Pareto better" moves. In the case of a move from point *A* to point *B*, individual 2 is made better off while individual 1 is no worse off. A move from point *A* to point *C* improves the welfare of individual 1 without harming individual 2. In moving from point *A* to point *D*, the welfare of both individuals is improved.

How about a move from *A* to *E* in figure 2.1? In this case, the Pareto criterion does not provide an answer because individual 2 is harmed by the move in which individual 1 gains. Most public policies in agriculture (and in other sectors) are similar to the move from *A* to *E* in that they benefit some people while disadvantaging others. An agricultural price support program, for example, benefits farmers at the expense of consumers and taxpayers. Therefore the Pareto criterion is of little or no help in the evaluation of actual public policies.

A number of theorists have attempted to devise a criterion for evaluating public policies which benefit some people at the expense of others. One widely discussed proposal is the compensation principle.

Compensation Principle

The compensation principle holds that a policy is an improvement if those who gain evaluate their gains at a higher figure than the value which the losers place upon their losses. Consider again the move from A to E in Figure 2.1. The compensation principle can be illustrated as follows. Determine the maximum amount individual 1 would pay rather than forgo the move from A to E. This might be, say, $200. Then find out how much individual 2 would be willing to pay to prevent this change— assume the amount is $100. If the former figure is larger, the compensation principle says that the move from A to E improves welfare since 1 could compensate 2 and keep some of the gain. The compensation principle does not require that individual 2 actually be compensated. (If individual 2 were actually compensated, the movement from A to E would be an improvement under the Pareto criterion.)

This seemingly plausible principle is based on an unacceptable implicit value judgment.[6] It involves a concealed interpersonal comparison. Even if individual 1 values his gain at $200 and individual 2 values his loss at $100, it does not follow that there is a net gain in moving from point A to point E. The compensation principle implicitly assumes that a dollar is worth the same to each individual. However, the $200 and $100 figures are *not comparable* and there is no legitimate way to make such interpersonal comparisons of utility. Consequently, unless compensation is actually made, the Pareto criterion is violated by public policies which benefit some people at the expense of others. Although the compensation principle is often used in welfare analyses of tariffs, price supports, and other government restrictions on competition, any such analyses inevitably involve invalid interpersonal utility comparisons.

Social Welfare Function

The "social welfare function" is another approach devised to analyze the welfare effects of policies that harm some people while benefiting others. The social welfare function is closely related to the indifference map approach of consumer theory. An indifference map is a method of describing an individual's preferences with a set of indifference curves. An indifference curve shows the set of market baskets yielding the same amount of utility or satisfaction. Thus, the consumer is indifferent about the set of market baskets on a given indifference curve. A social welfare function can be visualized as an indifference map ranking different com-

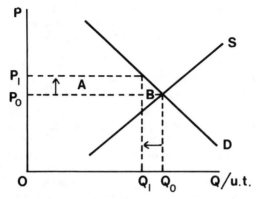

Figure 2.2. The welfare effects of production controls.

binations of utility to different members of society.[7] The broken line, u_1, in figure 2.1 represents one such level of utility. The social welfare function approach, however, is no panacea in the evaluation of public policies. In this approach, every point on the indifference map requires an explicit value judgment regarding the utility of one individual relative to the other. If such information were available, then the move from A to E in figure 2.1 would improve welfare because E is on a higher indifference curve of the social welfare function. Thus, this criterion for making welfare judgments is correct in one sense but of no practical use because there is no way to determine the required welfare judgments implicit in a social welfare function. Such utility comparisons between individuals inevitably involve value judgments, since no meaningful sum can be formed of the satisfactions provided for different people.

Cost-Benefit versus Constitutional Approach

Despite the problems inherent in meaningfully defining efficiency and equity under real-world conditions, these problems are often submerged in cost-benefit analyses. Empirical welfare analyses are frequently based on measurements of consumer surplus and producer surplus.[8] These measurements implicitly involve the use of the compensation principle.

Consider the welfare effect of an output restriction as depicted in figure 2.2 which increases price from P_0 to P_1 by decreasing output from Q_0 to Q_1. Area A is said to be a "transfer" from consumers to producers and the triangle B a "welfare cost" or "deadweight loss" of the amount by which the value of lost output (area under demand curve) exceeds the value of resources saved (area under supply curve).

These measurements based on market supply and demand curves inevitably involve interpersonal comparisons of utilities. It is assumed that a dollar is a dollar regardless of whether it is received or given up by consumers or producers (and regardless of which individuals are affected). Consequently, the measurement of areas *A* and *B* is subject to the same interpersonal utility measurement problems as those discussed above in connection with the compensation principle.

Similar problems arise in measuring the welfare effects of price supports, subsidized credit, import tariffs, marketing orders, and other government restrictions on competition in agriculture. Attempts are often made to justify the repeal of such restrictions in terms of the gain of utility of consumers at the expense of producers. Yet any such measurement of costs and benefits must involve interpersonal comparisons that, "to put it mildly, would be highly conjectural."[9] There is no legitimate way objectively to measure and compare the benefits afforded to or the harm endured by different groups of people, as F. A. Hayek emphasizes: "The childish attempts to provide a basis for 'just' action by measuring the relative utilities or satisfactions of different persons simply cannot be taken seriously . . . the whole of the so-called welfare economics, which pretends to base its arguments on inter-personal comparisons of ascertainable utilities lacks all scientific foundation. . . . The idea of basing coercive actions by government on such fantasies is clearly an absurdity."[10] The conclusion is that all policy recommendations involve value judgments.[11] For example, there is no value-free procedure to determine whether agricultural price support levels *should be* lowered or raised. In analyzing the effects of government restrictions on competition in agriculture, or in other areas, any defensible criterion must take into account the general utility of markets, and the fact that there is no principled philosophic difference between economic freedom and individual freedoms of other types.[12]

One possible alternative to cost-benefit analyses is to determine appropriate government policies at the constitutional level. If economic freedoms were legally protected, at least some of the objectives that narrowly focused interest groups attempt to achieve through the political process could be ruled out on constitutional grounds.

The proposed constitutional approach involves the adoption of self-denying ordinances that limit the objectives that individuals and groups attempt to achieve through political channels. In this approach, each potential government program is not considered on its own merits, but broad rules are laid down as to what government may do. The First Amendment, for example, adopts the general principle that "Congress shall make no law . . . abridging the freedom of speech." Milton and Rose Friedman have proposed the equivalent of the First Amendment to limit government power in the economic and social area—an "economic Bill of Rights."[13] Such a free-trade amendment would ensure that the right of people to buy and sell legitimate goods and services at mutually acceptable terms shall not be infringed by Congress or any of the states.[14] An economic-freedom amendment of this type would provide a touchstone in determining the legitimacy of government policies in agriculture and other sectors. Many of the current restrictions on competition in agriculture, including marketing orders for milk and oranges, import quotas for dairy products, and so on, are clearly inconsistent with economic freedom.

There is a growing concern in the United States about the appropriate functions of government and the effects of redistributive activities by narrowly focused interest groups on the political process. Increasingly, a balanced-budget amendment, presidential line-item veto authority, and other constitutional approaches are being discussed as possible ways of offsetting the overspending bias of modern democratic governments. (The problem of coping with this overspending bias is further discussed in chapter 5 which deals with public choice theory and agricultural policy). The constitutional approach assumes that a strong case can be made for free trade and voluntary exchange on the basis of the general utility of market exchange and the resulting enlargement of liberty of choice. Adam Smith, the father of modern economics, argued that a political system that defines and enforces individual property rights is broadly beneficial.

Although not all policy issues can be resolved on the basis of broad constitutional concepts, a change in the general climate of opinion as to the appropriate role of the state could have important implications for current agricultural programs. Most people in the United States place a high value on individual freedom. Thus it is ironic that the relationship between "human rights" and economic freedom has generally been ignored. A persuasive case can be made that prohibitions on mutually beneficial market exchanges are not fundamentally different from restrictions on First Amendment rights.[15] Ronald Coase argues that freedom of choice in making decisions among constantly changing employment, investment, and consumption opportunities is fully as important for most people as freedom of discussion and participation in government.[16] In fact, it may well be that the case for government intervention in the market for ideas is stronger than it is, in general, in markets for goods and services. Yet economic regulation is generally accepted while there is a strong predisposition against government restrictions of First Amendment rights.

In view of the importance of the provision of food, clothing, and shelter to the individual citizen, it is ironic that "human-rights" or ethical issues are so heavily discounted or ignored in discussions of price supports, marketing orders, import quotas, and other restrictions on economic competition. It has been argued, for example, that agricultural programs that restrict competition are "not authoritarian" because no production control program in agriculture "has been engaged in without a favorable vote by farmers."[17] The fact that an infringement of civil rights results from majority rule, however, does not eliminate the "human-rights" or ethical issue involved. Similarly, to the extent that economic rights are similar to First Amendment rights, the ethical issue is not removed by the fact that a plebiscite precedes compulsion in the case of the tobacco program, the peanut program, agricultural marketing orders, and other restrictions on competition.[18]

There is a relationship between economic freedom and political and individual freedoms. Where an individual works, the wage obtained or paid, how the money is spent, and the price charged for products sold are closely related to personal freedom. These choices are retained by the individual only when price signals rather than central direction are used to coordinate economic activity. Consequently, there is a great deal of evidence that economic freedom is a *necessary* condition for political and individual freedom.[19] Moreover, if one accepts the Coase view that economic rights are similar to First Amendment rights, the implications for price supports, marketing orders, import controls, and so on are manifest.

Rationale for U.S. Agricultural Programs

There are two competing hypotheses to explain government intervention in agriculture: the "public interest" (or "market failure"), and income redistribution.

Market Failure

The public interest justification holds that agricultural programs, instituted in response to market failure, are beneficial because they increase price and income stability arising from variability in farm product prices and yields. In the traditional welfare economics approach where real-world agricultural markets are measured against the competitive norm, "market failure" in the form of monopoly, market instability, imperfect information, and externalities is pervasive. As suggested earlier, however, market failure in the sense that real-world markets do not meet the conditions of perfect competition is not a sufficient reason to justify government intervention. Government programs also inevitably "fail" when measured against an idealized polity where there is perfect information and costless decisions, and political markets are always in equilibrium. The relevant comparison, of course, is between real-world markets and the real-world political process.

Income Redistribution

Income redistribution is another possible explanation for government intervention in agriculture. It may well be that the main motivating force behind agricultural policies has not been a desire for productivity growth and market stabilization, but rather a redistribution of wealth to commodity and other interest groups having the greatest political clout.[20] Why, for example, are domestic producers of cheese, butter, or sugar given protection against cheaper imports? Is it because dairy or sugar producers have low incomes (and these markets are unstable) or because they have effective political lobbies? The latter explanation appears to be more consistent with the evidence. In farm programs, the benefits are concentrated on a relatively small number of producers or landowners while the costs are widely diffused among taxpayers and consumers. More will be said in later chapters about this bias inherent in the political process which favors small groups at the expense of the public at large.

The conclusion is that the actual purpose of government programs in agriculture (and other sectors) may be quite different from the reasons indicated in the Congressional testimony and enabling legislation. Consequently, it is important not to merely *assume* that government programs are beneficial as is often done by individuals holding the "public interest" view of U.S. farm policies. In contrast to the conventional "market failure" approach, a view that agricultural policies are redistributionist is taken throughout this book. Before turning specifically to a description and analysis of U.S. farm policies, the nature of decision making in the political process—public-choice theory—will first be briefly described and specifically related to agricultural programs. The operation of the political process is shown to provide additional support for the redistributionist view of U.S. farm programs.

Summary

Agricultural programs in the United States have been justified on the basis of economic efficiency and equity considerations. Economic efficiency is concerned with the amount of output while equity is related to the way the output gets divided—income distribution. Since economic efficiency inescapably involves valuation, the concept provides little guidance in resolving public-policy issues.

The Pareto criterion which holds that a policy is Pareto better if one or more people are benefited without harming anyone is the most widely accepted criterion for making welfare judgments. However, the Pareto criterion is of little practical value since there are losers as well as gainers for all significant public policies. No satisfactory procedure has been developed to compare the costs and benefits of government policies which benefit one group at the expense of other groups.

The constitutional approach has recently been suggested as a possible alternative to cost-benefit analysis in the evaluation of government programs. In the proposed approach, the Constitution is the touchstone in determining whether a particular program is an appropriate government activity. This approach is rooted in the recognition that economic freedom is no less important than freedoms of other kinds. Although all policy questions cannot be resolved in this way, many current restrictions on competition in agriculture would be illegal if economic freedoms were given constitutional protection.

Market failure and income redistribution are alternative explanations for government intervention in agriculture. The conventional market failure view among agricultural interests has long been that U.S. farm programs are rooted in the public interest. There is a great deal of evidence, as shown throughout this book, that current farm programs are better explained by the success of agricultural groups in using governmental power to increase their own wealth.

Notes

1. Paul Heyne, *The Economic Way of Thinking* (Chicago: Science Research Associates, 1987), p. 120.

2. Thomas Sowell, *Knowledge and Decisions* (New York: Basic Books, 1980), p. 52.

3. E. C. Pasour, Jr., "Economic Efficiency: Touchstone or Mirage?" *Intercollegiate Review* 17 (1981): 33–46.

4. Harold Demsetz, "Information and Efficiency: Another Viewpoint," *Journal of Law and Economics* 12 (April 1969): 1–22.

5. James M. Buchanan, "Positive Economics, Welfare Economics, and Political Economy," *Journal of Law and Economics* 2 (October 1959): 125–138.

6. William J. Baumol, *Economic Theory and Operations Analysis*, 4th ed. (Englewood Cliffs, N.J.: Prentice-Hall, 1977), p. 530.

7. Ibid.

8. Jack Hirshleifer, *Price Theory and Applications*, 4th ed. (Englewood Cliffs, N.J.: Prentice-Hall, 1988), pp. 204–5.

9. Lionel Robbins, "Economics and Political Economy," *American Economic Review* 71 (1981): 8.

10. F. A. Hayek, *Law, Legislation and Liberty*, vol. 3: *The Political Order of a Free People* (Chicago: University of Chicago Press, 1979), pp. 201–2.

11. "Any attempt to construct a rigorous and universally applicable criterion for distinguishing what policy change is an economic improvement must founder on the problem of interpersonal comparisons. Where a policy change affects some persons favorably and others adversely, as is usually the case, there is no *a priori* way of weighing the net results." Baumol, *Economic Theory and Operations Analysis*, p. 526.

12. Robbins, "Economics and Political Economy," and Robert H. Bork, "A Lawyer's View of Constitutional Economics," in *Constitutional Economics: Containing the Economic Powers of Government*, ed. R. B. McKenzie (Lexington, Mass.: D. C. Heath, 1984), p. 228.

13. Milton and Rose Friedman, *Free to Choose* (New York: Harcourt Brace Jovanovich, 1980), p. 287.

14. William Breit, "Constitutionalizing the Regulatory Process: Comment," in *Constitutional Economics*, ed. Richard B. McKenzie (Lexington, Mass.: D. C. Heath, 1984), p. 210.

15. Ronald Coase, "The Market for Goods and the Market for Ideas," *American Economic Review* 64 (May 1974): 384–91.

16. Ibid.

17. Harold F. Breimyer, "Conceptualization and Climate for New Deal Farm Laws of the 1930's," *American Journal of Agricultural Economics* 65 (December 1983): 1156.

18. Jack High, "Is Economics Independent of Ethics?" *Reason Papers* 10 (Spring 1985): 3–16.

19. Milton Friedman, *Capitalism and Freedom* (Chicago: University of Chicago Press, 1962).

20. Bruce Gardner, "Agriculture's Revealing—and Painful—Lesson for Industrial Policy," *Backgrounder*, no. 320 (Washington, D.C.: The Heritage Foundation, 3 January 1984).

3

Government and the Economy:
Private versus Collective Choice

There are basically only two ways to coordinate economic activity: the market and central direction. A major issue in agriculture (as in all other sectors of the economy) is that of deciding which activities should be in the private sector and which should be conducted through the collective choice or political process. In order to make this decision intelligently, it is necessary to understand how the private and collective choice mechanisms operate.

Private Choice

Private choice relies to a great extent on market exchange. Although much of the coursework in economics deals with markets, the concept of a market is not easily defined. A market is not always a *place* where goods are sold but is rather a set of interrelationships involving supply and demand, a process of competing bids and offers.[1] The *market process* is fueled by the expectation of gains on the part of producers and consumers. Market choices serve to increase wealth because exchange is mutually beneficial. A key feature of market exchange is the lack of force or coercion. Since market exchange, by its very nature, represents a *voluntary unanimous agreement* by the parties involved in the transaction, informed exchange between individuals is a Pareto better move for each party. A purchase of a loaf of bread, for example, increases the expected wealth of both the purchaser and the seller.

Problems Arising from Private Choice

Despite the ostensible advantages of the voluntary nature of private choice, it is generally held to be beneficial to make some economic decisions through the collective-choice (or political) process. There are several situations, often described as examples of "market failure," where government action may be considered desirable in coordinating economic activity. Spillovers, public goods, an "unsatisfactory" income distribution, monopoly, market instability, lack of information, and high transaction costs are commonly cited examples.[2]

Problems of Private Property Rights

In some situations, it may be difficult to clearly define and adequately enforce property rights. The use of fertilizers or pesticides, for example, may create an externality or spillover problem in which an action by one farmer infringes on the property rights of others. The spillover problem is analyzed in more detail in chapter 17.

"Public goods" involve another type of property-rights problem. Public goods, by definition, are characterized by *nonrivalness* and *nonexcludability* in consumption. There is nonrivalness in the sense that any satisfaction that one consumer gets from a given amount of a public good does not detract from the enjoyment obtained from the good by other consumers. Nonexcludability is a characteristic of goods of this type in the sense that if a public good is provided to any one individual, additional consumers cannot be excluded from the benefits of the good through fees. National defense, for example, may be considered a public good insofar as it is impossible to protect one person from a foreign threat without, at the same time, protecting all other individuals.[3] If nonpayers cannot be excluded, individuals have an incentive to "free ride," i.e., to obtain the benefits of a good or service without contributing to its cost. The incentive for any one person to be a free rider is greater in large groups because each person may reason that the other beneficiaries will contribute enough to finance the good.[4] However, if all members of the community choose the free-rider strategy, there will be no production. Consequently, in this case where there is an incentive to "free ride," private production may not be feasible. The relevance of externality and public-goods ideas to current agricultural programs will be discussed later.

Distribution of Income

It is sometimes contended that the market system is unsatisfactory because the distribution of income (or resource ownership) may be very unequal. The "Edgeworth box" diagram is often used to show how exchange improves the allocation of consumption goods.[5] Consider the situation depicted in figure 3.1. In this "Edgeworth box" diagram, assume that the initial distribution of the two goods (X and Y) between the two individuals (A and B) is such that A has all of both X and Y. Although individual B has none of either good, the situation is Pareto optimal since any move along the contract curve (AB) would represent a decrease in welfare for individual A. That is, individual B cannot be made better off without reducing the welfare of individual A. The implication is that

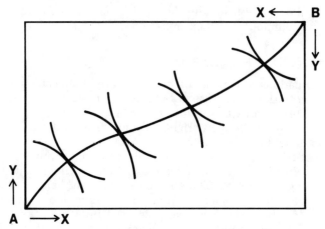

Figure 3.1. Economic theory and the distribution of income.

economic tools cannot be used to say how income *should be* divided. Even in the case of the stark distribution of income depicted in figure 3.1, economic theory cannot be used to justify redistribution.

The pattern of income in a market system is not likely to conform to any predetermined pattern, and since many people are unlikely to be satisfied with the market pattern of incomes, there is interest in ways to improve it. In the case of a voluntary transfer (charity), the redistribution of income presumably improves the welfare of the giver as well as the recipient. But an argument has been made that the "Pareto optimal" amount of re-distribution does not occur through private charity because charity yields benefits to others as well as to the donor. A number of studies have argued that charity should be viewed as a public good involving a consumption externality.[6] In this view, public-goods theory is held to provide a justi-fication for government transfer programs.

A strict application of public-goods theory, however, does not provide a rationale for governmental redistribution. First, the Pareto criterion pro-vides no guidance on policies that harm some people while benefiting others. Thus the idea that a particular government transfer program can be Pareto better is inconsistent as long as there is at least one person who opposes the redistribution. Second, voluntary transfers do not fit the public-goods framework. The nonrivalness and nonexclusion features of a public good are not met in the case of voluntary transfers. If exclusion is feasible, as it is in the case of private charity, the "free rider" problem does not arise. Thus, public-goods theory cannot be used to justify redistribu-tion.[7] This conclusion is merely a restatement of the underlying premise of chapter 2 that *all* distributional recommendations involve judgments of value.

Monopoly

Monopoly power is typically regarded as a major reason for government intervention. In the conventional neoclassical view of economic theory, the monopolist is defined as a single seller of a good for which there is no close substitute. Yet when subjected to close scrutiny this definition of monopoly cannot be sustained. If a good or service is defined narrowly enough, *every seller* is a monopolist since no other seller can precisely match the product and conditions under which the product is sold. On the other hand, there are substitutes for *all* goods and services.[8] Consequently, if a product is defined broadly, *no seller* is a monopolist.

If perfect competition is used as a norm, every price searcher (seller facing a demand less than perfectly elastic) is labelled a monopolist. This is not a realistic approach, however, since even the ten-year-old lemonade-stand entrepreneur can generally increase sales by lowering the price. Another possible alternative is to define monopoly on the basis of the elasticity of demand. If one attempts to define a monopolist on the basis of "market power" or the elasticity of demand, however, the classification must be arbitrary since market power defined in this way is a matter of degree.

Perhaps the most meaningful way to define monopoly is in terms of a grant of government power which restricts the ability of other sellers to compete.[9] The major source of monopoly or cartel power in agriculture (and in other economic sectors) in the United States today arises from government-sanctioned and enforced restrictions on competition. The tobacco, peanut, milk, and sugar programs are examples of government-enforced cartels in U.S. agriculture.

Market Instability and Lack of Information

Information is crucial in a smoothly functioning market process. Whether market participants would benefit from additional information, however, hinges on the costs and benefits of this information. Moreover, the costs and returns of acquiring information vary from person to person. Even if it were possible to acquire complete information, it would be uneconomic to do so. In the words of George Stigler, "information costs are the costs of transportation from ignorance to omniscience and seldom can a trader afford to take the entire trip."[10] It is economic for market participants and other decision makers to acquire more information only if the expected benefits exceed the costs. Thus, the fact that market participants are not fully informed does not imply that they have "too little" information. This topic of possible "market failure" due to information problems will be returned to in chapter 18, where government programs in agriculture designed to provide information, such as the Agricultural Extension Service and the Statistical Reporting Service of the USDA, are discussed.

A great deal of government intervention in agriculture has been justified on the basis of market stabilization. However, there is no way to eliminate market instability in a world of uncertainty. If government is to stabilize individual markets, planners must somehow overcome the information and incentive problems, described below, that are inherent in the collective choice decision-making process. Government stabilization policies, as emphasized in chapter 4, are controlled not by impartial and omniscient experts, but by elected and appointed governmental decision makers who, like the rest of us, make and implement policy in light of their own interests and in response to the incentives they face. It is stressed in chapter 4 that all governmental policies in a democratic society are significantly affected by the relatively short time horizons of governmental officials who face pressures to adopt policies that yield short-run benefits with costs that occur in the long run.[11]

The results of recent attempts by government to stabilize the entire economy provide little basis for optimism that government stabilization attempts will succeed. In the early 1960s, the argument was made that the federal government should "fine-tune" the economy to achieve a high level of aggregate demand by manipulating government expenditures and taxes. Twenty years later, the once high hopes for economic fine-tuning had been dashed on the shoals of economic and political reality. The evidence has convinced many people that the monetary and fiscal policies of the federal government, rather than stabilizing the level of economic activity, have had a major destabilizing effect.[12] If government is to stabilize agricultural markets, government officials must overcome the same kinds of problems faced in stabilizing the entire economy.

There are government actions, however, which would contribute to economic stability in agriculture. The government can create a climate to facilitate rather than impede the development of crop insurance, options markets, and other institutions that are helpful in dealing with weather and market risks, as discussed in chapter 15. However, there is a strong a priori case for decentralized competitive markets as the most effective means of coping with changing economic conditions. It should also be stressed that noninflationary monetary and fiscal policies at the national level are likely to contribute more to the stability of agricultural markets than stabilization policies designed specifically for agriculture (see chapter 15).

Transactions Costs

Transactions costs are those costs incurred in the process of voluntary exchange, including searching, advertising, inspecting, bargaining, and so on. High transactions cost is a major justification for collective action and the relative merits of private versus collective choice as the means of coordinating economic activity are influenced by the magnitude of these costs. In the case of services provided collectively, quite often it is not that the service *cannot* be provided through voluntary means. It is rather that the transactions costs of doing so are deemed to be too high. Consider the problem of privatizing police protection. The transactions costs of contacting individuals, collecting payment for services, and so on would often be quite high. There is also the problem alluded to above that individuals would have an incentive to "free ride" on the protection paid for by their neighbors. High transactions costs in such cases may make it impractical to exclude nonpayers from the benefits of police protection. In cases where the costs of excluding nonpayers are very high, collective action is often resorted to. In publicly financed police protection, for example, government supplies the service to everyone and pays for it with involuntary contributions (taxes).

Private Action versus Collective Action

The alternative to private decisions coordinated through decentralized markets is collective action coordinated through the political process. That is, central direction is the only alternative if market price signals are not used to coordinate economic activity. Government is unique among social institutions in that it is the only legal entity that possesses the power to secure cooperation through coercion. In contrast, cooperation is induced by offering people additional options in private choice.[13] The substitution of collective action for private action is often considered appropriate when there is "market failure" of the types discussed above. However, collective action is no panacea since there are also inherent problems in coordinating economic activity through the political process.

Undesirable Consequences of Collective Action

It is generally assumed that law and order and other traditional functions of government are necessary because of high transactions costs and the free-rider incentive. However, there is no consensus as to the necessity or desirability of such government intervention in the provision of information, in income redistribution, or in economic regulation. Government provision of information and regulation of voluntary exchange is particularly relevant to agricultural policy, since the development and dissemination of information to consumers and farmers has long been considered to be a major rationale for government involvement in agriculture.

The regulation of voluntary exchange in the form of price supports, interest subsidies, marketing orders, and other restrictions on competition has been at the heart of government efforts to increase incomes within agriculture. Collective action is, however, subject to problems similar to those described above in the case of private choice. In determin-

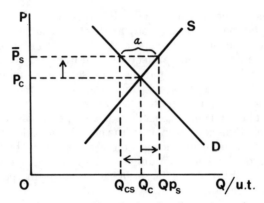

Figure 3.2. Upward-biased price signals create surpluses.

ing the appropriate role for government in agriculture, it is important to compare the operation of actual markets with real-world political institutions. This can only be done if the problems inherent in collective choice are taken into account in weighing the merits of government action, whether the issue is price supports, subsidized credit, soil conservation, or government-funded agricultural research.[14]

Information Problems

Information problems are endemic in the collective choice process because of the *separation of power and knowledge.* Market prices, reflecting demand and supply conditions, coordinate and transmit information to consumers and producers. In this way, the market system utilizes the detailed information that is contained in millions of minds more completely than is possible by any other known process. Much of the information incorporated in market prices simply cannot be articulated and conveyed to a central authority in statistical form.

Government intervention leads to a decrease in the volume and quality of information embodied in market prices and distorts the coordination process of the market.[15] Consider the supply-demand situation depicted in figure 3.2. When government raises the price of milk, sugar (or any other product) above the market clearing level (P_c) to P_s, the market begins to give out false or misleading signals. Producers are induced to produce "too much" (Q_{ps}) and consumers are induced to consume "too little" (Q_{cs}). The inevitable result, a surplus of amount a, is evidenced in U.S. agriculture by market surpluses of milk, wheat, corn, tobacco, and other products. Market prices provide correct signals to producers and consumers and properly ration goods and services only when prices are free to change in response to constantly changing economic conditions.

Incentive Problems

When decisions about resource use are made through the political process, problems also arise because of perverse incentives due to the *separation of power and responsibility*. Profits and losses provide the driving force for change and progress in a market system. Entrepreneurial decisions are guided by perceptions of profit opportunities, and only those firms survive that best anticipate market conditions. In contrast, there is no "bottom line" in the case of government enterprise or collective choice where political decisions are substituted for the discipline of the market. This point is especially apropos in the case of subsidized credit in agriculture discussed in chapter 16.

The public choice mechanism provides no reliable guidelines concerning the relative efficiency of various government agencies—there are no signals comparable to profits and losses of the market process. Moreover, there is a tendency toward overproduction of collectively provided goods and services because the goods are generally priced "too low." Whether the good is water, parks, schools, or services of the U.S. Department of Agriculture (USDA), consumers usually do not pay the full cost of services provided by government.

Pricing collectively provided goods and services below "cost" is not accidental. There is an advantage to political incumbents and to political employees in keeping prices low, since the law of demand applies to goods and services provided through government agencies just as it does for those produced in the private sector. Consequently, the lower the price of any government service, the larger the quantity of the service demanded and the larger the budget, number of jobs, and amount of political influence of the agency providing the service. Information provided by the Agricultural Extension Service to farmers, for example, is typically free. Thus, it is not surprising that there is usually a "shortage" of extension services (and of many other underpriced collectively provided goods and services).

Inability to Respond to Consumers with Different Tastes

Collectively provided goods such as national defense, education, the dairy program, and so on, are typically supplied at only one level and all taxpayers must contribute toward the provision of the program whether or not they use the service. This feature of collectively provided goods and services is fundamentally different from that of privately produced goods such as autos, clothing, and food, where the individual consumer has a choice, not only of whether to buy the good, but also of how much of the good to consume.

There is also an inherent inability of the collective choice process to respond to people with different tastes. Even if an individual fully agrees with the amount of public expenditures on agriculture, for example, he or

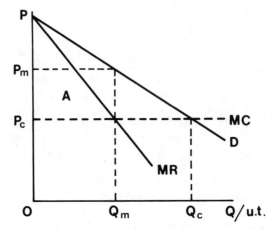

Figure 3.3. Cartels: why groups have an incentive to collude.

she may well disagree with how the budget is spent. One person, for example, may prefer more public expenditures on food assistance programs and less (or none) on price-support programs; another person may hold just the opposite view.

Restrictions on Competition

Government programs to reduce competition are frequently sought (and achieved) by various groups as a means of increasing their own wealth. This is particularly important in the case of agricultural programs discussed in later chapters of this book. Effective price support programs for milk, tobacco, sugar, and other products, for example, inevitably require restrictions on imports to prevent consumers from substituting lower-priced imports for higher-priced domestic products. There is increasing interest in the effects of farm programs, import restrictions, and other governmental policies that serve to increase the incomes of small groups at the expense of the public at large.

Rent-seeking Activity

The reason why producer groups have an incentive to restrict competition through collusion is shown in figure 3.3. The output under competitive conditions is OQ_c which is sold at the competitive market price OP_c. If the producers successfully form a cartel and restrict production to OQ_m, the cartel price is OP_m and profits are increased by the amount of rectangle A. However, each seller has an incentive to cheat on the agreement because the price received (OP_m) is higher than the cost of production (MC).[16] Thus, voluntary cartel arrangements are usually short-lived.

One way to enforce cartel agreements is through the use of legal sanctions. If a producer group can get a cartel agreement enforced through government sanctions, the chances of success are greatly improved. In reality, most successful cartel agreements and other restrictions on competition are administered or enforced by government. In addition to agricultural programs, examples of government-enforced restrictions on competition include labor unions, import restrictions, the Post Office, and occupational licensing.

The situation depicted in figure 3.3 provides an explanation for the widespread practice in which agricultural (and other) groups with narrowly focused interests attempt to use the power of the state to reduce competition and thereby increase income. "Rent seeking," a recently developed concept, is used to describe the resource-wasting activities that occur as individuals and groups seek transfers of wealth under the aegis of the state.[17] Large amounts of time and money are spent on lobbying activities, campaign contributions, and so on by teachers, farmers, auto workers, and other groups in attempts to influence the legislative process. Rent-seeking theory holds that the expected profits from legal restrictions on competition are likely to be largely competed away in rivalrous attempts to obtain and maintain the governmental assistance. It is possible for all of the potential gains (area A) to be dissipated through rent-seeking activities. (In this situation, how would the marginal cost curve including rent-seeking costs be drawn in figure 3.3?). Rent seeking or income redistribution appears to be a useful concept in explaining and predicting a great deal of government transfer activity in agriculture and other sectors of the economy.[18]

Despite the apparent importance of the rent-seeking phenomenon, the problem of identifying rent-seeking activities warrants more attention than it has received. All of the resources used by individuals and groups in obtaining and maintaining government activities cannot legitimately be regarded as rent-seeking waste. The lobbying and other resource costs necessary to achieve *beneficial* political activities will appear to be rent-seeking waste only if one compares the real-world political process with an idealized polity where there is perfect information and communication and where political markets are "in equilibrium." The issue of whether or not a particular governmental activity is beneficial hinges largely on one's view of the proper role of the state. The identification and measurement of rent-seeking waste poses essentially the same problems as those discussed earlier (chapter 2) relating to the identification and measurement of economic inefficiency.[19]

The Public Interest

The "public interest" typically is identified with the general welfare or the interests of the public at large. It is usually not possible to say, however, if a particular collective-choice outcome is in the public interest.[20] Political decisions almost always create losers as well as winners. The problem of determining whether such a policy is in the public interest is the same as that earlier discussed in the context of policy evaluation—it involves the problem of interpersonal utility comparisons. Moreover, although the term "public interest" is widely used to influence public opinion, the meaning of the concept is not clear since as previously discussed, the satisfactions provided for different people cannot be meaningfully summed.

Assuming that the public interest can be precisely defined, economists have devoted a great deal of effort to the question of whether such a thing as the public interest can exist.[21] Although this work was instrumental in winning a Nobel Prize for Professor Kenneth Arrow, it has little practical relevance for public-policy analysis. Public officials, as shown in the following chapter, do not have enough information about preference functions, production functions, and available resources to determine which policies would best serve the public at large. Furthermore, even if government decision makers could determine what actions are broadly in the "public interest," they would be unlikely to execute these policies because of perverse incentives in the political process.

While the "public interest" concept provides little guidance, decisions must be made about the role of government versus the market in coordinating economic activity. In choosing between alternative methods of organizing economic activity, it is important to avoid what Harold Demsetz calls the "nirvana approach"—the view that the relevant policy choice is between an ideal norm and an existing imperfect institutional arrangement.[22] Those who attack an existing market because it does not conform to the norm of "perfect competition" are guilty of committing the nirvana fallacy. The relevant policy choice is always among real-world institutions—all of which are imperfect.[23]

Summary

Goods and services may be provided through either the market or the collective-choice process. When property rights are not clearly defined, problems of externalities and public goods may arise in the market process. Other alleged problems associated with the provision of goods and services through private choice include an unsatisfactory distribution of income, monopoly, market instability, and insufficient information.

Provision of goods and services through collective action, however, is no panacea. There are also shortcomings and undesirable consequences of collective action including information problems, incentive problems, the inability to respond to consumers with different tastes, a tendency to restrict competition, and an inability by decision makers in the collective-choice process to determine which actions are in the "public interest."

The fact that market outcomes do not conform to the ideal of perfect competition does not imply that government intervention is warranted.

Imperfections are no less important in the political arena than in the market sector. A realistic choice about the extent of government intervention in agriculture (or in other sectors) must be based on a comparison of the real-world market process with the real-world political process.

Notes

1. Paul Heyne, *The Economic Way of Thinking* (Chicago: Science Research Associates, 1987), p. 144.

2. For a more complete discussion of the "undesirable consequences of private choice" see Peter H. Aranson, *American Government: Strategy and Choice* (Cambridge, Mass.: Winthrop, 1981), pp. 79–98.

3. David N. Hyman, *Public Finance: A Contemporary Application of Theory to Policy* (New York: Dryden Press, 1983), p. 128.

4. Ibid., pp. 128–30.

5. For a discussion of the Edgeworth-box analysis of the exchange process, see Jack Hirshleifer, *Price Theory and Applications*, 4th ed. (Englewood Cliffs, N.J.: Prentice-Hall, 1988), p. 387.

6. E. C. Pasour, Jr., "Pareto Optimality as a Guide to Income Redistribution," *Public Choice* 36 (1981): 75–87.

7. Ibid.

8. Heyne, *The Economic Way of Thinking*, p. 162.

9. Dominick T. Armentano, *Antitrust and Monopoly: Anatomy of a Policy Failure* (New York: Wiley, 1982), p. 42.

10. George Stigler, "Imperfections in the Capital Market," *Journal of Political Economy* 75 (1967): 291.

11. Heyne, *The Economic Way of Thinking*, pp. 520–521.

12. Ibid., chap. 19.

13. Ibid., chap. 14.

14. For a more complete discussion of the "undesirable consequences of collective choice" see Aranson, *American Government: Strategy and Choice*, pp. 98–113.

15. Paul Johnson, "Movement in the Market: Mobility and Economics in the Free Society," in *On Freedom*, ed. John A. Howard (Greenwich, Conn.: Devin-Adair, 1984), pp. 39–58.

16. For a discussion of cartels and the incentive for individual members to "chisel," see Hirshleifer, *Price Theory and Applications*, p. 251.

17. James M. Buchanan, R. D. Tollison, and G. Tullock, eds., *Toward A Theory of the Rent-Seeking Society* (College Station, Tex.: Texas A and M University Press, 1980).

18. "Regardless of the particular justification for agricultural policies, however, they are currently supported principally by what economists call rent-seeking behavior." Thomas Gale Moore, "Farm Policy: Justifications, Failures and the Need for Reform," *Federal Reserve Bank of St. Louis Review* 69, no. 8 (October 1987): 7.

19. E. C. Pasour, Jr. "Rent Seeking: Some Conceptual Problems and Implications," *Review of Austrian Economics* 1 (1987): 123–43.

20. Aranson, *American Government: Strategy and Choice*, p. 107.

21. Kenneth J. Arrow, *Social Choice and Individual Values*, 2nd ed. (New York: Wiley, 1963).

22. Harold Demsetz, "Information and Efficiency: Another Viewpoint," *Journal of Law and Economics* 12 (April 1969): 1–22.

23. James M. Buchanan, "The Achievement and the Limits of Public Choice in Diagnosing Government Failure and in Offering Bases for Constructive Reform," in *Anatomy of Government Deficiencies*, ed. Horst Hanusch (New York: Springer-Verlag, 1983).

4

Public Choice:
The Economics of the Political Process

Public-choice theory involves the application and extension of economic theory to the realm of political or governmental choices.[1] Methodologically, this economic theory of politics is individualist. Emphasis is placed on the actions of *individual* decision makers in the political process. Political events can be better explained by focusing on the actions of individual participants rather than on the actions of groups because groups, *as groups*, do not act. Any agricultural legislation, for example, occurs as the result of individuals acting in the political process. "In sum, groups do not live, cannot choose, and are unable to act apart from the lives, choices, and actions of the individual members who make them up."[2] Moreover, individual action is assumed to be purposeful and the decision maker is assumed to be the best judge of his or her own welfare. Although social welfare cannot be measured because utilities of different individuals are not comparable, social utility is viewed as the sum of individual welfares, rather than some imagined entity standing on its own.

It is recognized in the following analysis that individual participants in the political process are not motivated solely by pecuniary considerations. Moreover, there is no implication that public-choice theory can fully explain either political activity or how individual members of the political process will act in any specific situation. The theory is useful, however, in helping to explain collective-choice decisions at each level of government. The following analysis demonstrates how changes in costs and benefits, given other factors, can affect actions in different stages of the collective decision making process.

There are three branches in the American system of government: the legislative, executive, and judicial. These branches were designed to provide a system of checks and balances so that no branch would become clearly dominant. Moreover, it is through the interaction of these branches of government and the bureaucracy that public policies in agriculture and other areas are proposed, developed, adopted, and carried out (figure 4.1).[3]

Decision making occurs at each level in the political process (figure 4.1). Voters elect members of the legislature. The legislature enacts laws which

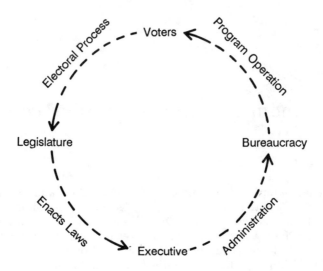

Figure 4.1. Model of the political process.

the executive administers. Legislation is actually implemented by the bureaucracy, i.e., government workers who staff the various public agencies but who are not subject to election by voters.

Individual Participation

The individual voter is confronted with a number of decisions about participation in the political process including such questions as: (1) should I vote? (2) how active should I be in political activities (including campaign contributions)? and (3) if active, should I run for office?

The act of voting itself cannot be explained on the basis of narrowly defined self-interest. The probability that an individual's vote will be decisive in any given election is minuscule. However, it is notable that Adolf Hitler was first elected head of the Nazi Party by only one vote.[4] Since voting involves a cost (mainly of time), the individual voter would choose not to vote on the basis of narrowly defined costs and benefits. Consequently, voting must be explained on other grounds: the individual voter might take an enlarged view of self-interest, receive satisfaction from participation in the democratic process, and so on.

Who are the activists in political activity? Both amateurs and professionals are active in the political arena.[5] Amateurs do not depend on politics for their economic livelihood. Professional politicians, on the other hand, may (and often do) depend on politics as their regular source of income. Consequently, when compared with amateurs, they are likely to be much more concerned with winning elections than with adhering to ideological principles. An amateur is more willing to support a probable loser because the outcome of the election has less effect on the amateur's economic interests. Consider the Mondale campaign in 1984. In areas of the United States where Mondale had little public support and other Democratic candidates minimized their ties to the national ticket, amateurs continued to campaign publicly for the ticket. Even if an amateur and a professional hold similar views, the actions and positions taken by the professional politician are more likely to be tempered by the views of the general electorate because of economic considerations.

Costs and benefits are also important in determining who runs for office. Although campaign funding is highly important to political success, the purpose of campaign contributions is not the same for all donors. The civics-book view is that political contributions resemble contributions to charitable organizations where the donor expects nothing in return. There undoubtedly are many small contributors who are motivated by altruism rather than by narrow self-interest.

There is a great deal of evidence, however, that the pecuniary motive is often important in political contributions.[6] Contributions may represent "extortion" by officeholders. That is, contributions may provide protection money or insurance against unfavorable legislation or from legislation which would take away current benefits. Dairy co-ops, for example, donated $1.3 million to 293 members of the U.S. House of Representatives from 1981 until the 1983 Dairy and Tobacco Adjustment Act was passed. This legislation not only maintained but extended the financial benefits of the dairy program by paying farmers to reduce milk production. Thus, contributions might also be viewed as "bribery"—as payoffs to achieve specific public-policy concessions. In the case of the dairy legislation, the outcome was a costly act resulting in some individual dairy producers receiving more than $1 million. As another example, the establishment of the Department of Education during the Carter Administration was widely viewed as a payoff for support given by the National Education Association during the 1976 presidential campaign.

The potential benefits of elective office at the local level are likely to be higher for lawyers, real-estate brokers, and Chamber of Commerce members whose political exposure can serve as self-advertising for their vocation or business. At the national level, political experience often pays off for ex-congressmen and high-level political appointees in the form of lucrative employment opportunities with business firms interested in gaining Washington contacts and acquiring knowledge of the political process as it affects their own business. At the local level, the ability to influence land-use zoning decisions, the location and timing of public works, property tax rates, and so on can provide immediate economic benefits.

Political Parties

Economic theory is also important in explaining the existence of political parties. Different parties have ideologies which provide low-cost

		Increased Economic Freedom	
		For	Against
Increased	For	Libertarian	Liberal
Personal Freedom	Against	Conservative	Populist

Figure 4.2. The relationship of economic and personal freedoms to liberal, conservative, libertarian, and populist ideologies.

information to voters. Party labels are analogous in some ways to product brand names such as GE, GM, and Toyota that provide valuable information to consumers. Similarly, the party labels Democrat, Republican, Libertarian, and Socialist reduce the cost to individual voters of obtaining information about the various candidates. The individual voter cannot expect to become well-informed about all candidates from which he or she must choose. However, since most candidates run on party platforms, the voter is likely to be able to determine a candidate's position on many issues solely on the basis of party affiliation.

William Maddox and Stuart Lilie separate questions of government intervention in the economy from issues involving civil liberties and propose a classification consisting of four ideological groups: liberal, conservative, libertarian, and populist (figure 4.2).[7] The traditional liberal-conservative dimension is increasingly inadequate in characterizing the ideological views of U.S. voters and politicians.

Legislative Branch

House and Senate members engage in three kinds of activities: advertising, credit claiming, and position taking.[8] In advertising, one key issue for any office holder or political candidate is how much to spend. In theory, the answer is clear if only monetary costs and benefits are taken into account. The politician can afford to spend up to the present value of the sum of the expected stream of discounted future returns. The uncertainties of the political process, however, mean that probability theory is of little value in making such choices. Both the chance of winning and the returns if elected are highly uncertain. Moreover, most candidates are not motivated solely by financial considerations. Indeed, some candidates such as Harold Stassen, a perennial candidate for President of the United States, run even when the expectation of winning is nil.

Credit claiming and position taking may be motivated to some extent by ideology but the desire to stay in office usually is the dominant influence. It is not unusual, for example, for a politician from a state with a strong agricultural constituency who is generally a staunch supporter of free enterprise to actively promote restrictions on competition for milk, tobacco, wheat, and other products. In fact, it is much more uncommon for the serious political candidate to place ideology over short-run political considerations.

Legislative activity is heavily influenced by the committee and seniority system of Congress. Agriculture is just one of many standing committees in the House and Senate. The person serving longest on the committee from the majority party is usually committee chairman—a position of added political clout and prestige. For many years, committee chairmen tended to be Southerners because of the dominance of the Democratic party in the South. Members of Congress from the South often were re-elected term after term so that Southern congressmen frequently attained seniority on Congressional committees. Southern congressmen have lost a great deal of influence on Congressional committees because the South is no longer a one-party region and because of changes in Congressional procedures.

Much of the power in Congress now resides in congressional subcommittees which tend to be organized along commodity lines in the House and along functional lines in the Senate. The eight Senate agriculture subcommittees are: Soil and Water Conservation; Agricultural Credit and Rural Electrification; Agricultural Production, Marketing and Stabilization of Prices; Agricultural Research and General Legislation; Rural Development Oversight and Investigation; Foreign Agricultural Policy; Nutrition; and Forestry, Water Resources and Environment. The eight House subcommittees are: Cotton, Rice and Sugar; Livestock, Dairy and Poultry; Wheat, Soybeans and Feed Grains; Tobacco and Peanuts; Conservation, Credit and Rural Development; Department Operations, Research and Foreign Agriculture; Domestic Marketing, Consumer Relations and Nutrition; and Forests, Family Farms and Energy.[9]

It is no accident that chairmen of committees and subcommittees in Congress tend to be from states where committee actions are important. That is, the chairman of an agriculture committee or subcommittee is likely to be from a state where agriculture is an important industry. However, interest in agricultural legislation by urban members of Congress has increased greatly since the 1960s following an increase in the scope of food assistance programs administered by the USDA.

The actions of decision makers in government agencies are influenced by the Congressional-electoral process. Reelection-minded congressmen have strong incentives to ensure that government agencies provide benefits to their constituents. The Congressional-bureaucratic system is a means to this end.[10] In return for electoral support from tobacco or dairy farmers, for example, a congressman from a tobacco or dairy state who is a member of the Congressional committee with jurisdiction over these USDA activities may provide a flow of benefits to his constituents. Moreover, a Congressional member of the relevant committee has an incentive to use a farm program for political purposes. This phenomenon is no less important in nonagricultural areas. Thus, congressmen often play a key role in agency decisions, and sanctions are likely to be imposed on those government bureaus that fail to provide congressional benefits. The conclusion is that the Congressional-bureaucratic system confronts government agencies such as the USDA with strong incentives to serve the interests of members of the affected Congressional committees.[11]

Members of Congress having different types of constituents often engage in log rolling (vote trading). This practice has become more important in agriculture with the increase in food assistance and other transfer programs favored by urban interests. For example, rural Congressman X may vote for the food-stamp bill of urban Congressman Y in exchange for Y voting for the agricultural price–support bill favored by Congressman X. Although vote trading is important and widespread, legal scholars disagree on its merits.

Lobbies or interest groups provide a way to bring together people of similar interests, to express their views to legislators, and to achieve legislation beneficial to particular groups. Farm organizations and commodity groups, for example, often lobby for or against legislation affecting agriculture. Lobbying groups may provide information as well as financial support to legislators. Depending upon the nature of their activities, lobbying groups are sometimes labelled as "pressure groups."

The Executive Branch and the Bureaucracy

The executive branch is charged with carrying out the laws enacted by Congress. The president influences legislation through his proposals made to Congress, support or opposition to bills, and use of the veto. Various cabinet departments, Agriculture, Defense, and so on, are charged with specific areas of responsibility. The president appoints the top administrators in the USDA and other agencies or bureaus, but the programs are administered by the bureaucracy. Although the top administrators change with a change in political administration, most of the government employees (e.g., 117,000 USDA employees) do not.

The key decision maker in the implementation of legislation and in economic regulation generally is the "professional public servant"—the bureaucrat. Bureaucrats are government workers not responsible for making public policy but rather for implementing policy decisions. The individual citizen's most frequent contact with government at all levels remains with bureaucrats. The ostensible functions of federal bureaus include supplying public goods, suppressing public ills, redistributing resources, controlling monopolies, and establishing property rights. Today, nearly one member of the work force in five is employed by some level of government.[12] Government bureaus confront decision-making problems unlike those faced by private firms. Most of these problems can be traced to the fact that there are no residual claimants in government bureaus. That is, there is no one in a government agency who personally gains when resources are used in ways that are most beneficial to the public at large.

It is sometimes suggested that employees who staff government agencies act to maximize social welfare without regard to their own utility, power, prestige, income, or vote appeal. In view of the large size of the government sector and the fact that individuals frequently move between the private and public sectors, there is little reason to assume that government employees are significantly different from an average cross section of the population having the educational qualifications required for that work.

Bureau employees are similar to other interest groups. It is to be expected, for example, that USDA personnel will actively defend and seek to expand government programs in agriculture. Bureau personnel are active in the electoral process, although the Hatch Act restricts federal employees from public campaigning. They are also important sources of information in Congressional hearings and for individual legislators.

What goals do decision makers in government bureaus pursue? Carrying out the "goals of Congress" is difficult because the goals are seldom clearly defined. Achieving the "public interest" is not feasible because the individual bureaucrat does not have the required information on consumer preferences, production possibilities, and available resources.[13] Moreover, even if decision makers in the collective-choice process could determine what actions were in the public interest, the incentive structure of the bureaucracy is not conducive to their following it.

What, then, are the goals of the bureaucrat? The bureaucrat, like other members of the political process, has a vested interest in staying in power and specifically in agency growth. In staying in power, it is important to minimize bureaucratic risk as a way of reducing criticism from without and, hence, bureaucratic strain. Thus, there is an incentive to institute policies yielding immediate benefits and to forgo policies involving potentially higher returns that involve more risk and a longer time horizon.

Consider the example of FDA (Food and Drug Administration) testing of new drugs. There are two costs associated with the introduction of a new drug: (a) lives lost (or damaged) through premature introduction, and (b) lives lost through excessive delay in introducing new drugs. The first cost is highly visible; the second cost is difficult to detect. Few people will condemn the FDA for lives lost due to the second cost, but sickness or death resulting from the use of a new drug will predictably evoke a public outcry. The result is that the FDA is likely to test drugs too much, if judged by a standard that is based on a realistic comparison of costs and benefits. In drug testing and in other areas, the political decision maker desiring to maintain power is well advised to minimize the probability of making detectable errors.

It is also helpful for a bureau head to maximize output of the agency that can be readily monitored—such as contacts made. One way to increase the demand for an agency's output is to offer the service to the public below the cost necessary to provide it. For example, USDA services such as those of the Agricultural Extension Service typically are heavily subsidized and priced below cost to farmers, homemakers, and other users of these services. This pricing bias in the collective choice process is likely to lead to a higher level of output than would be provided through private choice.

Members of government bureaus also benefit from agency growth. For the bureaucrat, salary, perquisites, public reputation, and patronage all increase with the size of agency budget. Thus, there is an incentive to maximize the bureau's budget. One way to increase the budget is to charge below-cost prices (as indicated above) to justify increased appropriations. Bureau officials also have an incentive to resist reductions in agency size. In responding to impending budget cuts, government officials are likely to sacrifice the services most highly valued by consumers rather than to make cuts which affect their own welfare. "Typically the immediate response of a public agency to proposed budget cuts is some variant of . . . the 'Washington Monument syndrome'. When faced with a budget reduction, the National Park Service immediately announced that such cuts could only be accommodated by closing the Washington Monument, the most popular tourist attraction in the nation's capital."[14] Even in periods of financial austerity, it is not uncommon to observe administrators in public agencies remodeling offices, adding new furniture, replacing carpeting, and so on.

Another way to maintain agency growth is to expand the bureau's jurisdiction or to maintain a service after the reason for the service no longer exists. Thus, there tends to be a ratchet effect that leads to growth of government agencies regardless of changes in economic conditions. It is predictable that decision makers in the political arena will not passively accept measures that increase competition or reduce the scope for collective choice. Thus, it is not surprising that Ronald Reagan's 1980 presidential campaign promise to abolish the Departments of Education and Energy was not kept. There is a vast group of administrators and employees who have a vested interest in maintaining and increasing the scope of activities of existing agencies.

It should be noted that agency decision making operates within the Congressional-bureaucratic system discussed above. Consequently, agency bureaucrats are, at least to some extent, beholden to a small number of congressmen sitting on the relevant oversight committees. Since congressmen having the most power over any particular bureau or agency evaluate the agency's performance through listening to their constituents, there are pressures for agencies to serve Congressional interests.[15]

Government Failure

A number of general shortcomings of the political process have already been discussed in contrasting private and collective choice (chapter 3).

Consider now some of the things that can go wrong in the political process itself. There is "government failure" at each stage of the collective-choice process.

Voting

A problem arises in delegating choice. Citizens do not usually vote directly on government policies. Instead, they vote for delegates who make policy choices. However, these delegates are elected on an infrequent basis—every two years in the House and every six years in the Senate. Thus, limited voting options erode the control of citizens over delegates.

There is also a bundling of issues in the electoral process as the same representative takes positions on many different issues. This bundling of issues poses a problem for the voter. A particular citizen, for example, may prefer the Republican candidate's position on national defense and the Democratic candidate's position on agriculture.

Political competition is highly imperfect. Candidates are tied to political parties and face pressures to run on the party platform. The situation with two major parties is analogous to duopoly in the market where there are only two sellers of a product. In contrast, the ideal political democracy would be perfectly responsive to the "will of the people." That is, there would be no problems because of lack of information, uncertainty, delegation of choice, and so on.

Problems also arise because democratic systems operate on the basis of majority rule. Political decisions are not consistent with the Pareto criterion because they always leave a minority of the electorate dissatisfied. Moreover, once a political decision is made, the same amount of the good or service is typically available to everyone regardless of differences in individual preferences. If everyone is provided, or is taxed to provide, a given amount of a specific good or service such as national defense or public education, many people will be frustrated. Log rolling, one way to take into account the intensity of minority preferences, is a very imprecise means to express the intensities of voter preferences. It should again be noted that the collective-choice process is fundamentally different from the market process in the ability to cater to minority tastes. In private choice, an individual is generally able to satisfy his preferences insofar as his budget permits, even though his tastes are markedly different from those of the average person.

Responsible Participation

There are also fewer incentives for responsible behavior in the political arena. We, as individuals, tend to act most responsibly when acting on our own behalf within well-defined property rights and liability rules. As a result, we are likely to spend more time in the process of purchasing an automobile than in investigating candidates before voting in a legislative,

Congressional, or presidential race. There is a good reason for doing so. The effort spent in investigating cars will likely make more difference to our own welfare than the time spent in finding out about various political candidates. Whereas a voter may rationally remain ignorant of political issues on the basis of narrowly defined costs and benefits, equivalent ignorance in market decisions is much more likely to impose severe penalties.

A comparison of private choice with the collective-choice process suggests that responsible behavior is closely related to the existence and enforcement of property rights. Nothing invites irresponsible conduct as much as resources "owned" by everyone—the common-property resource problem. This problem is inherent in government spending decisions. Since voters, politicians, and bureaucrats are engaged in spending the money of others, there is little incentive to economize. This problem is illuminated by the principle: *Nobody spends somebody else's money as carefully as he spends his own.*[16] This suggests that it may be advisable to extend property rights into areas that are now treated as communal property.[17]

Short-Run Focus of the Political Process

The long run for the politician (and for many bureaucrats) is the next election. Herman Talmadge, who served for ten years as Chairman of the Senate Agriculture Committee, graphically describes the short-run nature of the political process: "Most politicians live and breathe 24 hours a day in the hope of getting re-elected. They're politically motivated. Re-election means more to them than anything on the face of the earth except a death in their immediate families. And sometimes I think that if the family's not too close, the family would be secondary."[18]

The short-run nature of the political process explains the preference of politicians for programs where the benefits are immediate and the costs are deferred. It is politically unpopular, for example, to enact policies that would balance the federal budget. The costs of doing so are immediate while the benefits occur in the long run when current incumbents may be out of office. Similarly, programs to reduce benefit levels of Social Security, agricultural price supports, or other programs are considered to be politically unfeasible, especially in an election year. Indeed, as shown below, it is much more likely that incumbent politicians will attempt to manipulate government policies for short-run political purposes. The conclusion is that the quest for votes encourages politicians to take a short-run perspective. Consequently, there is no assurance that any non-optimal provision of public goods due to "market failure" will be solved through collective action. Instead, imperfections in the political process are likely to lead to too much of the goods and services being provided through the political process.

There is also evidence that the short-run focus of the political process creates economic instability. After analyzing elections from 1947 to 1976, Edward Tufte found a two-year political business cycle during which real income growth increased in eight of eleven election years as a result of increases in transfer payments. Tufte concludes that incumbent administrations manipulate short-run government policies affecting Social Security, veterans benefits, and so on in attempts to influence upcoming elections.[19] As shown in later chapters, short-run political considerations also loom large in the administration of agricultural programs.

Although the incentive structure of the political process quite often works against actions by politicians and bureaucrats that are in the best interest of the public at large, there is another reason why public officials do not act in the "public interest." It is impossible for any public official to do so, as previously indicated, because of limits on his information and conflicting interests of others. This leads even the most selfless decision maker in the political process to choose some feasible lower-level goal such as budget maximization.

Rationale for Economic Regulation

The problem of meaningfully defining the public "interest" is closely related to that of determining the rationale for government intervention. There is no consensus concerning the reasons for economic regulation by government. The conventional view has been that economic regulation in agriculture and other areas is instituted to protect the "public interest." This explanation does not appear to be valid for many programs in agriculture and other areas which benefit the few at the expense of many.

The "capture theory" is a distinctly different theory of economic regulation.[20] This theory holds that economic regulation is sought and initiated by the industry being regulated as a way to restrict competition and increase income. The capture theory appears to be relevant for much of the economic regulation initiated during the New Deal era by agencies such as the USDA and the Interstate Commerce Commission (ICC). However, it does not appear to be very helpful in explaining the spate of safety and environmental regulations instituted during the 1970s, including the Occupational Safety and Health Administration (OSHA) and the Environmental Protection Agency (EPA).

Conclusion

All of the preceding factors responsible for "government failure" can be traced to the two previously mentioned general problems inherent in the collective-choice process (see chapter 3). These problems warrant more emphasis. First, there are *incentive problems* caused by the *separation of power and responsibility*. Public officials are unlikely to economize because they neither bear the full costs nor reap the full benefits of their decisions. Cost saving, for example, is likely to adversely affect the public-agency decision maker's income and power. Thus, there is not the incentive to economize that is found under private ownership. Another frequently observed action resulting from perverse incentives is the mad scramble to exhaust the supply budget of a public agency near the end of the fiscal year. The budget in this case is treated as a common pool resource. "A common pool resembles one soda being consumed by several small boys each with a straw. The 'rule of capture' is in effect: ownership of the liquid is not established until it is in one's possession."[21]

This discussion is restricted to legal responses to economic incentives by public officials. As government grows, the opportunities and incentives for corruption also increase.[22]

Second, there are also *information* problems due to the *separation of power and knowledge*. Even if government agencies were run by selfless public servants dedicated to serving the public interest, they would be unable to do so. The secretary of agriculture, for example, has no objective way to determine the correct price support level for milk or the optimal amount of lending by the Farmers Home Administration (FmHA). These are income redistribution programs and, consequently, there is no value-free means to determine how much income should be redistributed—that is, how extensive and costly these and similar programs should be inevitably involves value judgments.

Improving the Collective-Choice Process

Recent presidents have attempted to make the federal bureaucracy more responsive to their administrations' policy agendas but have had little success. Many programs are mandated by Congress and beyond the immediate control of the president. Further, a president does not have the time to monitor the actions of the vast federal bureaucracy involving more than two thousand agencies. Thus bureaucrats are usually left largely on their own if they do not draw too much attention. Although no reform can eliminate the incentive and information problems inherent in government bureaus, there is increasing interest in possible measures to reduce the magnitude of these problems. "Privatization" refers to a range of measures designed to increase the role of market forces in the delivery of goods and services currently financed, produced, or regulated by government. The most common types of privatization involve contracting out or franchise arrangements, user charges, and so called load shedding in which government bows out and allows private producers to produce and offer goods and services directly to consumers. There is evidence that user fees, franchises, contracting out, and other privatization measures can improve current methods of financing and producing collectively provided goods and services.[23] However, none of these limited privatization procedures provide the incentive and informational advantages of production under decentralized competitive conditions.

Summary

Public-choice theory involves the use of economic principles to explain political decisions. Economic costs and benefits are important in decisions by the individual voter, by political candidates, by legislators, by the executive, and by the bureaucracy which administers and implements the laws enacted by the legislature. Just as markets work imperfectly compared to the ideal of perfect competition, the political process also "fails" when compared to the perfect polity.

Public-choice theory demonstrates why majority rule in a democracy does not guarantee results that are consistent with individual preferences. In voting, political competition is highly imperfect because of information problems, uncertainty, and delegation of choice. There is a short-run bias in the political process in favor of programs where benefits are immediate and costs are deferred. Finally, there are inherent information and incentive problems in the collective-choice process. Whereas price and profit signals induce economizing behavior by consumers and producers in decentralized markets, there are no comparable signals in public agencies. Votes and bureaucratic inducements provide no reliable signals concerning how much to produce or whether production is beneficial. The conclusion is that the presence of "market imperfections" including externalities, monopoly, lack of information, and public goods does not necessarily warrant government intervention. The relevant choice is always between imperfect institutional arrangements.

The theory of public choice emphasizes that problems similar to those affecting private choice are no less important in the collective-choice process. Furthermore, in the public sector there is no one in authority who personally gains by using resources in ways that are most beneficial to the public at large. The absence of residual claimants in government and the incentive to cater to special interest groups give rise to rent-seeking activities by individuals and groups with narrowly focused interests. There is increasing interest in contracting out, user charges, and other "privatization" measures as a means of reducing the magnitude of problems associated with the production and financing of goods and services that are provided through the collective-choice process.

Notes

1. For a good introduction to public-choice theory see James Gwartney and Richard E. Wagner, "The Public Choice Revolution," *The Intercollegiate Review* 23 (Spring 1988): 17–26.

2. Peter H. Aranson, *American Government: Strategy and Choice* (Cambridge, Mass.: Winthrop, 1981), p. 18.

3. Ronald D. Knutson, J. B. Penn, and W. T. Boehm, *Agricultural and Food Policy* (Englewood Cliffs, N. J.: Prentice-Hall, 1983), chap. 3.

4. Bernard Grofman, "Models of Voter Turnout: A Brief Idiosyncratic Review," *Public Choice* 41 (1983): 57.

5. Aranson, *American Government: Strategy and Choice*, p. 243.

6. Ibid., pp. 250–54.

7. William S. Maddox and Stuart A. Lilie, *Beyond Liberal and Conservative: Reassessing the Political Spectrum* (Washington, D.C.: The Cato Institute, 1984).

8. Aranson, *American Government: Strategy and Choice*, p. 356.

9. Source: Knutson, Penn, and Boehm, *Agricultural and Food Policy*, pp. 41–42.

10. Barry R. Weingast, "The Congressional-Bureaucratic System: A Principal Agent Perspective (with Applications to the SEC)," *Public Choice* 44 (1984): 147–91.

11. Ibid., p. 155.

12. Aranson, *American Government: Strategy and Choice*, p. 446.

13. William A. Niskanen, Jr., *Bureaucracy and Representative Government* (Chicago: Aldine-Atherton, 1971), p. 39.

14. James T. Bennett and T. J. Dilorenzo, *Underground Government: The Off-Budget Public Sector* (Washington, D.C.: The Cato Institute, 1983), p. 5.

15. Barry R. Weingast, "The Congressional-Bureaucratic System," pp. 149–50.

16. William C. Mitchell, "Fiscal Behavior of the Modern Democratic State: Public Choice Perspectives and Contributions," in *Political Economy*, ed. Larry C. Wade (Boston: Kluwer-Nijhoff, 1983), p. 89.

17. William C. Mitchell, "Efficiency, Responsibility, and Democratic Politics," in *Liberal Democracy*, ed. J. R. Pennock and J. W. Chapman (New York: New York University Press, 1983), p. 346.

18. Herman E. Talmadge, "Political Realities Affecting Agricultural Legislation," in *Farm and Food Policy: Critical Issues for Southern Agriculture*, ed. M. D. Hammig and H. M. Harris, Jr. (Proceedings of a Symposium, Clemson University, 2–3 June 1983), p. 85.

19. Edward R. Tufte, *Political Control of the Economy* (Princeton, N.J.: Princeton University Press, 1978).

20. George S. Stigler, "The Theory of Economic Regulation," *Bell Journal of Economics and Management Science* 2 (Spring 1971): 3–21.

21. Richard Stroup and John Baden, "Property Rights and Natural Resource Management," *Literature of Liberty* 2 (September–December 1979): 12.

22. Bruce Benson and John Baden, "The Political Economy of Governmental Corruption: The Logic of Underground Government," *Journal of Legal Studies* 14 (June 1985): 391–410.

23. E. S. Savas, *Privatizing the Public Sector* (Chatham, N.J.: Chatham House, 1982).

5

Implications of Public-Choice Theory for Agricultural Policy

Government policy in U.S. agriculture has changed dramatically over time. During the first 150 years following our country's independence, the federal government had relatively little influence on the production and marketing of goods and services. However, there was a dramatic increase in economic regulation during the Great Depression of the 1930s. Why do the programs instituted in response to the economic crisis existing at that time continue today? An understanding of the operation of the political process is helpful in answering this question. It is assumed throughout this book that the public policy process in agriculture is not fundamentally different from that in other areas. In this chapter, public choice theory is related specifically to the development of U.S. agricultural policy, and it is shown why similar pressures exist to overspend on agricultural programs as for programs in other sectors of the economy.

The Changing Agricultural Agenda

Productivity was the dominant theme of public policies directly affecting agriculture during the latter half of the nineteenth century when several important pieces of legislation affecting agriculture were enacted. The creation of the USDA in 1862 raised agriculture to cabinet status at the federal level. The Morrill Act of 1862 created the land grant college complex. The Hatch Act of 1887 provided funds to each state for agricultural research leading to the system of state agricultural experiment stations. The Smith-Lever Act of 1914 created the cooperative federal-state Agricultural Extension Service, and the Smith-Hughes Act of 1917 provided federal support for the teaching of vocational agriculture in high schools.

Prior to the Roosevelt administration in the 1930s, government programs in agriculture were small and seldom directly affected the individual farmer. Federal intervention in agriculture, however, increased dramatically during the Great Depression as President Roosevelt launched a host of "action programs" in agriculture, most of which are still in existence. The nature and effects of the various price support, production

49

control, credit subsidy, crop insurance, conservation, and other farm programs initiated at that time are the major focus of this work.

What brings about changes in the agricultural public policy agenda? A dramatic change in public policy is typically associated with an economic crisis. The "emergency" label was attached to almost every piece of early New Deal legislation enacted during the economic chaos of the Great Depression.[1]

Periodically new groups also arise to challenge the status quo. The challenge is often in the form of some attention-getting event or action. The modern environmental movement, for example, can be traced to the publication of Rachel Carson's book, *Silent Spring*, in the early 1960s. Again, the "hunger lobby" in the 1960s was important in increasing funds for food stamp and other food assistance programs.

Prior to the 1960s, the agricultural policy agenda was dominated by commercial agricultural interests. Since that time, traditional farm programs have been challenged by many groups including rural nonfarm residents, the poverty lobby, hired farm workers, minority groups, consumers, safety advocates, and environmentalists. The large increase in government expenditures for food stamp and other transfer programs and for safety, environmental, and civil rights legislation since the mid-1960s is a reflection of the effectiveness of these various groups in the public-policy process. During this period, many new programs affecting agriculture were enacted outside the usual agricultural policy process. Pesticide regulations, for example, were removed to a new agency, the Environmental Protection Agency (EPA). Agricultural safety became the concern of the Occupational Safety and Health Administration (OSHA). In addition, the interest of urban groups in agricultural programs increased as the food assistance portion of the USDA budget increased dramatically.

A model of the agricultural policy-making process is shown in Figure 5.1.[2] It emphasizes the fact that interest groups play an integral role in agricultural legislation.

There are several interest groups now heavily involved in determining the agenda for agricultural legislation.[3] First, there is the research and education movement which goes back to the pre–New Deal era. The USDA and state experiment stations associated with the land grant colleges are an important force. The public and private research establishment has a huge stake in agricultural research and in assessing the costs and benefits of various programs. The network of extension workers in every state associated with the land grant colleges is also important in maintaining support for the continuation and increase of government research, education, and extension efforts in agriculture.

Second, there are the groups supporting the price support, production control, and other farm programs inherited from the New Deal era. In this movement, individual commodity groups (e.g., the American Soybean Association) and farm organizations (e.g., the American Farm Bureau

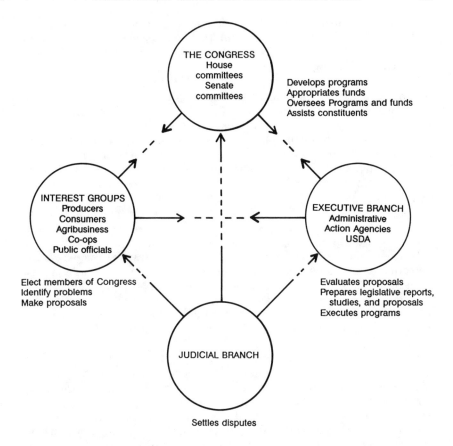

Figure 5.1. Model of the agricultural policy-making process.

Federation) continue to play important roles. Numerous political action committees (PACs) augment these professional farm groups which also frequently engage in lobbying activities.

Third, agribusiness groups, including farm supply and marketing cooperatives, are important political forces in maintaining government programs that stimulate farm production and thereby create a demand for their products and services.

Fourth, the network of county Agricultural Stabilization and Conservation Service (ASCS) offices which administer the price support and other farm programs is also important in ensuring grass-roots support for government intervention in agriculture.

A fifth group consisting of individuals interested in food stamps, environmental controls, and other consumer issues is also important in the legislative process affecting farm policies. Don Paarlberg coined the term "new agenda" to indicate this relatively new influence of small farmers, farm workers, the poor, racial minorities, consumers, and environmentalists, which he attributed to various "public-interest" advocates.[4] This group has a vast clientele and significant political clout as evidenced by the large increases in public expenditures on consumer, environmental, and poverty programs during the past twenty years. The impact of this group on the USDA agenda has increased at the expense of commercial agriculture. As one example, USDA expenditures for subsidized food programs have increased dramatically since the mid-1960s, in relative terms, when contrasted with outlays on price supports and other programs that more directly benefit commercial agriculture.

Finally, consumer and other groups that might be considered to represent the public at large are becoming more vocal. There is an increasing recognition that farm programs affecting wheat, corn, milk, peanuts, oranges, and other commodities benefit producer groups at the expense of consumers and taxpayers. Price support programs, as shown later, raise domestic prices of farm products and require import controls to prevent U.S. consumers from purchasing lower-priced imports. Domestic manufacturers who use price-supported products such as feed grains, peanuts, sugar, and so on as inputs in production are also frequently critical of farm programs.

In recent farm bills, vote trading between agricultural and urban interests has become more important. Agricultural interests have supported food stamps, minimum wages, solar energy development in agriculture, and other projects in exchange for urban backing for price supports and other farm programs. Despite the decrease in numbers of farms, commercial agricultural interests continue to get price support programs enacted that transfer income to them through government payments or higher product prices to consumers. The current political clout of the farm sector is surprising when it is realized that only about 3 percent of the population lives on farms. Moreover, the dairy, tobacco, sugar, wool, and several other price support programs only apply to a small section of the total farm population. How are these relatively small groups of farmers able to use government for their own ends?

Bias of Collective-Choice Process in Agriculture

In the previous chapter, it was shown why there is generally a systematic bias toward expansion of the role of government. The political process is oriented toward the short run and each government official has an incentive to maintain and increase the scope of his or her own agency. Moreover, the political process is biased in favor of activities which confer concentrated benefits on the few and impose widely dispersed and (often delayed) costs on the many. This description of the collective-choice process appears to be consistent with current agricultural programs.

Agribusiness

Consider the farmers and agribusiness groups who benefit from government programs affecting sugar, dairy, wheat, feed grains, tobacco, and other products.[5] When economic benefits to a small group can be achieved through political action, that group has an economic incentive to use the political process to obtain wealth transfers. For example, contributions by PACs to incumbent congressmen appear to have played an important role in the enactment of the Dairy and Tobacco Adjustment Act of 1983. Regardless of the reason for the enactment of this specific act, there is no doubt about the effectiveness of dairy producers, tobacco producers, peanut producers, and other groups in maintaining and expanding the role of government in agriculture.

The assistance provided by government to well-organized groups may occur in a number of different ways, including price supports, subsidies, tax relief, and protection from competition. The major types of government farm programs are described in later chapters. Product price supports are the most costly farm program in terms of government treasury outlays. However, it should be noted that there is a significant sector of agriculture, including many fruits and vegetables, poultry and livestock, in which there are no effective price support programs. This largely unregulated sector of agriculture accounts for about half to two thirds of U.S. farm production. Public-choice theory has been quite successful in explaining how small groups of agricultural producers are able to use the political process to increase their own wealth. This theory is much less useful in explaining why a sizable proportion of U.S. farmers and commodity groups have made little effort to restrict competition through political action.

The USDA

The USDA, a component of the executive branch of government, is a second important interest group directly involved in the policy process. The USDA is generally expected to represent farmers instead of the public at large. Indeed, the USDA mainly represented commercial farmers before and after World War II until the late 1960s. Since that time, the influence of consumer, environmental, and other groups on USDA policy has increased at the expense of commercial agriculture. In the Carter administration (1977–1980), the USDA actively cultivated the support of groups "favoring better nutrition, environmental protection and rural community development."[6] Regardless of the relative strength of the different groups influencing USDA activities, decision makers in the USDA have an incentive to expand the agency's role since salaries, power, and perquisites tend to be positively correlated with agency size. Consequently, USDA officials predictably seek to expand the range and scope of the agency's activities.

Congressional Committees

The legislative committees of Congress are a third interest group directly involved in the agricultural policy process. Farm state legislators tend to dominate the agricultural committees and subcommittees. Members of these committees tend to favor expanded government programs both because they typically represent districts where the commodities affected are important and because expanded programs increase their power and importance. This is not merely a matter of conscious wealth seeking or aggrandizement of power. Members of special interest groups generally have the ability to rationalize whatever is in their own interest as being also in the "public interest." Thus the tobacco program or the dairy program comes to be viewed by program proponents in tobacco and dairy production areas as beneficial to the legislator's own district and, indeed, to the entire nation. In addition to farm groups, the USDA, and congressional committees, various environmental and consumer groups also actively participate in the legislative process when proposed agricultural legislation impinges on food stamps, environmental issues, or other areas of concern.

The Breakdown of Budget Discipline

There is increasing public concern about the breakdown in budget discipline at the federal level and the huge federal budget deficits. The federal budget has been operating chronically in the red, with a surplus only in one year between 1964 and 1987. The federal budget deficit was $79 billion in 1981, $128 billion in 1982 and about $200 billion each year from 1983 to 1986.[7] These budget deficits occurred despite the adoption of a new budget process by Congress in 1974. This process consists of a budget resolution which sets the annual spending level based on revenue estimates, and "budget reconciliation," the process by which Congress presumably stays within the spending ceiling. Unfortunately, the process has not worked well, as evidenced by the huge federal deficits. Indeed, government expenditures increased from 22.1 percent of GNP in 1980 to 23.8 percent of GNP in 1986, suggesting that the Reagan administration was not successful in its attempt to reduce spending by the federal government.[8]

The budget deficits have occurred as government transfers have become more and more important. During the past fifty years, there has been a dramatic increase in the efforts by individuals and groups to obtain and maintain wealth transfers under the aegis of the state.[9] On the other hand, there has been a relative decrease in efforts devoted by individuals to production. This phenomenon is not restricted to agriculture. The dairy program, for example, is similar in this respect to a host of other programs including education subsidies, auto import quotas, and food assistance programs.

In achieving their objectives, groups use their lobbying power to influence governmental policy, thereby bringing about an increase in the complexity and scope of government. Mancur Olson argues that the effect of the increase in transfer-seeking activities by specialized pressure groups is gradually to strangle the economy.[10] Moreover, as special-interest groups become more important and distributional issues more significant, political life tends to be more divisive. These efforts by specialized pressure groups to achieve wealth transfers have intensified since the mid-1960s. The effect of these efforts on the political system is graphically described by F. A. Hayek: "So long as it is legitimate for government to use force to effect a redistribution of material benefits . . . there can be no curb on the rapacious instincts of all groups who want more for themselves. Once politics becomes a tug-of-war for shares of the income pie, decent government is impossible."[11]

Federal expenditures have also increased dramatically in agriculture; in fact during the 1980s USDA expenditures increased faster than federal expenditures generally. Outlays for price-stabilization programs alone increased from $4 billion in 1980 to some $26 billion in 1986. The ballooning treasury outlays in agriculture and other areas has created interest in ways to offset the inherent bias toward increasing government expenditures. The basic problem is that political decision makers have an incentive to treat the budget as a common-pool resource, which creates fiscal irresponsibility. The following analogy of the federal budget to a dinner check demonstrates the overspending bias inherent in the collective-choice process.[12]

The Federal Budget as a Common-Pool Resource

Suppose one hundred people go out to eat. Compare the likely behavior of each individual under two different situations. In the first procedure, each person pays his own bill; in the second the bill is divided evenly. Each individual has an incentive to spend more in the latter case since eating a one-dollar dessert under the check-splitting arrangement, for example, would cost the individual only one cent (rather than one dollar). This check-splitting arrangement in the collective-choice process leads to "pork-barrel" legislation in agriculture and other areas. Since the amount a legislative district will pay toward a dairy price-support program (or other federally funded project) is very small relative to its total cost, every representative in Congress has an incentive to obtain income transfers for farmers (and other special-interest groups) in his or her legislative district.

The analogy of the federal budget to a dinner check can be carried one step further. Suppose the check is to be divided evenly among the large group but the ordering will be done by committee so there will be separate committees for drinks, appetizers, entrees, salads, and desserts. Since each person is able to serve on the committee of his (or her) choice, lushes end up on the drinks committee, vegetarians on the salad committee, sweet-tooths on the dessert committee, and so on.[13] This arrangement further exacerbates the tendency toward overordering and overspending. The arrangement just described closely resembles the committee structure of the U.S. Congress.

The analogy of the federal budget to a dinner check is even closer if one assumes that the diner can use a special type of credit card in which the bill does not have to be paid if the diner loses his job or retires.[14] "Buy now—pay later" is very appealing to the representative primarily concerned with getting re-elected. The conclusion is that spreading the costs in small shares while concentrating benefits creates incentives for the continued expansion of government activity. As suggested earlier, the collective-choice process necessarily produces majorities and minorities, losers and winners, and a separation of cost and benefit calculations.

The congressional reforms of the 1970s which increased the powers of narrowly focused subcommittees of Congress have contributed to the problem of overspending. The powerful, narrowly focused subcommittees in agriculture (and other areas) encourage lobbying by commodity groups. The House Subcommittee for Livestock, Dairy and Poultry, for example, has maintained high dairy price supports in the face of a glut of surplus dairy products.

Reducing the Overspending Bias

What is the solution to this systematic bias toward expansion of the role of government in agriculture (and other areas)? Some political analysts view basic institutional and constitutional change as the only appropriate avenue for constructive reform and improvement.[15] Others deny the effectiveness of institutional and constitutional changes, contending instead that the problem is political.[16]

James Buchanan, a leading proponent of the constitutional approach, assumes that the rules of politics matter and that these rules determine the pattern of outcomes "almost independently of whom we may elect and who writes position papers offering policy advice."[17] In the constitutionalist approach, a necessary prerequisite to reform is to develop a wider recognition of the effects of organized groups that use governmental power to enhance their own wealth. The failure of a specific farm program, for example, will only rarely lead to its abandonment, since it will always be supported by one or more vociferous interest groups which benefit from the program. Hayek graphically describes the eventual result of these redistributive activities that result in an overspending bias. This trend of a continuing and progressive rise of the share of income controlled by government, "if allowed to continue, would before long swallow up the whole of society in the organization of government."[18]

Hayek's analysis is consistent with Olson's hypothesis that the re-distribution costs associated with the increase in specialized pressure groups as they expend resources to obtain and maintain government transfers is a key factor in the declining growth rate of nations.[19] Conse-quently, it might be argued that education is a necessary and sufficient condition to achieve meaningful reductions in government spending. Indeed, it is argued by some analysts that public recognition of the problem and public pressure for action are enough to eliminate chronic budget deficits.[20]

Even if the harmful long-run effects of efforts by individuals and groups to achieve income transfers are fully recognized, however, there is a "you-first" problem in limiting government activity. The dairy farmer, for exam-ple, is generally reluctant to start the process, even if recognizing the desirability of limiting transfer activity. As is the case for all other recip-ients of government largesse, the dairy farmer has an incentive to take the position: "I will give up my government aid if the aid to other groups also stops." But no one has an incentive to be first.[21] Indeed, the dairy farmer has an economic incentive to attempt to maintain the dairy program while favoring a reduction in the transfers received by steel workers, textile workers, school teachers, and other groups. The federal budget problem may eventually become so great, however, that the individual dairy farmer or other transfer recipient will agree to constitutional limits to programs benefiting him or her if others will also agree to do so.[22]

An analysis of different methods of limiting the harmful effects of narrowly focused interest groups in agriculture (and other areas) is be-yond the scope of this study. However, various constitutional measures, including a balanced-budget amendment, have been proposed to reduce the bias toward overspending by the federal government.[23] Constitutional restrictions affecting government spending might have an important psy-chological impact on members of Congress. Such measures however, are no panacea, since legislators are likely to find ways, such as off-budget spending, around statutory and constitutional roadblocks. As one ob-server noted, "The proposed statutes setting limits on expenditures . . . all have a glaring political weakness. Congress can, if it wishes, waive or override them."[24]

It is also possible that institutional changes in the congressional com-mittee system would be helpful in reducing the current bias which favors the interests of highly-organized small groups at the expense of the public at large. A system of random or rotating committee assignments in Con-gress, for example, is one possible change. Under a system of rotating committee assignments it would be less likely that dairy, tobacco, or other narrow interests would be able to use the political process to achieve programs that benefit the few at the expense of the many. Granting the president line-item veto power is another possible means of reducing the harmful effects of vote trading and "pork-barrel" legislation. However, by strengthening the power of the executive branch, this institutional change might enlarge the scope of government.[25] In sum, there is no consensus concerning the extent to which the spending and deficit problem is institutional and constitutional as opposed to political and educational.

Summary

Agricultural policies arise through the interaction of the three branches of government. However, public policies in agriculture have changed dramatically over time. From 1862 until the 1930s, the major goal of government efforts in agriculture was to increase productivity. During the Great Depression of the 1930s, a host of "action programs" was instituted in the midst of economic chaos. From the USDA's inception in 1862 until the mid-1960s, commercial agriculture dominated the agenda in federal agricultural policy. Since the mid-1960s, the influence of groups concerned about poverty, environmental, and safety issues has increased at the expense of farmers' and agribusiness interests.

There is a systematic bias toward expansion of the role of government in agriculture as in other areas. The interaction of interests from commercial agriculture, the USDA, and the legislative committees in the Congress tend to advance the interests of narrowly focused groups at the expense of the public at large. This phenomenon in agriculture and in other areas has led to a dramatic increase in government spending and rapidly increasing federal budget deficits.

Some political analysts contend that the solution to the overspending problem is institutional, while others contend that public education holds the key. Even if the public understands the problem, however, the incentive to overspend remains. A number of institutional and constitutional remedies have been proposed to offset the overspending bias at the federal level. At the legislative level, random or rotating committee assignments might be one way to reduce the influence of commodity groups on agricultural legislation. At the executive level, giving the president the power of line item veto might reduce the amount of pork-barrel and other spending that is not broadly beneficial. Finally, a constitutional limit on government spending such as the widely discussed balanced-budget amendment has been proposed as a way of limiting government expenditures.

It is not clear how effective any of these measures would be in limiting overall spending, or what the effect on specific programs would be. Indeed, it has been argued that representative democracy under majority rule is not likely to produce what the majority wants.[26] Rather it tends to produce what each of the interest groups making up the majority must concede to the others to get their support for what it wants itself. Despite the lack of consensus about the nature of the problem, interest is likely to remain high concerning possible ways of reducing the effects of narrowly focused special interests on the democratic process.

Notes

1. Robert Higgs, *Crisis and Leviathan: Critical Episodes in the Growth of American Government* (New York: Oxford University Press, 1987), p. 171.

2. Ronald D. Knutson, J. B. Penn, and W. T. Boehm, *Agricultural and Food Policy* (Englewood Cliffs, N.J.: Prentice-Hall, 1983), p. 36.

3. Don Paarlberg, "A New Agenda for Agriculture," chap. 12 in *The New Politics of Food*, ed. D. F. Hadwiger and W. P. Browne (Lexington, Mass.: D. C. Heath, 1978).

4. Ibid.

5. George P. Schultz, "Reflections on Political Economy," selection 32 in *The Economic Approach to Public Policy*, ed. R. C. Amacher, R. D. Tollison, and T. D. Willett (Ithaca, N.Y.: Cornell University Press, 1978).

6. Don F. Hadwiger, "Agricultural Policy," chap. 21 in *Encyclopedia of Policy Studies*, ed. Stuart S. Nagel (New York: Marcel Dekker, 1983), p. 513.

7. Office of Management and Budget, *Historical Tables: Budget of the United States Government, Fiscal Year 1988* (Washington, D.C.: U.S. Government Printing Office, 1987), p. 15.6(2).

8. Ibid., 15, table 3(2).

9. Edwin S. Mills, *The Burden of Government* (Stanford, Calif.: Hoover Institution Press, 1986).

10. Mancur Olson, *The Rise and Decline of Nations* (New Haven: Yale University Press, 1982).

11. F. A. Hayek, *Law, Legislation and Liberty*, vol. 3: *The Political Order of a Free People* (Chicago: University of Chicago Press, 1979), p. 150.

12. Richard H. Thaler, "Illusions and Mirages in Public Policy," *The Public Interest* (Fall 1983): 60–74.

13. Ibid.

14. Ibid.

15. James M. Buchanan, "Alternative Perspectives on Economics and Public Policy," *Cato Policy Report* 6 (January 1984): 1–5.

16. Norman J. Ornstein, "The Politics of the Deficit," chap. 11 in *Essays in Contemporary Economic Problems 1985: The Economy in Deficit* (Washington, D.C.: American Enterprise Institute, 1985).

17. Buchanan, "Alternative Perspectives," p. 5.

18. F. A. Hayek, *The Essence of Hayek*, ed. C. Nishiyama and K. Leube (Stanford, Calif.: Hoover University Press, 1984), p. 404.

19. Olson, *Rise and Decline of Nations*, p. 109.

20. Ornstein, *Politics of the Deficit*, p. 333.

21. Terry L. Anderson and Peter J. Hill, *The Birth of a Transfer Society* (Stanford, Calif.: Hoover Institution Press, 1980), p. 93.

22. James M. Buchanan, *Freedom in Constitutional Contract: Perspectives of a Political Economist* (College Station: Texas A & M University Press, 1977).

23. Richard B. McKenzie, ed., *Constitutional Economics: Containing the Economic Powers of Government* (Lexington, Mass.: D. C. Heath, 1984).

24. Dennis S. Ippolito, *Congressional Spending* (Ithaca, N.Y.: Cornell University Press, 1981), p. 250.

25. Ornstein, "The Politics of the Deficit," p. 331.

26. F. A. Hayek, *Law, Legislation and Liberty*, vol. 3, p. 134.

6

The Farm Problem and Economic Justice

Historically, the farm problem has been considered to be one of relatively low incomes and farm product prices. In large measure, the farm problem can be traced to the destabilizing effects of economic growth. During most of the past two hundred years the manufacturing and service sectors of the U.S. economy have been growing relative to agriculture. Since agricultural wage rates increased less rapidly than wage rates in the nonfarm sector, it is not surprising that agricultural interests perceived this difference as a "farm problem." Indeed, over the years many people have challenged the economic growth explanation of the farm problem, arguing that farm incomes are low because of a lack of "bargaining power."

There is also a great deal of interest in the concept of economic justice. The topic is ancient, but a number of economists and philosophers continue to work on the issue of how the economic pie *should* be divided. Some economists, recognizing that consumers are the main beneficiaries of agricultural progress, have argued for a general compensation policy to compensate farmers for losses associated with economic growth in the economy.[1] Before further consideration of problems relating to farm versus nonfarm income comparisons and economic justice, let us first consider two quite different explanations of the farm problem.

Economic Growth versus Market Power

There is a great deal of evidence that the farm problem is primarily due to economic growth.[2] Economic growth requires a shift of labor and other resources from agriculture to other sectors of the economy. In a market system, expected income is the primary means by which labor resources are allocated both within agriculture and between agriculture and other sectors. For resources to be bid away from agriculture in a decentralized market economy, it is necessary for incomes to be higher in nonagricultural sectors than in agriculture.

In U.S. agricultural programs, a great deal of effort has been devoted to

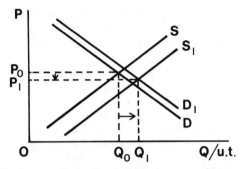

Figure 6.1. Why farm product prices tend to decrease with economic growth.

raising prices of farm products as a means of increasing farm incomes. With or without farm programs there has been chronic downward pressure on prices of farm products because supply tends to increase more rapidly than demand as economic growth occurs (figure 6.1). Mechanization, improved seeds, and the development of new pesticides and herbicides have increased supply through dramatic increases in agricultural technology. In 1950, farm employment was 9.9 million in a population of 152 million. By 1985, there were only 3.6 million farm workers in a population of 239 million.[3] The change in numbers of workers in nonfarm agribusiness firms providing inputs to agriculture and marketing farm products has been much less than the decrease in farm employment, but data on nonfarm agribusiness employment are not available. During the period from 1950 to 1980, farm numbers decreased from 5.4 million to 2.3 million, while average farm size increased from 215 to 445 acres per farm.[4]

The demand for farm products, which increases mainly due to increases in population and increases in consumer income, has not increased to the same extent as the supply of farm products. Demand increases due to population growth are gradual. Demand shifts due to increases in consumer income hinge on economic growth and the income elasticity of demand for farm products, which is low relative to that for nonfarm products. This suggests that a smaller and smaller part of the household budget will be spent on food as economic growth occurs.[5]

The demand for farm products at the farm level is also generally considered to be quite inelastic with respect to price, although the demand for a number of farm products is becoming more elastic as the export market for farm products increases in importance. The implications of this increase in elasticity of demand for domestic price-support programs are discussed in chapter 14. When demand is highly inelastic, a small increase in output can result in a large decrease in price. Moreover, the more inelastic is demand, the larger the price decrease when the supply of a product increases relative to demand. The combination of an inelastic demand for farm products and supply increasing faster than demand is important in any historical explanation of the U.S. "farm problem."

Market power has been suggested as an alternative explanation of the farm problem. The New Deal action programs of the 1930s were based on the idea that farmers are dispersed and weak while the rest of the economy is either monopolized, or has the ability to "administer" prices without regard to the basic underlying supply and demand conditions. It is sometimes held that farmers are at a disadvantage in terms of bargaining power within the agricultural sector, both in buying inputs and in selling farm products. Instead of attempting to increase competition among the allegedly monopolistic agribusiness firms, however, there was (and continues to be) a deliberate government policy of restricting competition in agricultural product markets. That is, government-organized producer cartels were formed to raise prices of cotton, tobacco, milk, peanuts, and other products above their competitive market-clearing levels.

In reality, the level of farm product prices in the absence of government programs has little if anything to do with lack of market power or bargaining power by farmers. As shown in chapter 7, the New Deal measures instituted to restrict competition were not limited to agriculture. That is, the concepts "market power" and "administered prices" in practice have little significance aside from prices set and/or enforced by government. The "free-rider" incentive is typically strong enough to negate the effects of voluntary cartels since each firm has an incentive to cheat on any voluntary agreement to restrict output as a means of increasing price.[6] Moreover, even if a group of sellers were able to effectively restrict production, price cannot be set independently of demand. In summary, the evidence does not support the market-power explanation of the farm problem.

Farm versus Nonfarm Incomes

The idea that wages should be equalized between different economic sectors is inconsistent with the role of price signals in a competitive market economy. If public policies were instituted to equalize wages in each sector for comparable units of labor, there would be little incentive for labor to adjust in response to changing economic conditions. Despite this fact, there has been, and continues to be, a great deal of interest in farm/nonfarm income comparisons. Although it is easy to make such comparisons, it is difficult to make them meaningful, as the following analysis shows.[7]

Why Do Incomes Vary?

In general, incomes vary between individuals due to differences in the quantity and quality of resources owned. Indeed, much of the observed

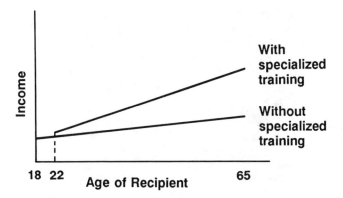

Figure 6.2. Incomes vary because of differences in education and experience.

variation in incomes can be explained by a life-cycle theory of education and job experience (figure 6.2). Individuals who invest in post–high school education expect to have a different time profile of income. Income is lower (or negative) during the training period, and then, on average, rises faster than the income of individuals not acquiring additional education and training. Thus, there will always be a "natural" amount of income inequality due to differences in age, education, and training.

Studies have shown that a great deal of the variation in incomes between individuals can be explained by the life-cycle model of income. Although cross-sectional studies show incomes to be highly unequal between individuals, these differences, to a considerable extent, reflect different positions of individuals in their lifetime income earning profile. The income of a recent college or university graduate, for example, is likely to be considerably less than the income of an individual with similar education who also has (say) twenty years experience (figure 6.2). Similarly, the income of the high school graduate at age forty-five is expected to be less, on average, than that of the college graduate. The observed income differences, however, tend to disappear when one takes into account the costs of education and the value of experience. Stated differently, much of the observed inequality in incomes which shows up at any given moment in time disappears when adjustments are made for differences in education, training, and experience.

Most income distribution data fail to take account of the dynamics that affect individual incomes over time. When these factors are taken into account, there is a remarkable degree of movement by individuals and families within the American income distribution even among the richest and poorest segments of the population. A study of changes in family incomes from 1971 to 1978 found that "only about half of the best-off Americans in 1971 were still the best-off in 1978, and only about half of the poorest Americans were still poor."[8] The study indicated that most

Table 6.1.   Median Money Income of Farm versus Nonfarm House-
              holds.

	1945	1955	1965	1975	1985	1986
Farm population ($/year)	1,291	2,111	4,122	10,845	21,903	23,650
Nonfarm population ($/year)	2,595	4,840	7,060	13,829	29,356	30,997
Farm as a percent of nonfarm	49.7	43.6	58.4	78.4	74.6	76.3

SOURCE: U.S. Department of Commerce: Bureau of the Census, Money Income and
Poverty Status of Families and Persons in the United States (Washington, D.C.: U.S.
Government Printing Office, various years).

significant income changes follow some major change in family situation
such as divorce, death, marriage, children leaving home, and so on. The
income streams of many people are characterized by years of high and low
earnings and sudden changes in family size. The conclusion is that static
distributions of income that do not take these factors into account are
likely to be highly misleading.

Comparing Farm and Nonfarm Incomes

Farm incomes, on average, appear to be somewhat lower than nonfarm
incomes. Median money income for the farm population was 76 percent
of that for the nonfarm population in 1986 (table 6.1). On the basis of this
measure, there has been a dramatic improvement in farm income since
1945 (table 6.1). There are a number of problems, however, in making
income comparisons of this type.

First, the concept of "average farm income" has little meaning since
income per farm operator family varies widely depending on farm size.
About half of all farms have sales of less than $10,000, and account for
only about 3 percent of total agricultural product sales (table 6.2). On the
other hand, the largest 4 percent of farms with annual sales of more than
$250,000 account for almost 50 percent of total agricultural product sales.
If the almost half of the farms that are noncommercial rural residences are
not counted as farms, the resulting income statistics would show the farm
sector to have higher incomes, on average, than the nonfarm population.[9]
On small farms, most family income is now derived from nonfarm
sources. In 1984, for example, farmers with farm sales of less than $20,000
per year, on average, obtained all of their disposable income from off-farm
sources.[10] The conclusion is that discussions of "average farm income"
are generally highly misleading because the farm is not the primary
source of income for many farmers, including most small farmers.

Second, any meaningful comparison of farm and nonfarm incomes must take differences in worker productivity due to differences in age, education, and experience into account. If these differences are not accounted for, observed income differences have little economic meaning. Income comparisons such as those presented in table 6.1 make no adjustments for these factors. Thus, it may be that much of the closing of the farm/nonfarm income gap over time is due to a relative increase in the productivity of farm workers.

Third, farming is capital-intensive and returns to farmers' business capital comprise a higher share of their "income" than for the nonfarm population. Much of this income is not included in USDA income statistics of the farm sector. During the inflationary conditions of the late 1970s, for example, owners of farm assets received huge increases in wealth as prices of land and other farm assets increased. During the 1980s, in contrast, owners of farm assets incurred losses in wealth as prices of farm real estate decreased by as much as 50 percent in some areas of the United States. A meaningful comparison of farm versus nonfarm incomes must take such changes in real wealth into account.

Fourth, cost of living and tax differences must be taken into account. Money incomes must be adjusted for differences in cost of living, capital gains, and taxes in making comparisons of real incomes for farmers versus nonfarmers. Generally, the real income level for a given money income is somewhat higher in rural areas because of income-tax advantages, including consumption of home-produced products. D. Gale Johnson has estimated that farm per capita disposable income of 75 to 80 percent of nonfarm income would provide an equivalent return to farm resources.[11]

Finally, nonpecuniary aspects of employment play an important role in the decisions of some farmers to enter or to continue farming. The satisfaction gained from working in the outdoors and of being one's own boss may be high enough to substitute for a substantial amount of money income.

When all of these factors are taken into account, there is no persuasive evidence that incomes are now lower in agriculture. Regardless of the

Table 6.2.   Farms and Production by Sales Class Groups, 1985

SIZE GROUP	SALES CLASSES	NUMBER OF FARMS	PERCENT OF PRODUCTION
Rural Residences	Less than $ 10,000	1,164,000	2.8
Small Family Farms	$ 10,000–$ 40,000	473,000	7.5
Family Farms	$ 40,000–$250,000	544,000	40.9
Large Family Farms	$250,000–$500,000	66,000	16.6
Very Large Farms	$500,000 and up	27,000	32.2

SOURCE: U.S. Department of Agriculture, *Economic Indicators of the Farm Sector, 1985* (Washington, D.C.: U.S. Government Printing Office, 1986).

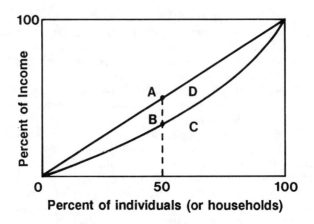

Figure 6.3. The Lorenz curve.

relative position of incomes in agriculture currently, attempts both now and in the past have been made to increase agricultural incomes by increasing farm product prices. The result of increasing incomes by agricultural price supports is predictable. When product prices are increased, small farmers are affected relatively little since the benefits of higher prices vary with sales. It has been estimated that the largest 10 percent of farms get more than half of the benefits of farm programs while the smallest 10 percent of the farms receive less than 10 percent.[12] Even though the effects of various government programs vary widely even for farms of a given size depending upon crops produced, the conclusion holds that large farms receive most of the short-run benefits.

Income Inequality and Economic Justice

Even if incomes are adjusted for differences in worker productivity due to age, education, and experience, income differences will remain.

The Lorenz Curve

The Lorenz curve is a technique providing information on the distribution of incomes, but it does not take these productivity differences into account (figure 6.3). In this approach, income recipients are ranked from lowest to highest, and against their cumulative number the cumulative percentage of income received is plotted.[13] The straight line from the southwest corner to the northeast corner of the rectangle represents a perfectly uniform distribution of income in the sense that every individual (or household) would have the same income. At point A, for example, 50 percent of the individuals get 50 percent of the income, or the division of the economic pie is perfectly equal. This, of course, is not what one expects to find in the real world. The actual distribution of incomes is consistent with a Lorenz curve convex to the southeast corner. In the unequal distribution of incomes depicted in figure 6.3, the lower 50 percent of individual income recipients get less than half of the income (point B).

The Gini coefficient (G) for a Lorenz curve is a measure of degree of inequality of income distribution.

$$G = \frac{\text{Area } D}{\text{Area } C + \text{Area } D}$$

The straighter the Lorenz curve, the closer G is to zero and the more equal incomes are. Where the necessary information is available to compute it, the Gini coefficient provides a measure of the equality of incomes.

A Lorenz-curve analysis was used in analyzing the distribution of direct payments in 1982 by farm size to producers for wheat, feed grains, and cotton. As expected where payments are related to output, the benefits accrued disproportionately to larger producers. The Gini ratios ranged from .458 for barley to .619 for cotton and averaged .596.[14]

It should be emphasized that a Gini coefficient provides no information as to whether incomes or farm income payments are different from what they should be. The problem of determining what incomes "should be" is essentially the same as that of describing the distribution of incomes consistent with "economic justice."

Economic Justice

The concept "economic justice" focuses on the question of what is meant by a "just" distribution of incomes. Much of the discussion about the distribution of incomes implicitly assumes that a more equal income distribution is more "just." If this were the case, the ideal would be a perfectly equal distribution of incomes. Such an ideal might be defensible in a world where goods and services did not have to be produced and the only economic problem was the distribution of goods and services. Indeed, much of the discussion of economic justice implicitly assumes that production and distribution are distinct economic activities so that income distribution has no influence on the production of goods and services. In reality, of course, production and distribution are not distinct activities but are instead integral parts of the same economic process. The way the economic pie is divided (the size of factor shares) has a crucial influence on the size of the economic pie (the amount of goods and services produced). What would happen to output, for example, if there were no connection between work and financial reward and if every worker were to receive the same income regardless of the amount of work done? The effect on output of goods and services is obvious. If the instructor announced on the first day of class that everyone would get the same grade regardless of class performance, how would the students' effort and incentives be affected? Few people would contend that a system where there is no connection between work and reward is just.

Although the term "economic justice" is widely used, F. A. Hayek concludes that the phrase has no meaning in a free society.[15] The fates of different individuals in a decentralized market economy do not conform to a generally acceptable principle of justice. That is, there are no rules of individual conduct yielding a pattern of incomes that would appear just, and there is no test by which we can determine what is "socially just." Consequently, the appeal to "economic justice" provides no guidance in deciding what the relative remunerations of a farmer, a lawyer, or the inventor of a life-saving drug should be.[16] Thus, the concept economic justice (or social justice) is empty in a competitive system where each person is allowed to use his own knowledge for his own purposes, since nobody's will can determine relative incomes or prevent them from being determined partly by accident. The belief that a just distribution of incomes can be objectively determined assumes away information problems and ignores the coordination and informational role of market prices.

Moreover, any attempt to impose anyone's concept of economic justice through the political system must conflict with economic freedom—the right of individuals to engage in mutually beneficial exchange. It is not possible to preserve the voluntary nature of the competitive system while imposing upon it some "socially just" pattern of remuneration by an authority with power to enforce it.[17]

The issue of "economic justice" is essentially the same as that of the "just" wage. Philosophers have struggled for centuries with the meaning of the concept of a "just" wage or income. The analogy between economic outcomes and games is helpful in thinking about "just" or "fair" incomes (or wages). The fairness of a game is typically evaluated on the basis of rules. If the rules of a game are clearly stated, known and accepted in advance, and impartially enforced, the outcome of the game is usually considered fair. Thus, the outcome of a game is not used as a test of the game's fairness. The fact that the Nebraska football team typically defeats most of its opponents, for example, does not suggest that the games it plays are unfair. Similarly, justice or fairness in the economic area should not be judged on the basis of economic outcomes. It can be argued that the outcome of the market process, as in the case of a game, is neither just nor unjust, because the results are not intended nor foreseen and depend on a multitude of circumstances not fully known by anyone. In another sense, wages and prices from decentralized competitive markets are "just" in the same sense that outcomes of fair games are just.[18] There is increasing interest by political economists and philosophers concerning the significance of "competitive" prices and the decentralized market system, both in the production of goods and services and in maintaining individual and political freedom.[19]

Summary

There are two competing explanations for the "farm problem": economic progress and a lack of bargaining power by farmers. The weight of the evidence suggests that the farm problem in the United States can be traced to economic growth. As economic growth occurs, agriculture decreases in importance relative to other sectors of the economy. Historically, higher incomes have been the means by which labor resources were bid away from agriculture in a developing economy. Increases in technology over time have also increased the supply of farm products more rapidly than demand, placing chronic downward pressure on farm product prices.

Although farm incomes in the United States have, on average, traditionally been low relative to nonfarm incomes, there is no consensus that farm incomes are lower today. Meaningful farm versus nonfarm income comparisons are difficult to make, because of differences in farm size, worker productivity, cost of living and tax differences, and nonpecuniary aspects of employment. Income equality does not imply "economic justice." While it is easy to determine that incomes of individuals vary widely, income differences do not necessarily imply that incomes are "unjust." Indeed, the concept of economic justice appears to have no precise meaning in a free society where individuals are able to use their resources for their own purposes. Moreover, it is not possible to preserve free markets while imposing upon it any "socially just" pattern of remuneration.

Much of the discussion related to differences in individual incomes assumes that production and distribution are separate and distinct economic activities. In reality, incomes are received by resource owners in the operation of the market process. Consequently, the remuneration received by resource owners affects resource use and, consequently, the amount of production.

Notes

1. E. C. Pasour, Jr., "Economic Growth and Agriculture: An Evaluation of the Compensation Principle," *American Journal of Agricultural Economics* 55 (November 1973): 611–16.

2. Hendrik S. Houthakker, *Economic Policy for the Farm Sector* (Washington, D.C.: American Enterprise Institute, 1967).

3. U.S. Bureau of the Census, *Statistical Abstract of the United States: 1986* (Washington, D.C.: U.S. Government Printing Office, 1985).

4. U.S. Department of Agriculture, *Agricultural Statistics* (Washington, D.C.: U.S. Government Printing Office, 1965 and 1985).

5. Engel's Law holds that the income elasticity of demand for farm products is less than one.

6. E. C. Pasour, Jr., "The Free Rider as a Basis for Government Intervention," *Journal of Libertarian Studies* 5 (Fall 1981): 453–63.

7. Mark Lilla, "Why the 'income distribution' is so misleading," *The Public Interest* 77 (Fall 1984): 62–76.

8. Ibid, p. 70.

9. David H. Harrington, "Income and Wealth Issues in Commercial Farm and Agricultural Policy," *Increasing Understanding of Public Problems and Policies—1984* (Oak Brook, Ill.: Farm Foundation, 1984), p. 148.

10. *Economic Report of the President* (Washington, D.C.: U.S. Government Printing Office, 1986), p. 132.

11. D. Gale Johnson, "Agricultural Policy Alternatives for the 1980s," in *Food and Agricultural Policies for the 1980s*, ed. D. Gale Johnson (Washington, D.C.: American Enterprise Institute, 1981), p. 189.

12. D. Gale Johnson, "The Performance of Past Policies: A Critique," chap. 2 in *Alternative Agricultural and Food Policies and the Farm Bill*, ed. Gordon C. Rausser and K. R. Farrell (Berkeley, Calif.: Giannini Foundation, 1985), p. 32.

13. George J. Stigler, *The Theory of Price*, 4th ed. (New York: Macmillan, 1987), p. 293.

14. U.S. Senate, *The Distribution of Benefits from the 1982 Federal Crop Programs*, S. Prt. 98-238, 98th Congress, 2nd Session (Washington, D.C.: U.S. Government Printing Office, 1984), p. 41.

15. F. A. Hayek, *Law, Legislation and Liberty*, vol. 2: *The Mirage of Social Justice* (Chicago: University of Chicago Press, 1976).

16. Chiaki Nishiyama and K. R. Leube, *The Essence of Hayek* (Stanford, Calif.: Hoover Institution Press, 1984), pp. 77–78.

17. Ibid., p. 68.

18. John Hospers, "Justice versus Social Justice," *The Freeman* 35 (January 1985): 24. Hospers defines a just wage as "the wage that one's services can command on a free market." Ibid., p. 19.

19. See Robert Nozick, *Anarchy, State and Utopia* (New York: Basic Books, 1974); Hayek, *The Mirage of Social Justice;* and James M. Buchanan, *Freedom in Constitutional Contract: Perspectives of a Political Economist* (College Station: Texas A & M University Press, 1977).

7

The Role of Government
in U.S. Agriculture

This chapter deals with the roots of current farm programs, the initiation of these programs, growth in farm programs over time, and possible explanations for the growth of government in the United States.

Roots of Current Farm Programs

Current farm programs are firmly rooted in legislation enacted during the Great Depression or the New Deal era, but the basic approach can be traced to earlier years. The McNary-Haugen two-price plan of the mid-1920s, for example, had the goal of raising farm product prices in the domestic market above those of the world market through the use of export subsidies. The required subsidies were to be financed through assessment of a processing or handling tax. Under the McNary-Haugen plan, a government export corporation would buy wheat and other products as a way of increasing domestic farm prices. These surplus farm products were then to be "dumped" in international markets and reimports restricted by tariffs. Five McNary-Haugen bills were introduced from 1924 to 1928 but none of them were enacted into law. However, the principal features of these bills were adopted in the New Deal legislation of the following decade which provided for the financing of export subsidies out of tariff receipts.

The Capper-Volstead Act of 1922 was another important precursor of current farm programs. This act marks the beginning of the modern cooperative movement. The act gives producers the legal right to act together in jointly marketing their products. Thus, members of co-ops enjoy a favored status when contrasted with other business firms which are legally prohibited from such collusive activity by antitrust laws. Without the act, many of the market activities currently engaged in by agricultural co-ops would be violations of either the Sherman Antitrust Act or the Clayton Act which restricts mergers. Co-ops presumably do not maintain their exemption when they engage in predatory market product to achieve "undue price enhancement." However, enforcement is entrusted to the Secretary of Agriculture rather than the Department of Justice.[1] Moreover, it is not clear what activities are forbidden and no Secretary of Agriculture has found an example of undue price enhancement by agricultural marketing co-ops. During recent years, however, milk, navel orange, and other co-ops have faced legal challenges from other quarters. Marketing orders and other co-op activities are described in more detail in later chapters.

The Federal Farm Board was the most immediate forerunner of New Deal action programs in agriculture. The board was created in 1929 by President Hoover who envisioned the farm problem as one of temporary overproduction and low prices. The basic idea was to raise prices of wheat, cotton, and other products by government purchase and storage of the products until some future period of production deficits. The board first attempted to support farm prices through a government-sponsored grain storage program. However, the board's budget was soon exhausted, with little effect on prices, and President Roosevelt abolished the Federal Farm Board in 1933.

The Agricultural Adjustment Act of 1933 and the Great Depression

Historically, the agricultural policy agenda prior to 1933 focused on measures to increase production and to maintain competitive markets. Federal intervention on a massive scale was initiated during the Roosevelt New Deal, and there was a pronounced change in program goals as the USDA under Secretary of Agriculture Henry Wallace developed a host of new action programs. Instead of increased production and competitive markets, the Agricultural Adjustment Act (AAA) of 1933 established the goals of "parity" prices and incomes in agriculture. The objective was to raise farm product prices (and farm incomes) above the free-market level. Specifically, the goal of the parity price approach was to raise product prices so that a physical unit of a particular product (pound, bushel, and so on) had the same buying power that prevailed during the base period of 1910 to 1914.

The 1933 AAA was enacted during the depths of the Great Depression, which occurred during the decade from 1929 to 1939. The Great Depression was a period of economic chaos and massive economic contraction. During a three-year period, stock (equity) prices lost nine-tenths of their value, real GNP decreased by one-third, industrial production was reduced by one-half, and unemployment reached 25 percent of the labor force. The overall level of prices fell by 9 percent in 1931 and 11 percent in 1932. In agriculture, this was a period of $.05 per pound cotton and $.30 per bushel corn.[2] In evaluating the appropriateness of the government policies instituted at that time, it is helpful to understand why the Great Depression occurred.

Cause of the Great Depression

The conventional wisdom has been that the Great Depression happened without a cause. In this view, the market economy is inherently unstable and the Great Depression was merely a severe manifestation of this instability. Thus, it is frequently argued, the government must intervene in agriculture and other areas to regulate and stabilize the economy. However, there are strong reasons for doubting this conventional explanation of the beneficial effects of government intervention during the Great Depression.[3] Contrary to what has been taught to generations of students and future policymakers, there is a great deal of evidence that government intervention in the form of high tariffs, high taxes, restrictive monetary policies, and policies to maintain wages and prices either caused or greatly exacerbated the economic chaos prevailing at that time.[4] The Smoot-Hawley Tariff Act enacted in 1930, for example, raised tariffs to the highest levels in the twentieth century—52.8 percent on an ad valorem basis. Restrictions on imports mean reductions in exports, and it was to a large extent because of this protectionist legislation that U.S. farm exports were reduced by two-thirds from 1929 to 1933. The protectionist trade policies were especially damaging to agriculture because of its heavy dependence on exports and the inelastic demand for farm products. The result was that farm prices plunged, many farm loans turned bad, and farm foreclosures mounted.

A purchasing-power theory of wages during the Great Depression had a profound effect on public policy. Under this mistaken theory, depressions occur where the share of income received by workers is too small. Since low wages lead to underconsumption, according to this purchasing-power theory, maintaining wages was seen as the appropriate policy during the Great Depression.[5] Thus, the U.S. government actively resisted the downward adjustment of wages and prices at a time of critically high unemployment. While President Hoover merely "jawboned" to keep wages up, President Roosevelt enacted the National Industrial Recovery Act (NIRA). The general thrust of the act was to suppress competition in whatever form it might take. The NIRA, for example, empowered the president to approve "codes of fair competition" which applied cartel-type codes on an industry basis and legally prevented wages and prices from falling.[6] A spate of wage increases followed at the bottom of the severe depression as a result of these policies. Thus, the price support policies in agriculture were consistent with the NIRA and other attempts by government to suppress competition and to maintain high prices.[7] The theory that falling prices were causing the depression and that government-enforced cartels would hasten recovery was as mistaken in agriculture as in other sectors.

Monetary and fiscal policies also contributed to the economic chaos. The Hoover administration enacted the biggest percentage increase in taxes in peacetime history in 1932, and President Roosevelt hiked taxes in 1935 and routinely thereafter. By 1938, the corporate tax rate had gone from 11 to 19 percent and the top income tax rate from 24 to 79 percent. The Federal Reserve reduced the money supply by one-third from 1929 to 1933, a period of severe economic contraction, and increased the discount rate by 2 percent in 1932.[8]

In summary, the government policies during the Great Depression of high tariffs, high taxes, monetary mismanagement, and political manipulation of wage rates and prices could hardly have been better designed to bring about economic stagnation or to prevent economic recovery. The programs instituted to restrict competition in agricultural markets were consistent with the collectivist thrust of the NIRA and other New Deal initiatives instituted to remedy supposed market failures. "The incredible aspect of these actions is that they were justified by the belief that the private sector was responsible for the Great Depression."[9]

New Deal Measures in Agriculture

A broad range of New Deal programs were instituted to deal with the farm problem. Included were programs providing for:

Production controls and price supports
Subsidized food distribution
Export subsidies
Subsidized farm credit
Conservation of land and water resources
Crop insurance and disaster payments
Expanded agricultural research and extension services

Programs in all of these areas are still in effect although many changes have been made since the programs began. The remainder of this book is devoted to an analysis of U.S. farm programs and policies, including a description of major changes in the programs over time. Not all of the programs listed above are consistent either in their objectives or in their effects. Agricultural research, for example, is designed to increase technology, which tends to decrease product prices. Price support programs, on the other hand, are designed to increase product prices. The more effective the research and extension programs, the more costly it is to support product prices at any given level. Other examples of inconsistent policies will be discussed in later chapters.

The Growth of Government in U.S. Agriculture

Evidence of Growth

There was a dramatic increase in government involvement in U.S. agriculture during the Roosevelt New Deal era. USDA expenditures increased from less than $172 million in 1929 prior to the New Deal to $1.2 billion in fiscal 1935 (table 7.1). The USDA outlays as a percentage of the total federal budget increased markedly in the 1930s, declined during World War II, rose again following the end of the war, and slowly declined until 1970. The USDA budget as a percent of the total federal budget increased from 4 percent in 1970 to 6 percent in the early to mid-1980s, even as the total U.S. budget was rising at an unprecedented peacetime rate. As shown in chapter 20, increases in food and nutrition programs were responsible for much of the USDA budget growth from 1970 to 1980. The large increase in USDA outlays since 1980 has been in price support programs.

The growth in USDA expenditures since World War II has been dramatic, measured on either a per farm or a per farm worker basis. On a per farm basis, expenditures in nominal terms increased from $523 in 1950 to $23,826 in fiscal 1987 (table 7.1). It should be noted again that there was a pronounced increase in the food stamp and other food assistance programs during this period.

USDA employment increased continually from 1929 to 1980, as the number of farms and farmers decreased. USDA employment rose most rapidly during the New Deal era from 1929 to 1935. Employment increased continuously following World War II until 1980, trended downward through 1986, and increased slightly in 1987.

The growth in USDA classified by general purpose of expenditure is presented in chapter 20, following a discussion of the various programs. While outlays for stabilization of farm prices and incomes have increased dramatically since 1980, these outlays have varied widely over the years depending upon price support levels, weather, export sales of farm products, and so on. There have also been pronounced upward trends in outlays for food and nutrition programs and in rural development and credit programs. This pattern of growth in USDA activities is consistent with public-choice theory. In the classic expansion pattern of bureaucracy, the USDA, having outgrown the area it was originally designed to aid, has moved into tangential areas such as rural recreation, community facilities, urban nutrition, and so on.

Changes in the relative importance of farm program expenditures also reflects the changing pressures of various groups on the USDA over the years. The main thrust of the action programs instituted during the New Deal era was income support to commercial agriculture. The USDA was dominated by commercial agriculture until the 1960s, as described in chapter 6, when the influence of nonfarm groups became much more important. During the Carter administration (1977–1980), the influence of various consumer and environmental groups on the USDA agenda increased at the expense of commercial agricultural interests. Although the pendulum swung back toward commercial agriculture to some extent during the Reagan administration, the influence of commercial agriculture on USDA activities is unlikely to be restored to its previous position of dominance.

So long as government expenditures on agricultural programs were viewed as in the "public interest," these programs were subject to relatively little criticism. More and more, however, consumer groups are challenging marketing orders for milk, oranges, and other products; the sugar program; the tobacco and peanut programs; and other farm programs which benefit a relatively few agricultural producers at the expense of the public at large. Agricultural programs are increasingly being viewed as income redistribution programs rather than "public interest" activities.

Reasons for Growth of Government Farm Programs

A number of factors are important in the growth of government farm programs. The fact that benefits are highly concentrated and costs are widely diffused is important in understanding increases in wealth by various groups achieved through the political process. However, opportunities to achieve wealth transfers through the political process are not new. Why have groups of farm producers and other narrowly focused special interests begun to rely more and more on the political process over time rather than on market opportunities as a means of enhancing their own wealth? Why did federal expenditures as a share of GNP increase from 2.5 percent in 1929 to almost 25 percent in 1986?

A number of other explanations for the growth of government have been cited. First, there is the notion that a modern industrial economy must have an expanding government sector because of the increased complexities of modern life.[10] This factor, although seemingly plausible, has limited explanatory power since regulation of public health and environmental externalities accounts for only a small part of what the government actually does. In agriculture, for example, price supports and credit subsidies and most of the other activities in which government is engaged have little or no connection with the increased complexity of the economy.

The "public-goods" model is a second and closely related justification for the growth of government. In the case of public goods, it is argued, government coercion is required to overcome the free-rider problem. However, this explanation has little relevance for most expenditures on agricultural programs. While it may be important in the case of agricultural research and educational programs (chapter 18), the outlays for farm price supports, agricultural credit subsidies, and food assistance cannot be explained on the basis of public-goods theory. Indeed, in the case of marketing orders and other government-enforced cartel-type activities, government is used to negate the effects of beneficial free riders who would in the absence of government sanctions ensure competitive market conditions.

Table 7.1   USDA Expenditures and Employment, 1929–1987.

	USDA EXPENDITURES					USDA EMPLOYMENT		
DATE	TOTAL (BILLIONS OF DOLLARS)	PERCENT OF TOTAL FEDERAL BUDGET	PERCENT OF NET FARM INCOME	PER FARM (DOLLARS)	PER FARM WORKER (DOLLARS)	TOTAL[a] (THOUSANDS)	PER THOUSAND FARM WORKERS	PER THOUSAND FARMS
1929	0.2[b]	5	3	31	17	24.4	2	4
1935	1.2	19	23	179	96	85.1	7	12
1940	1.4	15	31	223	129	81.9	7	13
1945	2.3	2	18	385	213	82.0	8	15
1950	3.0	7	22	523	299	84.1	8	15
1955	4.6	7	41	966	552	85.5	10	16
1960	5.4	6	47	1,367	763	98.7	14	25
1965	6.9	6	53	2,056	1,230	113.0	20	34
1970	8.4	4	58	2,848	1,857	116.0	26	39
1975	15.6	5	61	6,188	3,609	121.0	28	48
1980	34.8	6	172	14,303	9,393	129.1	35	53
1985	55.5	6	181	24,299	17,817	117.8	38	52
1986	58.7	6	157	26,513	20,158	113.1	39	51
1987	49.6	5	NA	23,826	NA	117.1	NA	54

SOURCES: Column 1 from Office of Management and Budget, Historical Tables, Budget of the U.S. Government; all other columns from U.S. Department of Commerce, Statistical Abstract of the United States.

[a] Total paid civilian employment.

[b] More than 50 percent of expenditure was for road construction, an item not reported in later USDA budgets.

Third, there has been a change over time in ideology—in the public perception of the appropriate role of government. Prior to the New Deal era, there was a consensus that the role of government should be mainly limited to its protective functions. This attitude is shown in the view expressed by President Grover Cleveland about a congressional appropriation in 1887 of $10,000 for seed-grain to assist drought-stricken farmers in Texas. Cleveland considered it wrong to use public funds to indulge a benevolent and charitable sentiment. He vetoed the appropriation with the message that "the lesson should constantly be enforced that though the people support the Government the Government should not support the people."[11]

During the past fifty years, constitutional restraints on the exercise of government power have broken down as individuals and groups have come to feel that government should be the problem-solver of last resort. Government has increasingly become a vehicle for accommodating the demands of narrowly focused special interests rather than protecting the interests of the general public.

Emergency or economic crisis is another explanation for the growth of government in agriculture and other sectors of the economy. In U.S. history, the most significant crises have taken two forms: war and business depression.[12] As mentioned earlier, the AAA of the New Deal represented a large increase in the role of government in U.S. agriculture. It was argued that the individualistic approach of the market was unable to cope with the economic crisis and that government planning was required in agriculture and in other sectors of the economy. Thus, the AAA and other New Deal measures were justified on the basis of economic emergency and Congress attached the emergency label to almost every bill it enacted.[13] It is significant that expansions of state power justified on the basis of emergency conditions often do not disappear when the crisis is over. The New Deal measures enacted to deal with the economic crisis in agriculture, for example, remain largely intact fifty years later.

There is no simple answer to the question of why government intervention has increased in U.S. agriculture. It is likely, as in many other areas of economic activity, that there is no single reason for the dramatic growth of farm programs during the past fifty years. However, the growth of government spending generally appears to be related to the erosion over time of the constraints on the powers of the federal government but largely unrelated to the political party in office. A recent study found no significant difference in the growth of real total federal spending in the United States from one party to another during the period since World War II.[14]

Summary

Although government programs in agriculture have roots in the Mc-Nary-Haugen two-price plan, the Capper-Volstead Act, and the Federal Farm Board, almost all current farm programs have a direct link to the

New Deal era. During the Great Depression, a host of action programs involving price supports, credit subsidies, export subsidies, subsidized food distribution, crop insurance, and conservation were launched to deal with the economic chaos in U.S. agriculture.

The conventional wisdom has been that the Great Depression resulted from a failure of the market process and that massive government intervention was necessary to stabilize agriculture and the rest of the economy. There is a considerable amount of evidence, however, that government policies of high tariffs, high taxes, monetary mismanagement, and political attempts to maintain high wages and prices either caused or greatly exacerbated the chaotic economic conditions of that era.

The record of government programs in agriculture since the New Deal era is consistent with the predictions of public-choice theory. The programs instituted at that time to deal with emergency conditions have been maintained and increased over time, seemingly regardless of economic conditions. USDA employment and expenditures have increased dramatically since the 1930s even as the number of farms and number of farmers were decreasing and farm income was increasing relative to nonfarm income. Although the USDA has mainly represented commercial agriculture since the agency was founded in 1862, the influence of environmental and consumer groups in agency decisions has increased considerably since the mid-1970s. More and more, it is recognized by consumer groups and the general public that income redistribution is a major reason for U.S. farm programs. However, other factors including a change in public opinion as to the appropriate role of the state may also be important in the growth of government in agriculture (and other sectors).

Notes

1. Bruce L. Gardner, *The Governing of Agriculture* (Lawrence, Kan.: The Regents Press of Kansas, 1981), p. 48.

2. The Consumer Price Index in 1933 was 38.8 (1967 = 100). In 1986 it was 327.6.

3. Christian Saint-Etienne, *The Great Depression, 1929–1938* (Stanford, Calif.: Hoover Institution Press, 1984).

4. Ibid., p. 38

5. Daniel J. B. Mitchell, "Wage Flexibility in the United States: Lessons from the Past," *American Economic Review* 75 (May 1985): 36–40.

6. Robert Higgs, *Crisis and Leviathan: Critical Episodes in the Growth of American Government* (New York: Oxford University Press, 1987), p. 178.

7. Benjamin M. Anderson, *Economics and the Public Welfare* (Indianapolis: Liberty Press, 1979).

8. Alan Reynolds, "What Do We Know About the Great Crash?" *National Review*, 9 November 1979, pp. 1416–21.

9. Saint-Etienne, *The Great Depression*, p. 41.

10. Robert Higgs, "The Sources of Big Government," *Intercollegiate Review* 20 (1984): 23–33.

11. Quoted in Alan Nevins, *Grover Cleveland: A Study in Courage* (New York: Dodd, Mead, 1933), p. 332.

12. Higgs, *Crisis and Leviathan*, p. 30.

13. Ibid., p. 171.

14. William A. Niskanen, "The Growth of Government," *Cato Policy Report* 7 (July–August 1985): 8–10.

8

Price Supports, Parity, and Cost of Production

The basic idea of the farm price support programs launched during the 1930s, as explained in the previous chapter, was that wages and prices should be kept high in a period of falling prices. In agriculture, farm product prices were deliberately raised above the market clearing price. The problem of how high to set prices of wheat, cotton, tobacco, and other farm products then arose. That is, should product price be set at OPs_1, OPs_2, or at some other level (figure 8.1)? This chapter describes the parity-price and cost-of-production approaches to setting price supports. It also analyzes price setting to increase market stability and emphasizes why there is no economically defensible means of setting price support levels.

Parity Price

The parity-price concept was developed as an objective and seemingly defensible basis for determining price support levels for farm products. Parity was defined as the price which gives a unit of the commodity the same purchasing power in the current period that it had in the period 1910–1914. This base period in the computation of parity prices for farm products was not arbitrarily chosen, as one might predict from public-choice theory. The period 1910–1914 is known as a "golden period" of agriculture because prices received when compared with prices paid by farmers were highly favorable during that era. Indeed, the 1910–1914 base period used during the 1930s to define a "fair price" was the most favorable to agriculture since the Civil War.[1]

The objective of the parity-price approach for farm products is quite simple. For example, if a bushel of wheat would buy (say) a shirt in the period from 1910 to 1914, then to be at parity a bushel of wheat should be priced so as to buy a shirt today. (This example assumes that the price of shirts has increased at the same rate as the price of goods and services generally.) In computing the parity price according to this original formula, the price of wheat in the base period was multiplied by the "parity index," the current Index of Prices Paid by Farmers for Commodities and

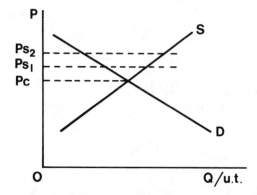

Figure 8.1. The price support level is arbitrary.

Services, Interest, Taxes, and Wage Rates expressed on the 1910–1914 = 100 base. For example, the price of wheat in the period 1910–1914 was $.88 per bushel. In 1985, the annual average prices paid index (as computed by the USDA) was 1121.[2] Thus, the 1985 parity price for wheat computed by the original parity formula was $1121 \times (\$.88) = \$9.86$ per bushel. The actual price of wheat averaged only $3.16 per bushel during the 1985 crop year.[3] During the period since the 1930s, farm product prices generally have been considerably below the parity level.

Farm product prices have seldom been supported at 100 percent of parity, even when price supports were based on the parity concept. Indeed, a great deal of debate over farm policy during the 1940s and 1950s was concerned with the appropriate "level of parity." That is, the agricultural policy debate quite often was concerned with whether the price of wheat, milk, or another price-supported product should be supported at 75 percent, 80 percent, 90 percent, or some other proportion of parity.

It is fully predictable that an effective price support based on parity, or any other standard, will inevitably create surplus problems. Thus, a watering-down of the parity approach occurred because of problems created by surplus production. In addition to supporting prices at less than 100 percent of parity based on the original definition of parity, the parity formula itself has been changed over time.

The parity formula was "modernized" in 1948 as follows:

"New" Parity Price = (Adjusted Base Price) (Parity Index).[4]

$$\text{New Parity Price} = \frac{Pi(t_{\overline{10}})}{PRI(t_{\overline{10}})} \cdot PPI(t_1)$$

Where:

$Pi(t_{\overline{10}})$ = a ten-year average price for commodity i (based on ten most recent complete calendar years).

$PRI(t_{\overline{10}})$ = a ten-year average of the index of prices received by farmers for all commodities (based on corresponding 120 months average).

$PPI(t_1)$ = current monthly index of prices paid (parity index—1910–1914 = 100).

The moving average in the new parity formula effectively lowers parity prices for commodities which have been trending downward more rapidly than farm prices generally and raises the parity price for products whose recent prices are stronger than the aggregate (as measured by the prices-received index). This process also permits parity prices to be calculated for commodities that were not widely grown in 1910–14 (e.g., soybeans).[5]

The use of parity in farm programs over time has been greatly reduced. However, the USDA now calculates parity prices for 142 commodities.[6] Moreover, although the 1985 farm bill does not mention the term, the permanent legislation that provides the basis for farm programs when the 1985 act expires, and farm programs not covered by the act, do rely on parity price measures.[7] The parity index is used in formulas that determine the support prices for wool, tobacco, and quota peanuts. Permanent legislation for dairy, wheat, and other basic commodity price support programs requires the USDA to base price supports on parity prices if temporary legislation expires. Monthly parity prices are also required in administering some marketing orders involving quantity controls, including navel oranges and lemons.[8]

Shortcomings of the Parity-Price Approach

There are a number of problems associated with the use of the parity concept. First, parity prices hinder the functioning of the market process. They assume both that farm product prices and input prices were in the proper relationship in the 1910–1914 base period and that this relationship remains the same over time. However, there is no logical reason for tying current price relationships to any particular historic time period. Market price at any point in time is determined by the interrelationship of supply and demand, and there is no reason to expect the supply and demand for any particular product today to bear the same relationship to other goods and services that it did from 1910 to 1914 (or in any other historical time period). Indeed, relative prices in a market system are constantly changing in response to changing demand and supply conditions. By adopting a historical base period, the parity formula freezes an otherwise self-adjusting price mechanism.

Furthermore, in tying price relationships to a base period, parity fails to allow for differences in changes in productivity over time. For example, increases in output per hour of labor since 1965 have been greater in poultry than in vegetable production. Thus, there has been more downward pressure over time on poultry prices because of increasing supply. Consequently, a price support program based on parity prices during this period, other factors being constant, would have created larger surplus problems for poultry than for vegetables.

Similarly, parity fails to allow for differences in changes in demand over time. If the demand for chicken increases relative to pork, other factors being constant, the price of chicken will increase. If prices of these products were supported at parity on the basis of 1910–1914 relationships, the surplus problem would be more acute for pork.

Second, and closely related, parity prices products out of foreign and domestic markets, resulting in either surpluses or production controls. Thus, parity prices that raise prices are inconsistent with free trade, domestically and internationally.

Third, parity prices may have only a small effect on the incomes of some farmers since incomes are determined by quantity produced and price. A parity price for wheat, for example, will have little effect on the producer who has few bushels of wheat to sell. Thus, even if all farm products were supported at 100 percent of parity, many small farmers would continue to have relatively low net farm incomes.

Finally, the problem of selecting the appropriate level of parity price is similar to that of determining the long discredited "just price." When price is raised above the market clearing level as in figure 8.1, there is no objective procedure for determining what the price should be. That is, when market price signals are consciously ignored through the use of price supports, credit subsidies, and so on, setting prices involves judgments of value. Even though the results are highly flawed, the parity approach, given the base period, does provide an objective procedure for computing "parity prices" for farm products. In this approach, however, there is no objective basis for selecting any particular base period or, once the base period is selected, for setting prices at 70, 80, 90, 100 (or any other) percent of parity. The problem of determining the level of price supports is the same as for all other income redistribution policies that benefit some people at the expense of other people.

Cost of Production

The shortcomings of the parity price approach in setting price support levels led to another approach in the 1970s. The Food and Agriculture Act of 1977 embraced cost of production as the primary guide in determining the level of farm product price supports. Cost of production, however, is no more defensible than parity as a procedure for determining what the level of product prices should be.

First, consider the problems in measuring cost as it influences entrepreneurial choice. Choice is influenced by opportunity cost, the value of the highest sacrificed alternative associated with any action. For example, the cost to a farmer of using land in corn production is the value of the land if used in the best alternative use, say soybeans. However, the expected return to land in soybeans depends upon soybean price, yield, and production expenses. Different producers will make different estimates of costs and returns and of the return to land in soybeans. Jones, for example, may anticipate a return to a land of $25 per acre when using land in soybeans. Smith, being more optimistic about future soybean yields, may anticipate a return of $40 per acre to land in soybeans. Under these conditions, the opportunity cost per acre of land to produce corn is $25 for Jones and $40 for Smith. These are the relevant costs for Smith and Jones to impute to land in producing corn, whether the land tended is owned or rented.

Land is not unique in this respect. Different farm operators will also make different estimates of the value of machinery, buildings, and other durable resources in alternative uses. Thus, the opportunity costs of these resources will vary widely from farm to farm.

The preceding discussion illustrates a basic principle. Opportunity cost is subjective, and there is no reason to expect the opportunity cost of resources for Farmer Jones to be the same as for Farmer Smith.[9] Moreover, the outside observer has no way to determine or measure the opportunity cost that influences the producer's decision.

Secondly, different producers will generally appear to have different costs on the basis of accounting records. In the North Carolina Dairy Records Program, for example, the net cost of production in 1984 was about twice as high for the highest-cost 10 percent when compared with the lowest-cost 10 percent of enrolled dairy farms.[10] Hence, any effective level of price support selected for a farm product is likely to be above the costs reported by some farmers and below the costs reported for others.[11]

This observed variation in accounting costs between farms is not necessarily caused by differences in opportunity costs but may be merely due to differences in the accuracy of the reported data or to lags in the capital market in revaluing specialized resources. Competition in the capital market tends to force expected outlays at the farm level toward expected product price.[12] If product price is supported above the market level, costs tend to rise to equal product price. Thus the third shortcoming of cost of production as a basis for price supports is the capitalization problem.

This phenomenon is illustrated in figure 8.2. When product price is increased above the market level to OP_s, prices of land, rights to produce, skilled workers, and other specialized resources are bid up so that production outlays tend to equal product price. In this way, the income-earning potential of land, allotments, and so on is converted into increased prices of these resources. This process by which the income-earning potential of an asset is converted into the value of the asset is described as capitalization. The capitalization process ensures

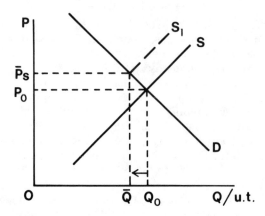

Figure 8.2. Increased product prices are capitalized into higher production costs.

that a price support program that increases price will tend to cause outlays to rise to equal price—and supply to shift to the left (figure 8.2).

If there are specialized inputs such as land, labor, and allotments, cost cannot be determined independently of demand or product price. Consider the example of land. Assume that land is the only specialized resource and that there are only two kinds of land, good land and average land. When expected product price is $E(P)$, there is initially a return ("rent") to the superior land indicated by the rectangle A (figure 8.3). The fact that good land is expected to be more productive causes the income earning potential to be converted into higher land prices. The lure of expected profits provides the entrepreneurial motivation for prices of more productive inputs to be bid up. Consequently, competition causes land users to bid up the price of good land high enough so that the expected return to superior land is no higher than for other investments of similar risk. The added return is capitalized or converted into increased land values so that production costs on good land (and average land) tend to equal product price. Thus an increase in demand or price of corn results in increased prices of land and other factors specialized to corn production.

The fact that cost cannot be determined independently of demand or product price when there are specialized resources is highly important for U.S. agricultural policy. Consider the economic effects of a policy to dramatically increase the price of corn to (say) $10 per bushel. The above analysis suggests that the price of land and other specialized corn growing resources would be bid up so that costs would also tend to equal $10 per bushel (figure 8.4). That is, the prices of land and other specialized resources vary with corn price and competition creates an incentive for the price of these resources to be bid up high enough to make price equal to cost regardless of how high the price is set.

The conclusion is that cost of production is not a defensible basis for agricultural price supports.[13] Any effective price support will affect the cost of production. A price support will bring about an increase in the price of specialized resources even if the price support is effective only some of the time. If a price support is effective only one year out of five, for example, it will still increase cost of production. Furthermore, under real-world conditions of specialized resources, there is a ratchet effect if price supports are based on costs of production. An effective increase in the support price will inevitably increase cost of production (figure 8.2). If, in turn, price support levels are based on costs, the increase in cost would cause the price support level to increase, which would then lead to higher costs, and so on.

The preceding analysis suggests that regardless of the method used to increase product price, price supports affect resource allocation and result in higher prices of land, allotments, and other specialized resources. Thus if price supports are set high enough to be effective, the allocation of resources will be affected. There is no way to devise a system of effective price supports that does not distort the pattern of resource use. Furthermore, when price is arbitrarily raised above the competitive market clearing level, there is no defensible procedure for determining the appropriate level of price support.

Cost of production as a basis for setting price supports was de-emphasized in the 1981 farm bill. However, a National Agricultural Cost of Production Standards Review Board was established by the 1981 legislation to review annually the cost of production procedures used by USDA in price support programs. The 1985 farm bill extended the life of the board until 1990.

Price Setting to Increase Market Stability

Increased market stability is often cited as a rationale for agricultural price supports. The argument is made that operation of markets for farm

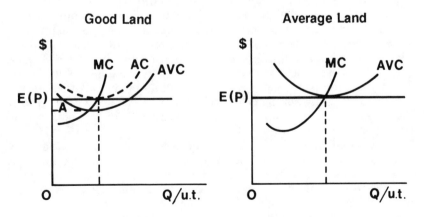

Figure 8.3. The advantage of good land is capitalized into higher costs.

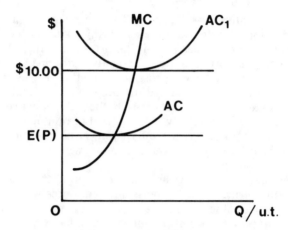

Figure 8.4. When product price is increased, costs tend to rise to equal expected
price.

products might be improved if price supports were set at or below equilibrium price levels as a means of decreasing market instability. If the
price support level were set at the competitive market clearing price level,
for example, risks associated with downside price movements would be
decreased. Recognizing that governmental officials in the real world seldom or never attempt to set agricultural price supports in this way, let us
consider the potential of such price setting to increase market stability.

If price setting is to increase market stability, government officials must
cope with the information and incentive problems inherent in collective
decision making (chapter 3). There is an information problem in setting
prices to increase market stability because there is no way to know before
a crop is planted what the market clearing price will be. Indeed, as
markets throughout the world for farm products become more interdependent, market prices for U.S. farm products are influenced more and more
by supply and demand factors in other countries. And, abstracting from
the perverse incentive problems that are endemic to the political process,
there is no reason to think that information about supply and demand
conditions will be more accurately assessed by government officials than
by market participants, say as reflected in futures prices for farm products.

Moreover, if price setting is to increase market stability without distorting resource use, it is important that prices be set correctly. If product
prices were set above the market clearing level, any increase in market
stability would be at the expense of increased cost of production as the
benefits of higher prices are incorporated into higher resource prices, as
described above. And the price support need not be set high enough to be
effective each year for the postulated capitalization effect to increase
prices of land and other specialized resources.

If, as suggested above, prices were set low enough to have no influence on product prices, market instability might be reduced without distorting resource use. However, such stabilization schemes, though interesting intellectual exercises, are of little practical significance. Even if government officials could obtain the information necessary to ensure that price supports will be set at or below market clearing levels, the incentives in the political process are such that they would be highly unlikely to do so. Indeed, government farm programs as implemented through the political process generally distort resource use, and as shown in chapter 15, are likely to decrease rather than to increase market stability. After taking these information and incentive problems into account, the conclusion is that market stability is no more defensible than parity or cost of production as a rationale for agricultural price supports.

Summary

The agricultural price support programs initiated during the 1930s deliberately raised product prices above market clearing levels. The concept of parity price was first used in setting price support levels for farm products. A parity price for any product was designed to give the product the same purchasing power on a per unit basis that it had during the base period 1910–1914. Although the parity formula was later modified, the inherent problems of this approach have not been resolved. Parity prices hinder the operation of the price mechanism in the market system. There is no reason to expect the price of any product today to bear the same relationship to other prices that it had in some historical time period. Product price is determined by supply and demand conditions and relative prices constantly change over time as economic conditions change. Although parity is still used as a rallying cry by some farm groups, the concept has been largely abandoned in U.S. agricultural price support programs.

In the Food and Agricultural Act of 1977, cost of production was taken as a guide in determining the level of price supports. There are two major shortcomings of this approach. First, cost as it influences choice is subjective and there is no way for the outside observer to measure the costs which influence individual decisions. Second, in a world of specialized resources, cost cannot be determined independently of demand or product price. If product price is supported above the market clearing level, prices of land, allotments, and other specialized resources will be bid up so that there is a tendency for cost to rise to the level of product price, regardless of how high price is set. That is, the benefits of price support programs are largely capitalized into higher prices of land and other specialized resources. Cost of production is no longer the key factor in determining the level of price supports.

The search for a defensible basis for setting the level of price supports will predictably fail. The problem of how high to set the level of price support is essentially the same as that of other measures to redistribute income. Redistribution through legislated price supports can no more be justified on the basis of economic theory than can any other income transfer. Any attempt to justify the setting of agricultural prices above the competitive market level involves interpersonal utility comparisons and value judgments which are "essentially incapable of scientific proof."[14] Moreover, price setting to increase market stability is not feasible because of information and incentive problems that are inherent in the political process.

Notes

1. Harold G. Halcrow, *Food Policy for America* (New York: McGraw-Hill, 1977), p. 11.

2. U.S. Department of Agriculture, *Agricultural Statistics* (Washington, D.C.: U.S. Government Printing Office, 1985).

3. Ibid.

4. Loyd D. Teigen, *Agricultural Parity: Historical Review and Alternative Calculations*, AER No. 571 (Washington, D.C.: U.S. Government Printing Office, 1987), p. 7.

5. Ibid.

6. Ibid., p. 5.

7. Ibid., p. 10.

8. Ibid., p. 11.

9. James M. Buchanan, *Cost and Choice* (Chicago: Markham, 1969).

10. G. A. Benson and S. R. Sutter, *1984 Dairy Farm Business Summary and Business Evaluation Workbook*, North Carolina State University, Agricultural Extension Service, AG-39, June 1986.

11. Clifton B. Luttrell, "Farm Price Supports at Cost of Production," *Federal Reserve Bank of St. Louis Review* 59 (December 1977): 2–7.

12. Milton Friedman, *Price Theory* (Chicago: Aldine Publishing Company, 1976), p. 146.

13. E. C. Pasour, Jr., "Cost of Production: A Defensible Basis for Agricultural Price Supports?" *American Journal of Agricultural Economics* 62 (May 1980): 244–48.

14. Lionel Robbins, "Economics and Political Economy," *American Economic Review* 71 (1981): 9.

9

Market Models and Overview of Production Controls and Marketing Quotas

Three main types of government intervention have been used to support (raise) agricultural product prices since the New Deal action programs were instituted in the 1930s. Most of the price support programs currently in effect fall into one or more of these categories.

Price Supports Alone

The simplest type of price support program is one where the government merely sets price (on the basis of parity, cost of production, or some other criterion) above the market clearing level. If the price is set at OP_s as in figure 9.1, there will be surplus production. In a pure price support program of this type, the government presumably acquires the surplus produced at the policy-determined price. The acquisition cost to taxpayers is the amount of surplus (A in figure 9.1) times the support price OP_s. The real cost is the acquisition cost plus storage cost less whatever the government sells the stocks for.

This model is applicable to the current U.S. dairy program (see chapter 11). In the dairy program, Congress sets the level of price support. Milk price is then supported by a standing offer by the Commodity Credit Corporation (CCC) to buy enough milk products (dry milk, butter, and cheese) to raise milk price to the support level.

Surpluses are inevitable and fully predictable when government uses price supports to raise farm product prices above competitive levels. For example, the U.S. government has acquired huge stocks of dairy products under the dairy program. In 1985, the government owned 2.6 billion pounds of butter, cheese, and dry milk—about 11 pounds for every person in the United States.[1] The U.S. government has also purchased large amounts of wheat, feed grains, cotton, and other products at various times during the past fifty years in the operation of other price support programs.

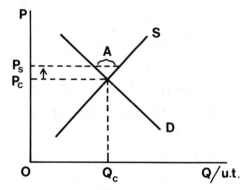

Figure 9.1. Price supports without quantity restrictions.

Price Supports with Restrictions on Output or Input Use

Price supports inevitably lead to increased production, thereby creating an incentive for further government involvement through programs to control production.[2] A price support program alone is likely to be costly to taxpayers. The treasury cost, of course, hinges on how high the price support is set above the market clearing price. One way for the government to reduce the cost to taxpayers is to restrict the quantity of the product produced or marketed. If production were restricted to OQs as in figure 9.2, the support price OPs would be achieved without there being any surplus production. As shown below, however, resource use is distorted, regardless of whether production is reduced by restricting the use of inputs or by limiting output.

Acreage Allotments and Output Quotas

At various times since the 1930s, acreage allotments have been used in price support programs for cotton, corn, wheat, tobacco, peanuts, and other products. Restricting the use of land, however, negates the most productive pattern of resource use that would occur in an unhampered market, thereby distorting input use and increasing production costs. If a farmer's use of land is restricted through an acreage allotment, for example, other inputs, including fertilizer and pesticides, will be substituted for land. When input use is distorted in this way, marginal cost per unit of output is higher than it would be in the absence of the constraint on resource use (figure 9.3).

The effectiveness of acreage allotments in restricting production is undermined both by increases in production technology and by the substitutability of other inputs for land. In the tobacco program, for example, as technology increased and other inputs were substituted for land, to-bacco yields under acreage allotments increased from 1,083 pounds per acre in 1944 to 2208 pounds in 1964. Thus, to restrict production to the desired level during this period, acreage allotments had to be reduced again and again.

In 1965, the tabacco program was changed so that production was restricted by a marketing poundage quota as well as acreage allotment. A marketing quota specifies the number of pounds that a producer can sell in a given year. The peanut program is another that involves the use of marketing quotas. Marketing quotas are a much more effective means of restricting production than restrictions on input use. As shown below, however, marketing quotas also distort the pattern of resource use and increase the cost of production.

Market Value of Allotments and Quotas

Acreage allotments and production or marketing quotas are, in one sense, artificial factors of production. When production or marketing is restricted, the *right* to produce or sell acquires a value. In general, the demand for any productive input is derived from the demand for the product that it produces.[3] There is a derived demand for acreage allot-ments or marketing quotas just as there is for other inputs. (Since the economic effects of acreage allotments and output quotas are very similar, the following analysis is limited to production or marketing quotas.) If the government specifies the number of units which may be sold and, hence, produced, the right to produce can be viewed as a factor perfectly inel-astic in supply (figure 9.4). The demand for the quota is determined by conditions in the product market. Competition will cause the annual rental value of the quota to tend to equal the difference between product price and the cost of production, excluding the quota cost. The market value of the right to produce and sell tobacco quota is the present value of

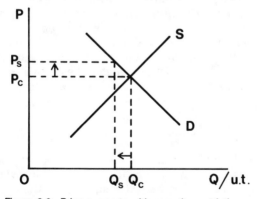

Figure 9.2. Price supports with quantity restrictions.

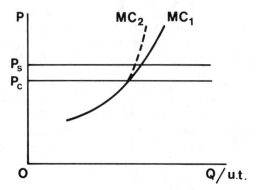

Figure 9.3. Production cost is increased when land use is restricted.

the stream of expected annual quota rents. This assumes that quota is the only specialized resource. In reality, land and other factors are not completely specialized so that some of the product price increase would be capitalized into prices of land and other specialized factors. This value of the quota in the product market corresponds to the rental value of the quota in the quota market. The higher product price is above nonquota production costs (supply) at the mandated level of output, the more valuable the right to produce and the greater the rental value of quota.[4]

The value of the right to produce, as described above, is capitalized into the market price of quota. Consequently, price support programs that restrict production through quotas and allotments increase production costs for owners or renters of quota. If a nonquota owner rents (or buys) quota to obtain the right to produce, production outlays are increased. If the owner uses the quota, it is an opportunity cost. Moreover, the more production is restricted, the higher the quota or allotment price. During the heyday of the flue-cured tobacco program, for example, the per acre rental value of the marketing quota often exceeded $1000 per year in low-cost production regions. The difference between tobacco price and nonquota cost is greater in low-cost production regions, and so is quota value. Stated differently, the lower are nonquota production costs, the higher the derived demand for this input and the higher the quota price for any given level of marketing quota.

Voluntary Diversion of Land

The voluntary diversion of land played an important role in the Soil Bank of the 1950s and is important in current cotton, wheat, and feed grains programs. In the Soil Bank program, a part of the Agricultural Act of 1956, farmers were paid to take land out of production. The basic idea was to take land out of production on a long-term basis as a way of reducing the output of farm products. The Soil Bank, a response to the surplus production created by price supports, was viewed as an alternative to acreage allotments and marketing quotas. Sections of farms and entire farms were removed from production for periods ranging from three to fifteen years. While participation was voluntary, the diverted land of participating farmers had to be maintained in soil-conserving uses. During the period from 1961 to 1972 an average of 12 percent of U.S. farmland was enrolled in the Soil Bank program.[5] The annual cost of the program reached a peak of almost $1 billion in 1971. In addition to cost, another objection was the effect of the program on rural businesses and institutions in communities where farmers placed whole farms in the Soil Bank.

Moreover, paying farmers to leave productive land idle is not consistent with efficient resource use. The Soil Bank program induced farms to shift large amounts of land from more productive to less productive uses. The land was idled not because its use was unprofitable but rather to reduce surplus production created by government price support programs. Large amounts of valuable output, as valued at world market prices, were foregone in idling millions of acres of productive farm land in this way.

The overall objective of farm programs involving the voluntary diversion of land is the same as for mandatory acreage allotment programs: to reduce production and increase product price. The basic difference is that in voluntary diversion programs producers respond to economic incentives rather than to legal coercion. Farmers obtaining price supports under current cotton, wheat, and feed grain programs, in which participation is optional, must set aside some specified amount of land in conservation uses. The effect of land diversion programs on product supply is depicted in figure 9.5. Supply shifts to the left since there is less land in production and producers are induced to combine inputs in less productive ways. The nature and effects of current price support programs involving volun-

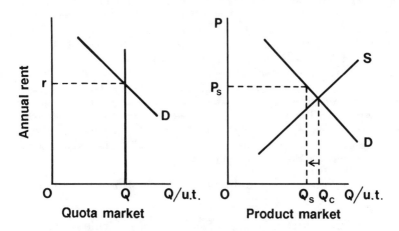

Figure 9.4. Rental value of production quota is derived from product market.

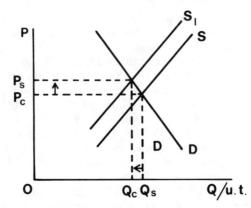

Figure 9.5. The effect of land diversion programs on product supply, output and price.

tary land diversion programs will be explained more fully in the following chapter.

Compensatory Payments

Price supports involving the use of compensatory payments were popularized in the "Brannan Plan" of the late 1940s. Charles Brannan was Secretary of Agriculture in the Truman Administration. The compensatory-payments approach is illustrated in figure 9.6. Product price is supported at a level OPs. At this price, producers will produce the amount OQs.

In the compensatory-payment approach, the government does not purchase the amount that consumers do not buy at OPs, the price support level. Instead, the amount produced (OQs) is sold by producers at whatever price will clear the market (OPm). A government subsidy of OPs − OPm per unit of product produced is then paid to producers. The total subsidy is (OPs − OPm).OQs. Producers know in advance what price they will get but not how much of this price will be received through the market and how much through government payments.

The compensatory-payment approach is used today in the case of cotton, rice, wheat, and feed grain programs where a "target price" is guaranteed by paying producers the difference between the target price and the market price (or the loan rate). These government outlays are referred to as "deficiency payments." The income redistribution effects of the target price approach and its effects on domestic and international markets for farm products are described in chapters 10 and 14.

History and Operation of Production Control Programs

Production controls were a key feature of the Agricultural Adjustment Act of 1933. As indicated previously, the AAA was one of many anticompetitive New Deal measures that restricted production, set prices, set wages, restricted imports, and so on.

Production Controls

Under the AAA of 1933, acreage allotments restricted farmers to planting only a specific number of acres of particular crops such as rice, wheat, cotton, peanuts, and tobacco. A national acreage allotment for a crop was set at a level that would meet anticipated domestic and export consumption. The national allotment was then apportioned among individual farms based on historical plantings of the crop. As indicated above, the effectiveness of the mandated reduction in land use was reduced as farmers withdrew the poorest land from production and tended the allotted acres more intensively. Other production control measures received a great deal of criticism. For example, farmers were paid to plow up cotton, and the government, in a widely publicized and much criticized program, bought up pigs and killed them to reduce the supply of pork.

The AAA of 1933 was declared unconstitutional by the U.S. Supreme Court in 1936. Although President Roosevelt lost this battle, production controls were soon incorporated in other farm legislation. The Soil Conservation and Domestic Allotment Act of 1936 combined conservation with production controls. The Agricultural Marketing Agreement Act of 1937 provided for agricultural marketing orders which have been and continue to be widely used for milk, oranges and other fruits, vegetables, and specialty crops. Finally, the AAA of 1938 became the pattern for subsequent farm programs involving production controls. This Act provided price supports and production controls for "basic crops"—wheat, corn, cotton, rice, peanuts, and tobacco. Price support levels were set, at the discretion of the secretary of agriculture, between 52 and 75 percent of parity. Marketing quotas were binding upon all producers if two-thirds of the producers holding production allotments voted for quotas in a referendum. In the early years, price support programs generally involved man-

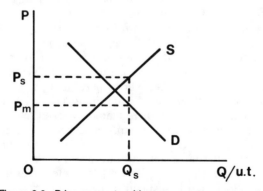

Figure 9.6. Price supports with compensatory payments.

datory controls for all producers once the program was approved in a producer referendum. Currently, the tobacco program, the peanut program, and marketing orders are mandatory control programs in this sense. Since the early 1960s, there has been a shift toward voluntary production controls. The decision as to whether to participate in current wheat, cotton, and feed grain programs, for example, is made by the individual producer. Production controls were removed during World War II as commodity prices increased because of the war. Postwar food problems in Europe and Asia (and the Korean War) kept demand strong so that surpluses were not a major problem into the early 1950s. The Agricultural Act of 1949 gave the secretary of agriculture authority to lower price support levels, and price supports were decreased from 1953 to 1960, during the Eisenhower Administration. However, surplus problems mounted in the mid-1950s due to increases in technology which brought increased pressure for government intervention. The 1949 Act also provided for acreage allotments and marketing quotas if approved by two-thirds of the voting producers. This Act was the last permanent farm legislation enacted into law. All subsequent farm bills have been amendments to the 1949 Act and specify an expiration date, and if replacement legislation is not enacted before the expiration date, provisions of the 1949 Act become effective.

The CCC and Nonrecourse Loan Program

The New Deal price support programs led to surplus production and government storage of agricultural products. The Commodity Credit Corporation (CCC) was created as a companion policy of the AAA in 1933. It was created to provide for loans and storage when production was "too large." The CCC, although created as a temporary agency, continues to serve as the government's arm for acquisition, storage, and sale of surplus commodities. Within the USDA, the CCC retains responsibility for providing the financial and storage functions related to price and income support programs. The CCC has no operating personnel. Its activities are carried out through the staff and facilities of ASCS (an agency of USDA) and it borrows directly from the federal treasury.

The CCC employs two measures to increase price: direct commodity purchases, as in the dairy program, and nonrecourse loans. The nonrecourse loan continues to be the major program instrument used in price support operations for grain, cotton, peanuts, and tobacco.

In a nonrecourse loan, a farmer who is participating in a price support program obtains a nine-month loan from the CCC by pledging a quantity of commodity as collateral. Loans are made at a fixed rate per unit called the loan rate which varies from year to year according to current legislation. A farmer may store the product in his own or in commercial facilities. Loans are made to the farmer without recourse, that is, no recourse is available to the lender (the government). The farmer obtaining a loan may elect to repay the loan within a specified period and regain control of the commodity or default on the loan. If the loan rate is above the market price and the borrower defaults, ownership of the commodity passes to the CCC, satisfying the loan obligation. Commodities obtained by the CCC on defaulted loans become the property of the government and are held in CCC storage until released on the market or otherwise disposed of. The CCC loses on such transactions, unless bailed out by war or other exigencies, since it must generally dispose of goods at market prices below loan rates.

The nonrecourse loan provides a ready source of capital which permits the producer to store the commodity and delay marketing, thus retaining the potential to obtain a higher price later in the marketing season if price increases above the loan rate. If the loan is redeemed, the producer must repay the loan plus interest based on a subsidized interest rate. Since the subsidized interest rate has tended historically to make CCC loans a cheap source of credit when compared with funds from commercial sources, farmers have sometimes placed grain under loan even when harvest prices were above the loan rate.[6]

Changing Role of CCC Loans

Historically the loan rate tended to place a floor under the market price. The Food and Security Act of 1985 changed the role of CCC loans through the introduction of marketing loans and generic payment-in-kind (PIK) certificates.[7] With the marketing loan provision, a producer is allowed to repay the loan at either the original loan rate or at the current market price, whichever is lower. This effectively divorces the loans from their role as a market price support mechanism and is equivalent to an export subsidy. Marketing loans were mandated for cotton and rice but they are discretionary for feed grains and wheat. The USDA elected not to use marketing loans for the latter commodities in the 1986, 1987, and 1988 farm programs.

As further explained in chapter 10, the USDA has also used generic PIK certificates, cash equivalent ownership rights to CCC commodities, to avoid paying benefits in cash. The use of generic PIK certificates is another way of reducing market prices of commodities below loan rates.[8] If, for example, a farmer receives $1,000 value in PIK certificates, the amount of commodities received from CCC stocks or under CCC loans is determined by the market price rather than the loan rate. The use of marketing loans and PIK certificates means that commodities placed under loan are not effectively isolated from the market, and product prices may be reduced far below the loan rates. The implications of the use of marketing loans and generic PIK certificates for international trade are further discussed in chapter 14.

Mandatory versus Voluntary Production Controls

Over the years, the extent to which farmers have been free to choose to participate or not to participate in production control programs has varied a great deal. In the early years, most production control programs were voted on by farmers. This is still true in the case of the tobacco program, the peanut program, and some marketing orders. Wheat, feed grain, and cotton production control programs, however, are now operated on a voluntary basis in the sense that the individual producer has the option of whether to participate in these programs. The producer who does not sign up and comply with program provisions is not eligible for price supports.

The fact that a plebiscite precedes compulsion in the case of mandatory production control programs does not remove the coercive aspect of these programs. The minority of producers who oppose a mandatory program are required to participate just as in any other government program operated on the basis of collective-choice decision-making procedures. A watershed in the freedom by individual farmers to participate in farm programs occurred during the Kennedy administration of the early 1960s. The Food and Agricultural Act of 1962 gave the President power to impose mandatory production controls following approval by two-thirds of the producers. The controls were not to be on acreage but on the pounds or bushels sold. In a 1963 wheat referendum, mandatory controls were soundly defeated.[9] Most of the production control programs since that time have been on a voluntary basis with farmers paid to participate.

It should be emphasized that the distinction between voluntary and mandatory production control programs is not as clear-cut as implied by the preceding discussion. The voluntary versus mandatory distinction as used in discussions of agricultural policy typically refers only to decisions by farmers as producers of the product involved. All price support and production control programs are inconsistent with the competitive market process. That is, there is a fundamental incompatibility between effective domestic agricultural price support policies and free trade. When the domestic price of any product is raised above the world price, imports must be restricted to prevent domestic users from buying the lower-priced product abroad. The plebiscites conducted in the operation of farm programs do not include the much larger number of taxpayers and domestic and foreign consumers who bear the costs of the programs.

Summary

Three different types of product price support programs have been used in U.S. agriculture. In the case of price supports alone, price is supported above the market level, and the government buys the surplus created by the support program. If the price support is effective, the government outlay required to operate the program is likely to create pressures to raise product price through restrictions on production. Product output can be reduced either by restricting input use or by controlling output directly. Both acreage allotments and marketing quotas have been widely used in the operation of U.S. price support programs. When output is restricted, the means of controlling production acquires a value. Increases in product prices resulting from price support programs are capitalized into prices of land, allotments, and other specialized resources, thereby increasing production costs.

In the compensatory payments approach, producers are permitted to produce as much as they wish at the supported price. The quantity produced is sold at a price that will clear the market. Producers then receive a government subsidy for the difference between the market price and the support price.

Price support programs lead to government purchase and storage activities for agricultural products. The CCC is the government agency responsible for the financing of surplus removal. In a nonrecourse loan, the farmer obtains a loan from the CCC by pledging an eligible commodity as collateral. The farmer may either repay the loan within a specified period and regain control of the commodity or default, in which case ownership passes to the CCC.

The long-run effect of price supports on product price will be different from the short-run effect. The initial effect of price support programs is to increase prices of farm products. The raising of product prices, however, holds resources in agriculture that would otherwise have been reallocated to more productive uses. These excess resources increase supply, thereby placing downward pressure on product prices—or increased pressure on the federal treasury to finance price support programs.

The production control programs operated in conjunction with price support operations in the New Deal era were mainly mandatory for all producers once the programs were approved in a farmer referendum. Currently, the individual producer must participate if production controls are approved by two-thirds of the producers in the case of tobacco, peanuts, and marketing orders. Since the early 1960s, producer participation in most other production control programs has been on a voluntary basis for domestic producers. All effective price support programs are inconsistent with the competitive market process, however, as they inevitably impede mutually voluntary exchange and distort markets through accompanying import quotas, export subsidies, and other restrictions on competition.

Notes

1. U.S. Department of Agriculture, *Agricultural Statistics 1986* (Washington, D.C.: U.S. Government Printing Office, 1987), p. 454.

2. Ronald D. Knutson, J. B. Penn, and W. T. Boehm, *Agricultural and Food Policy* (Englewood Cliffs, N.J.: Prentice-Hall, 1983), p. 208.

3. Gary S. Becker, *Economic Theory* (New York: Alfred A. Knopf, 1971), p. 135.

4. This topic is further discussed in chapter 10 in connection with the tobacco program.

5. Knutson, Penn, and Boehm, *Agricultural and Food Policy*, p. 218.

6. Bruce L. Gardner, *The Governing of Agriculture* (Lawrence, Kan.: The Regents Press of Kansas, 1981), p. 24.

7. Steven R. Guebert, "Changing Role of CCC Loans," *Agricultural Situation Report* (McLean, Virginia: Farm Credit Administration, Feb. 6, 1987).

8. Joseph V. Kennedy, "Generic Commodity Certificates: How They Affect Markets and the Federal Budget," *Choices* 2 (1987/3): 14–17.

9. Luther Tweeten, *Foundations of Farm Policy*, second ed. (Lincoln: University of Nebraska Press, 1979), p. 469.

10

Production Controls and Current Price Support Programs

A number of price support and production control programs continue to be based on restrictions on land use. Although participation in price support programs for cotton, rice, wheat, and feed grains is voluntary to the individual producer, the participating producer must restrict land use to receive program benefits. There is no restriction of this type for participants in the soybean, sugar, wool, or honey programs. In the case of the tobacco program, participation is mandatory and production historically has involved stringent poundage and/or acreage controls. Participation in the peanut program, historically quite similar to the tobacco program, is now optional to the producer. The operation of both types of price support programs—optional and mandatory participation—is discussed in this chapter.

Programs where Participation Is Optional

Price support programs for cotton, rice, wheat, and feed grains are tied to voluntary reductions in land use. The current acreage-reduction feature of these programs was first introduced in 1970. Each new farm bill has brought changes in price support levels, but the operation of these programs remains basically unchanged. In this chapter, the way these programs operate is described without discussing the numerous program changes that have occurred since 1970 or the complexities of programs for individual commodities.

Acreage Reduction

The acreage-reduction feature of current cotton, rice, wheat, and feed grain programs requires that a certain percentage of a farmer's cropland must be taken out of production in return for the farmer's right to receive program benefits. In 1987, for example, the maximum allowable planting was 80 percent of the farmer's base acreage for feed grains and 72.5 percent for wheat. Under the 1985 farm bill, the base acreage for a particular farmer in any year is based on the average acreage devoted to the crop during the preceding five years.

Price support and income support payments provide incentives for producers to participate in wheat, rice, cotton, and feed grain programs. Since producer participation is optional, program benefits must be large enough to offset the farmer's foregone income from producing on the acres set aside. The producer not only loses production from the acres taken out of production but also incurs the cost of planting a cover crop in placing the land in a "conservation reserve." In some cases, the cost of idling land has been offset to some extent by direct diversion payments. In 1986, for example, participating corn producers received a diversion payment of $.73 per bushel for 2.5 percent of their base acreage of corn. Farm commodity programs are administered within USDA by the Agricultural Stabilization and Conservation Service (ASCS).

Target Prices and Deficiency Payments

The concept of "target price" was first used in the Agriculture and Consumer Protection Act of 1973. In this compensatory-payment approach, the target price is the effective price support level in implementing wheat, cotton, rice, and feed grain programs. When the market price falls below the target price, participating producers receive direct government payments, referred to as "deficiency payments." The deficiency payment rate per unit of product is generally equal to the difference between the target price and the higher of the loan rate or the market price. Deficiency payments are based on the national average market price received by farmers for the entire marketing year, but some of the deficiency payments may be made to farmers earlier as "advanced payments." The deficiency payment on a farm is determined by the payment rate, program acreage, and the "farm program payment yield," which is based on historical yields for the farm. There is a maximum $50,000 payment limitation "per farm" for deficiency payments. This restriction, other payment limitations, and associated enforcement problems are discussed in chapter 12.

The 1985 farm bill significantly reduced loan rates for the period 1986–1990 to make U.S. farm products more competitive in international markets. However, target prices were reduced little. Thus, U.S. farmers are more beholden to government than ever before for their income under the 1985 farm bill.

Magnitude of Deficiency Payments

The deficiency payment rate varies, depending upon the relationship between the target price, the loan rate, and the market price.[1] If the market price, Pm, is above the target price, Pt, the price support is ineffective and no deficiency payment will be made (figure 10.1). Price support levels, however, are usually set high enough to be effective. Consider the situation depicted in figure 10.2 where the market price is above the loan rate

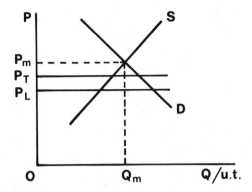

Figure 10.1. Target-price approach where price support is ineffective.

but below the target price. In this case, the target price OP_T results in an output of OQ_T which clears the market at a price OPm. Here the "deficiency payment" would be based on the difference between the target price and the market price. Thus, the total government deficiency payment would be $(P_T - Pm) \cdot OQ_T$

Eligible producers have the option of obtaining a commodity loan from the CCC at the loan rate. The loan rate for a particular commodity varies between regions and varies from year to year. Thus participating producers have an incentive to place the commodity under loan to the government if market price is expected to be below the loan rate. However, the market price conceivably can fall below the loan rate either through the use of "generic" PIK certificates or "marketing loans" (described in chapter 14), or if a large number of producers elect not to participate in the price support program and are ineligible for CCC loans (figure 10.3). In that situation, deficiency payments of $(P_T - P_L) \cdot OQ_T$ would be made to eligible producers. For participating producers electing to place commodities in the nonrecourse loan program, the price received would be the loan rate plus the deficiency payment. In the absence of "marketing loans" (which are not available for most commodities), or widespread use of "generic" PIK certificates, the situation depicted in figure 10.3 is unlikely to occur because the 1985 farm bill has induced almost all farmers to participate in government programs.

Effects of Target-Price Program on Output and Market Price

Input use is distorted in target-price programs because productive land is diverted to lower-valued uses (conservation reserve). Thus, one effect of the target-price approach is to decrease product supply.[2] The possible effects on output and market price are shown in figure 10.4. The supply curve under the price support program is S_1. If the target price is P_T, the

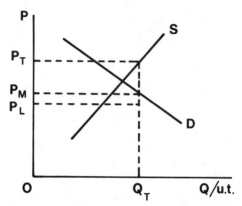

Figure 10.2. Target-price approach where market price is above loan rate.

quantity of output is OQ_T, and OP_M is the market clearing price for this output level. How does this price compare with that in the free-market situation? The target price is clearly above the competitive price level because the free-market supply curve lies to the right of S_1.

The relationship of market price and output under the program to the corresponding free-market levels depends upon the extent to which supply is decreased because of the program. Output may be reduced if the decrease in supply due to set-aside acreage is large. If free market supply conditions are as indicated by S_3 (figure 10.4), for example, output would be lower under the price support program than under a free market.

It is more likely, however, that the target price system leads to *increases* in output. If the decrease in supply because of the program is not large, say from S_2 to S_1 (figure 10.4) and the target price is well above the free-market level, output is likely to increase. Target prices that bring about increases in production have the effect of suppressing the world price. Under this condition, U.S. production is subsidized through deficiency (and diversion) payments to the detriment of producers in other countries. That is, the target-price approach in this case can be viewed as an indirect means of subsidizing exports (this issue is further discussed in chapter 14).

On the other hand, target-price programs that increase domestic prices above world prices stimulate production in other countries. Indeed, the overall effect of price supports implemented through the target-price approach has generally been to decrease the U.S. share in world markets. In the absence of export subsidies, it is the loan rate relative to world market prices that determines U.S. exports of farm products. If the loan rate, which historically has constituted a floor under domestic market prices, is above world prices, then U.S. products will not be competitive in world markets.

The loan rates for U.S. commodities prior to the 1985 farm bill often provided an incentive for producers in other countries to increase their output. The U.S. price support loan rates in effect provided an umbrella for farmers in other countries, enabling these producers to undersell U.S. farmers while the U.S. government supported the market. Thus, G. Edward Schuh's conclusion may be valid about farm programs prior to 1986: "if we were to set out to design a system that would cause us to lose market share, we would be hard pressed to design a better one."[3] The 1985 farm bill instituted "marketing loans" and generic PIK certificates and increased direct export subsidies to make U.S. farm products more competitive in world markets (see chapter 14).

Payment-in-Kind (PIK) Programs

The Payment-in-Kind program was initiated in 1983. It did not replace but merely supplemented existing price support programs for wheat, cotton, rice, and feed grains. Instead of receiving cash payments as an inducement to remove land from production, participating farmers were paid in actual farm commodities for land taken out of production. The "surplus" commodities paid to farmers were from government controlled stocks. The stated objectives of the PIK program were to reduce production, reduce surplus stock holdings, and avoid increased budget outlays. The terms of the program were highly attractive to cooperating farmers. The payment rate on land not planted was 80 percent of average production for feed grain and cotton and 95 percent for wheat.

The PIK program was the most massive and costly acreage reduction program in the history of U.S. farm policy.[4] More than 69 million acres were idled in 1983 by the PIK programs, and farmers received commodities with a book value of about $9 billion.[5]

Large producers were the major gainers from the program. The $50,000 ceiling on price support payments to any one farmer was lifted and some farmers received PIK payments of more than $1 million.

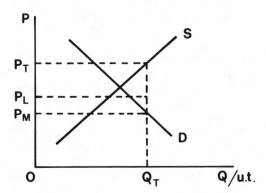

Figure 10.3. Target-price approach where market price is below loan rate.

Agriculture and the State

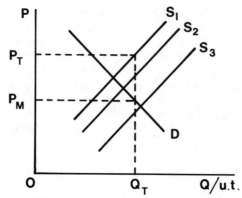

Figure 10.4. Effect of target-price and acreage-reduction program.

The PIK program provides a good example of government programs having effects that cannot be foreseen, which, in turn, create pressures for new programs to deal with these unanticipated consequences. The PIK program reduced sales of farm equipment, fertilizer, and other agricultural inputs, disadvantaging firms selling those inputs. Congress then made agribusiness firms eligible for subsidized Farmers Home Administration (FmHA) loans. A new program administered by the Small Business Administration was also initiated. This program offered low-interest loans to businesses in counties with heavy PIK participation that could prove PIK reduced their income by stipulated amounts over a six-month period.

The PIK program also adversely affected consumers and purchasers of affected farm products. Livestock and poultry producers, for example, were harmed by the PIK program because of sharply higher feed costs. By restricting production and increasing prices, the PIK program also reduced exports of U.S. farm products. Moreover, although PIK was effective in reducing government stocks of surplus commodities, it did nothing to reduce long-run production incentives.

"Generic" PIK certificates, initiated in the 1985 farm bill, were used as a substitute for a portion of the direct cash payment in making advance deficiency payments for wheat and feed grains. These certificates could be redeemed for wheat, feed grains, rice, or milk. However, the USDA permitted the certificates to be sold by any holder, and some PIK recipients found that selling the paper yielded a higher cash return than selling the underlying commodities. The premium apparently was related to bumper harvests and the short supply of storage space.[6] The storage space problem made the PIK certificates all the more valuable because they could be redeemed for storage space as well as surplus commodities. That is, producers in a tight storage situation could acquire certificates in order to redeem regular CCC loans, and thus move such commodities into the market.

Farmer-Owned Reserve

The farmer-owned reserve (FOR) for wheat and feed grains was introduced in the late 1970s by the Carter administration. It was designed to stabilize prices and to provide increased supply assurance to domestic and foreign customers.[7] The FOR is, in effect, a loan extension in which the CCC provides annual storage payments. Under the current program, the loans are made for three years and may be extended "as warranted by market conditions."[8] These reserve loans require market prices to rise to a certain level before they can be repaid. Whenever the market price for the commodity has reached the "release price," the secretary of agriculture may increase the interest rate on loans to encourage producers to redeem their loans and market their grain. The release level is set at 140 percent of the regular loan rate or the target price, whichever is higher.[9] The upper limit on the amount of grain placed in the reserve is specified as a percentage of the estimated total domestic and export use during the marketing year.[10] Producers are penalized if they redeem their wheat or feed grain loans when reserve stocks are below the upper limits and market prices are below the release level.

The FOR program represents federally-managed subsidized holding of grain stocks by farmers. Storage subsidies include reduced-interest loans and storage payments. Loans may be called in prior to the maturity date only if the secretary determines that emergency conditions require that the commodities be made available.[11]

The operation of the farmer-owned reserve program faces the same questions as other government programs to manage reserve stocks. The basic question is whether the farmer (and other private entrepreneurs) or the government is better able to make storage decisions. Storage decisions made through the collective-choice process are subject to the problems described earlier. Information about future demand is not known, so all storage decisions involve uncertainty. However, there is no reason to expect the public official to have more accurate information about current and future market conditions than actual market participants. Furthermore, the private entrepreneur, with his own funds at stake, has a greater incentive to make the best use of available information. When storage decisions are made through the political process, short-run political considerations are likely to dominate economic considerations. The massive government stocks of dairy products acquired through the dairy program are a good example.

There is also a closely related question of why storage of food and fiber products *should* be subsidized. Storage operations will be undertaken to the extent that private entrepreneurs think storage will be profitable. When storage operations are subsidized, more of the product is stored than is warranted on the basis of market information available when the storage decision is made. Moreover, if the amount of farm products stored in the United States increases, storage of these products is discouraged in importing countries. In summary, when information and incentive problems are taken into account, there is no reason to think that storage decisions made through the collective-choice process will improve on storage decisions made by private entrepreneurs operating in decentralized markets.

Other Programs

Soybeans

Although there is no target price as for wheat, rice, cotton and feed grains, soybean price is supported through loans and purchases. The price support level for soybeans in the past has generally been low enough to be ineffective. The loan rate was $5.02 per bushel for the 1987 soybean crop, which was the minimum rate under the 1981 farm bill. For 1988–90 crops, the support price (loan rate) will be based on a five-year moving average of market prices.[12] The loan rate so determined may be reduced by no more than 5 percent in any year (but not below $4.50 per bushel) to "encourage domestic use and exports."[13]

Sugar

The 1985 farm bill continues the sugar program for domestically grown sugarcane and sugar beets through 1990. The sugar program holds the domestic wholesale price of raw sugar considerably above the world price. In October 1987, for example, the domestic price was more than three times the world price.

How are sugar imports discouraged when domestic prices are so much higher than world prices? Import quotas, fees, and duties of various kinds have been used in the past. Now, restrictions consist solely of country-by-country import quotas. These quotas, though quite valuable, are allocated free of charge to sugar exporting countries.

The 1985 farm bill directs the Secretary of Agriculture to use non-recourse loans in supporting sugar prices. Import quotas are to be set at a level that will permit the USDA to operate the program "at no cost to the government" by preventing accumulation of CCC stocks to sugar.[14]

The absence of taxpayer cost, however, does not imply that the sugar program is costless. Producers benefit by the difference between domestic price and world market price. These benefits in the 1982–1983 fiscal year averaged $98,000 per sugarcane farm and $43,000 per sugar-beet farm.[15] Although the benefits are highly concentrated to the ten to fifteen thousand sugar producers, the costs are highly dispersed among the 240 million U.S. consumers. Since the average consumer uses only about one hundred pounds of sugar per year, it is easy to see why individual sugar producers are more concerned with maintaining the sugar program than sugar consumers are in abolishing it. Although consumers bear the cost of the program through higher sugar costs, the cost per consumer is quite small.

Support for the sugar program is not limited to domestic sugar producers. The sugar program is highly beneficial to the corn-based sweetener industry, and the Washington lobbyists for corn refiners are highly effective advocates for sugar price supports.[16]

Wool and Mohair

The 1985 farm bill extends the National Wool Act of 1954 through 1990. Under this program, the price of wool and mohair is supported through loans, purchases, and other operations, using the CCC as the implementing agency. The government makes up the difference between the price support level and the market price in "incentive payments" to farmers. In 1983, for example, the price support was about two-and-a-half times the market price.[17] Thus the wool program is highly costly to taxpayers. A tariff on wool imports is a key ingredient in the wool program because the price support level greatly exceeds world price. The wool policy is, as one might expect, largely a product of the wool industry.[18] A variety of justifications has been offered for the wool program. However, all appear to be consistent with the rent-seeking theory of government action.

Wool production has declined markedly in the United States during the past thirty years in spite of government efforts to aid wool growers. Domestic consumption of wool has declined to less than half the level of the early 1960s and domestic production is less than one-third of consumption.[19]

Honey

The 1985 farm bill, after much debate, extended the honey program and set the loan rates for 1986 and 1987. The loan and purchase levels for 1988–90 crops will be the rate from the previous year reduced by 5 percent, but the level cannot be less than 75 percent of the average price received by producers in the preceding five crop years.[20] The operation of the honey nonrecourse loan program is similar to that for wheat and feed grains.

The honey price support program has become more expensive as the government acquired increasing quantities of honey. The honey support price has been greater than the world price and imports of honey have increased.[21] Since honey is not protected by stiff import barriers, the cost of high price supports shows up as treasury costs instead of higher honey prices to consumers. The original rationale of the honey program was to ensure an adequate supply of honeybees for crop pollination purposes.

However, this rationale is not valid since producers of seed or fruit crops to which bee pollination is essential pay for or supply their own honeybees for this purpose.[22]

The Tobacco Program: Participation Mandatory

Both the peanut and the tobacco programs have marketing quotas. Tobacco has had strict production controls since the 1930s. The programs for peanuts and tobacco will be discussed separately because the programs are now quite different.

Why is government policy so important in tobacco production?[23] Although the harvested acreage of tobacco amounts to less than one-half of one percent of total U.S. cropland, tobacco has a high value per acre. The gross revenue from tobacco, totaling $3500 to $4000 per acre, is ten to twenty times larger than that from corn. Tobacco is also an important regional crop. In North Carolina, for example, tobacco accounts for about one-third of gross farm receipts. Moreover, within the tobacco production region many farmers and land owners have an interest in tobacco production. Tobacco is grown in twenty-one states on about 200,000 farms. An additional 350,000 quota holders have a stake in the tobacco price-support program.[24] The political clout of tobacco producers, as described below, is also affected by the way in which the tobacco program operates.

There are several different themes in tobacco policy. These include: (1) restrictions on smoking in public places, (2) efforts to reduce consumption generally, and (3) producer price support programs. The first two will be only briefly described.

There are increasing efforts to restrict smoking in public places, including work areas, airplanes, and restaurants. Most of the impetus for this legislation is at the local or state level, and it is too early to determine what the long-run effects will be.

A second theme of attempts to reduce consumption has a much longer history. Sumptuary taxes have been imposed on tobacco products since colonial times. If the demand for tobacco products is inelastic, a high tax rate may generate large revenues with relatively little effect on consumption of tobacco products. "In 1983, an estimated $8.9 billion in taxes was collected—$4.7 billion by the Federal Government and $4.2 billion by state and local governments. Thus, taxes collected amounted to more than 2.5 times tobacco farm sales."[25]

Efforts to reduce consumption have intensified since 1964 when the Surgeon General of the United States issued a report attacking smoking.[26] Radio and TV cigarette advertising has been banned in the United States and health warning labels are required on cigarette containers.[27] Although cigarette use has been trending downward in the U.S., per capita cigarette consumption appears to be increasing on a world-wide basis.[28]

There has been a great deal of criticism of the tobacco program. The tobacco program is facing increasing pressures not only because of the health problems associated with tobacco use but also because of the program's effects on tobacco exports. At the end of World War II, the U.S. share of flue-cured tobacco exports exceeded 60 percent. By 1985, that percentage was down to 22 percent.[29] The price support program in the U.S. has indirectly subsidized the production of tobacco in Canada, Brazil, India, and in other countries that are major competitors of the United States in tobacco production.

Production Controls and Price Supports

Efforts in the United States to increase tobacco price by restricting production can be traced back to the 1600s. However, an effective producer cartel for tobacco was not achieved until the AAA of 1933. Although the tobacco price support program has been modified over time, the program today is very similar to the program of the 1930s.[30] In the beginning, the tobacco program had price supports with strict production controls on land use. A national acreage allotment was determined and allocated among individual farmers. With prices supported above the competitive level and farmers able to sell legally all of the tobacco produced at the supported price, fertilizer, pesticides, and other inputs were substituted for land. Therefore, allotments had to be cut again and again to maintain prices and prevent a buildup of storage stocks. Since 1965, tobacco producers have also been subject to poundage marketing quotas. The price support level, originally based on parity, was adjusted from year to year by the Prices Paid Index from the early 1960s until the Tobacco Reform Act of 1986 was passed.

The loan and storage features of the tobacco program are operated using grower–owned and operated cooperatives. For flue-cured tobacco, the Flue-Cured Tobacco Cooperative Stabilization Corporation (Stabilization) takes control of all tobacco that goes under loan. At the time of the sales auction, Stabilization pays the farmer for tobacco going under loan with money borrowed from the CCC. Stabilization then stores the crop and arranges for sale to private buyers.

In response to widespread public criticism of government expenditures on the tobacco program, the "No Net Cost" Tobacco Act of 1982 established a producer-supported fund to repay the government for program outlays (except for administrative costs). Growers were assessed fees in 1984 and 1985 but the assessment fund was not large enough to cover expected losses and it became clear that the program was not financially viable. Thus events did not work out as expected, and the "no net cost" approach led to a federal bailout of the tobacco program in 1986.

The Tobacco Reform Act of 1986 reduced the average level of price supports by about 20 percent and established a formula for setting support prices based on a moving average of past market prices and on the USDA index of prices paid by tobacco farmers.[31] Major domestic buyers are now required to estimate purchases for the upcoming crop year in the

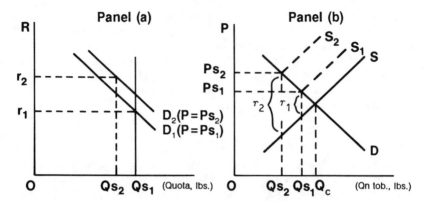

Figure 10.5. Tobacco quota rental price is derived from product market.

spring. The secretary of agriculture then sets the quota based on these data and export projections with an adjustment for inventory levels and other market conditions.[32]

The Tobacco Reform Act of 1986 provided for the sale of large unsold stabilization inventories from previous crop years at greatly discounted prices, resulting in a loss to the CCC. This act thus clearly amounted to a government subsidy to rescue the "no net cost" tobacco program.[33]

Quota Price—How Determined

The demand for tobacco quota is derived from the demand for tobacco. Since the quota, or the right to produce and sell tobacco, does not enter the production process except as it constrains output, the demand for quota reflects the residual revenue, taking into account the cost of all other factors. Assume tobacco price is supported at the level OPs_1 (panel b, figure 10.5) This price is consistent with the output level OQs_1. The rental value of the quota is the difference between product price and nonquota production costs as represented by the supply curve (amount r_1 in panel b, figure 10.5). This quota value is shown in the quota market as having an equivalent annual rental value of or_1 (panel a, figure 10.5). Thus the value of the quota is determined by tobacco price and the nonquota costs of production.

If the amount of quota is reduced, say to OQs_2, product price increases to OPs_2. Alternatively, it is necessary to reduce production to OQs_2 if the market price is to be increased to the price support level OPs_2 without incurring a surplus. As the amount of quota is reduced and product price increases, quota value rises and factors with upward-sloping supply curves receive lower returns. The demand for quota increases from D_1 to D_2 as product price increases (panel a, figure 10.5). Thus, all things being equal, quota rental price is higher the higher tobacco price is supported above the competitive level.

Tobacco must be produced in the county to which the quota is assigned, but the quota can be rented in place or sold within county lines. 1982 legislation, for the first time, provided authority for owners of flue-cured tobacco allotments and quotas to sell these rights. However, allotments and quotas may be sold for use only to other active producers in the same county.[34] As of 1987, owners can no longer rent out tobacco allotment. Owners must produce their own quota, rent it in place, or sell the quota.

The preceding discussion provides an explanation for the fact that rental prices for quota vary from county to county. Quota rental values are higher in the lower-cost production areas. In figure 10.5 (panel b), for example, the supply curve would lie to the right of curve SS in a lower-cost county. In this case, the difference between the support price, say OPs_1, and supply would be greater and so would quota rental value.

The market value of tobacco quota can be explained by capital asset pricing theory. If the tobacco program were expected to last forever, the quota value would be determined by the capitalization formula

$$PV = \frac{A}{i}$$

Where:
PV = Present value of a pound of quota
A = Annual rental price per pound of tobacco quota
i = Discount rate

In reality, there is a great deal of uncertainty about the future of the tobacco program. This uncertainty is reflected in higher discount rates and reduced market prices for tobacco quota.

Transitional Gains Trap

The capitalization of increased product prices into prices of quotas and other specialized resources gives rise to what has been referred to as a "transitional gains trap."[35] The producers who were assigned allotments when the tobacco program was initiated received a windfall gain. The right to produce tobacco—the tobacco acreage allotment—immediately acquired a value because production was legally restricted. However, the fact that the allotment acquired a value also meant that production costs were increased (panel b, figure 10.5). After the program was begun, the farmer who wished to produce tobacco had to either own tobacco allotment or rent it from another owner. If allotment is rented, the cost is direct. If the producer tends owned allotment, its use has an opportunity cost. Thus, one effect of the tobacco program has been significantly to increase production costs.

When increases in price supports lead to increased prices of allotments, quotas, and other specialized resources, the individuals owning these resources at the time prices increase receive the benefits. Later producers, however, receive little or no benefit since the higher product prices are offset by higher production costs. The conclusion is that the gain from price supports is transitory or a once-and-for-all windfall.

Moreover, once a price support program is begun, there is no way to abolish the program (return to competitive markets) without imposing windfall losses on owners of quotas and other specialized resources— many of whom are not the ones who received the original windfall gain. This "transitional gains trap" problem where the value of the right to produce is capitalized into higher production costs is inherent in price support programs of all types.

The Peanut Program

Peanut production is in some respects quite similar to tobacco production. Both are high value crops important on a regional basis, and both programs are binding on all producers if at least two-thirds of the producers voting in a referendum approve it. The peanut program was begun in the 1930s and peanut acreage allotments lasted until 1977. At that time, acreage allotments were replaced with poundage quotas.

The peanut program is now a two-price plan. Peanuts produced for edible use in the domestic market are supported above the competitive level. Under the 1985 farm bill, the price support rate is equal to the preceding year's price "adjusted for changes in the cost of peanut production (excluding land), but in no event more than 6 percent above the previous year's supported price."[36] Peanut growers are allocated quotas based on the expected consumption of peanuts in the domestic market. Only quota holders are entitled to price supports. A grower may produce peanuts in the absence of a quota, but there are strict controls on the use of peanuts not produced under quota. Quota holders and other producers may produce nonquota peanuts in unlimited amounts but receive the market clearing price for these "additionals" which must be exported or crushed into oil and meal. Peanuts marketed for domestic edible use in excess of the farm poundage quota are subject to a penalty equal to 140 percent of the support price.

Peanut quotas (like tobacco quotas) may be sold or leased within but not between counties. The peanut price support program increases cost of production for the same reasons that the tobacco program does. The restriction on movement of quotas across the county or state lines prevents the shifting of production to the most profitable production regions. The barriers to mobility also lead to huge disparities in productivity between production regions. For example, peanut yields in Georgia average more than double those in Texas.[37]

In the operation of the two-price plan, import restrictions virtually prohibit imports of edible peanuts. If this were not done, lower-priced imports would be substituted for the higher-priced peanuts produced under price supports for the domestic market. Thus the program represents a transfer of income from consumers who must pay higher prices for edible peanuts to holders of peanut quotas.

Summary

A number of price-support programs continue to be based on restrictions on land use. In the case of cotton, wheat, rice, and feed grain programs, participation is voluntary from the standpoint of the individual producer. Farmers are induced to participate by a compensatory payments program which assures the producer of a "target price." The cost of participation to the eligible producer is a mandatory reduction in the amount of land planted. The diverted land must be placed in an approved conservation use. The target price, if effective, is above the competitive level, but the amount of production may be less or more than under the free market, depending upon the amount of diverted acreage. These price support programs, based on voluntary diversion of productive land to less productive uses, are expensive to taxpayers, and are inconsistent with free trade.

Participating producers receive "deficiency payments" when the market price falls below the target price. Eligible producers also have the option of obtaining nonrecourse loans. The farmer-owned reserve for wheat and feed grains is an extension of the initial nine-month nonrecourse loans in which the CCC provides annual storage payments. The farmer-owned reserve implicitly assumes that private entrepreneurs would store "too little" in the absence of this federally–managed and subsidized storage program.

Price support programs are also operated by the CCC for soybeans, sugar, wool, and honey. The sugar program is the most costly of these programs. Although the treasury cost is small, import quotas have been used to raise domestic sugar prices some three times above world market levels in recent years.

The government–sponsored and sanctioned tobacco production cartel is subject to the same criticism as other cartels. The tobacco program now faces added pressures due to the health effects of tobacco use. Increasingly, questions are being raised about the role of government in tobacco production. While the Surgeon General and other government agencies are attempting to reduce tobacco use, the USDA subsidizes research in tobacco production. In one sense, it is ironic that various groups are challenging the tobacco price support program for health reasons, since elimination of the tobacco program would surely reduce the price of tobacco products and lead to an *increase* in the amount of smoking.

The elimination of the tobacco (or peanut) program would also abolish the value of tobacco (or peanut) marketing quotas. The effect would be a reduction in cost of production, with costs being reduced more in low-cost production areas where quota values are highest. There is a "transitional gains trap" in the case of the tobacco, peanut, wheat, cotton, and other price support programs. Present producers do not benefit appreciably from the programs once program benefits have been capitalized into higher costs of allotments, land, and other specialized inputs, but owners of land, quotas, and other assets would incur substantial windfall losses if the programs were terminated.

Large farms receive larger gains from farm programs because deficiency payments and other benefits are usually associated with amount of output. Indeed, farm program payments go primarily to farmers whose incomes are far above the median household income in the United States. This paradox, the effect of increased asset prices on producers versus asset owners, and attempts by farmers to circumvent payment limitations are further explored in chapter 12.

Notes

1. Ronald D. Knutson, J. B. Penn, and W. T. Boehm, *Agricultural and Food Policy* (Englewood Cliffs, N.J.: Prentice-Hall, 1983), p. 222.

2. The Food Security Act of 1985, by legislating target prices to 1990, may also reduce uncertainty about farm product prices. If uncertainty is reduced, farmers will produce more at a given price than they would without the price guarantees. If there is an increase in supply, it will offset some of the decrease in supply associated with the land set-aside features of the price support system. Geoff Edwards, "U.S. Farm Policy: An Australian Perspective," *Federal Reserve Bank of St. Louis Review* 69, no. 8 (October 1987): 20–31.

3. G. Edward Schuh, "U.S. Agriculture in the World Economy," in *Farm and Food Policy: Critical Issues for Southern Agriculture*, M. D. Hamming and H. M. Harris, Jr., Proceedings of a Symposium, Clemson University, June 2–3, 1983, p. 69.

4. Fred H. Sanderson, "A Retrospective on PIK," *Food Policy* 8 (May 1984): 103–10.

5. Ibid., p. 106.

6. David Rapp, "PIK Certificates Prove Popular with Farmers and Lawmakers," *Congressional Quarterly* 44 (September 13, 1986): 2139–42.

7. Knutson, Penn, and Boehm, *Agricultural and Food Policy*, p. 224.

8. Lewrene K. Glaser, *Provisions of the Food Security Act of 1985*, AIB Number 498 (Washington, D.C.: ERS, USDA, 1986), p. 36.

9. Ibid.

10. Ibid.

11. Ibid., p. 37.

12. Barbara C. Stucker and Keith J. Collins, *The Food Security Act of 1985: Major Provisions Affecting Commodities*, Economic Research Service, U.S. Department of Agriculture, Ag. Info. Bulletin No. 497 (Washington, D.C.: U.S. Government Printing Office, 1986), p. 8.

13. Ibid.

14. Ibid., p. 10.

15. Economic Research Service, Sugar: Background for 1935 Farm Legislation, AIB Number 478 (Washington, D.C.: U.S. Department of Agriculture, 1984), p. 37.

16. Michael Fumento, "Some Dare Call Them . . . Robber Barons," National Review, 13 March 1987, pp. 32–38.

17. James Bovard, "A Subsidy Both Wooly-Headed and Mammoth," Wall Street Journal, 17 April 1985.

18. Harold G. Halcrow, Agricultural Policy Analysis (New York: McGraw-Hill Book Company, 1984), p. 149.

19. Ibid.

20. Glaser, 1985 Food Security Act, p. 32.

21. Report to the Congress, Federal Price Support for Honey Should Be Phased Out, GAO/RCED-85-107 (Washington, D.C.: General Accounting Office, 1985).

22. Ibid., p. ii.

23. Several different kinds of tobacco are grown but flue-cured and burley account for more than 90 percent of total production. Economic Research Service, Tobacco: Background for 1985 Farm Legislation, AIB Number 468 (Washington, D.C.: U.S. Department of Agriculture, 1984), p. 1.

24. Ibid., p. 26.

25. Ibid., p. 1.

26. Paul R. Johnson, The Economics of the Tobacco Industry (New York: Praeger, 1984).

27. A recent study concludes that successive restrictions on advertising have tended to undermine improvements in cigarettes while doing nothing to reduce smoking. John E. Calfee, "The Ghost of Cigarette Advertising Past," Regulation 10 (Nov.–Dec. 1986): 235–45.

28. Johnson, Tobacco Industry, p. 66.

29. Ibid., p. 100, and USDA, Tobacco Outlook and Situation Report Yearbook (Washington, D.C.: U.S. Government Printing Office, 1987).

30. Daniel M. Sumner and Julian M. Alston, Consequences of Elimination of the Tobacco Program, Bulletin 469 (Raleigh: N.C. Agricultural Research Service, 1984).

31. Daniel A. Sumner, "A Study of the Recent History and a Projection of Budget Costs of the 'New' Tobacco Program," Paper presented at Annual Meeting of American Agricultural Economic Association, Reno, Nevada, July 27–30, 1986.

32. Ibid.

33. Ibid.

34. Economic Research Service, Tobacco, Background for 1985 Farm Legislation, p. 24.

35. Gordon Tullock, "The Transitional Gains Trap," Bell Journal of Economics 6 (Autumn 1975): 671–78.

36. Barbara C. Stucker and Keith J. Collins, The Food Security Act of 1985: Major Provisions Affecting Commodities, AIB Number 497 (Washington D.C.: ERS, USDA, January 1986), p. 9.

37. "Goober Madness at the USDA," Regulation 9 (Jan.–Feb. 1985): 6–8.

11

Cooperatives and Marketing Orders

Historically, there has been a widespread opinion that farmers suffer because of a lack of bargaining power. This attitude is related to the fact that the farmer's share of the consumer's dollar has decreased over time as processing and marketing services for food products increased. Middlemen are often blamed for many of the farmer's woes. Farm income is thought to be lower because of the profits earned by middlemen as farm products move from the farm to the consumer. Thus, farmers and farm organizations have long sought ways to increase the share of the consumer's food dollar received by farmers. This chapter presents an analysis of cooperatives and marketing orders—marketing institutions designed to increase farmers' bargaining power and to reduce the role of middlemen in the marketing of farm products.

Marketing and Supply Cooperatives

The underlying idea of a cooperative is that it provides a way for a voluntary association of individuals to avoid dealing with profit-seeking firms.[1] The basic objective of a co-op is to reduce or eliminate middleman margins. A group of farmers may band together in buying inputs or in marketing products. In marketing co-ops, quite often there is also a goal of increasing price by controlling supply.

Co-ops are owned and controlled by member patrons and operated on a nonprofit basis. The co-op share of farm-level marketing activity increased from about 20 percent in 1952 to abut one-third in 1980.[2] In 1984, there were 3,514 farm marketing co-ops and 2,136 farm supply co-ops in the United States.[3]

Capper-Volstead Act

The co-op movement began in the early 1800s in the United States, when dairy producers in Connecticut attempted to act together as a group in churning and marketing butter. The establishment of co-ops was an important activity of all the major farm organizations. However, the modern co-op movement received a major impetus with the passage of the

Capper-Volstead Act in 1922. The act, which establishes conditions under which an organization might be defined as a co-op, attempts to increase the bargaining power of farmers by protecting co-ops from the antitrust provisions of the earlier Sherman and Clayton Acts. Although "undue price enhancement" by co-ops is forbidden, enforcement is entrusted to the secretary of agriculture rather than the Department of Justice. In view of the subjective nature of the concept "undue price enhancement," it is not surprising that no secretary of agriculture since 1922 has found an instance in which a co-op was guilty of this practice. When prices are raised above free-market levels, it is a matter of opinion as to whether price has been "unduly" increased.

In the early 1980s, the Justice Department, the Federal Trade Commission, the General Accounting Office, and the Executive Office of the President expressed concern about the effects of co-op activities. While the Capper-Volstead Act gives co-ops the right to form a common marketing agency, the extent to which co-ops can legally control the production of their members is uncertain. It is clear that without the act many of the co-op marketing activities would be in violation of federal antitrust laws. Co-ops, for example, are allowed to engage in information-sharing activities that would almost certainly violate antitrust laws if done by a group of investor-owned firms. Cooperatives such as those involving marketing orders for milk and navel oranges which significantly increase consumer prices are facing increasing public pressure.

Incentive Problems

It is held by some economic analysts that "most cooperatives are unable to compete with the large investor firms."[4] When a co-op attains any significant scale of operation, the absence or weakness of economic incentives is likely to create management problems. Although co-ops must have full-time employees and hired management, management functions in most co-ops are in the hands of people who are not residual claimants. The residual claimant of a proprietary firm is the owner. He or she reaps the profits or bears the losses of managerial decisions. In an investor-owned firm, there is a market for corporate stock. Consequently, equity prices in an investor-owned firm, unlike equity prices in a co-op, reflect the market's assessment of the firm's long-run prospects. There is also a market for corporate managers. Hence, market signals in investor-owned firms provide important information in monitoring management, despite the separation of ownership and control.

In a co-op, on the other hand, management does not stand to gain or lose depending upon success of the firm, at least to the same extent, as in a typical investor-owned firm. Thus, there is a separation of power and responsibility in the co-op and the attendant incentive problems. The goals of co-op managers will vary, but it is predictable that when decisions are made by those who are not residual claimants, decision makers will manage in a way that lowers the present value of the co-op's stream of future residual returns.[5]

The residual claimants of a co-op's earnings are its members. When a new member purchases equity in a co-op, unlike the purchase of corporate stock, no right to future residual co-op earnings is acquired and no right to sell the equity is acquired.[6] The rights to future residual earnings belong to future patrons. Upon admission to membership in a co-op, a new member-patron acquires the same rights to the organization's residual cash flows based on patronage as those held by existing members. Since co-op residual claimants can capture the benefits of investment decisions only over the time horizons of their expected membership, there is a general tendency to favor investment decisions with short payoff horizons.[7] In view of the inherent incentive problems in the co-op form of business enterprise, the question arises: why do co-ops survive?

Tax Treatment of Cooperatives

A key to co-op survival appears to be the tax treatment afforded patronage refunds.[8] Patronage refunds are not counted as income to the co-op and are therefore not taxed but are taxed as personal income to the co-op members. Earnings retained in the business after they have been allocated to members' accounts are not taxable to the co-op, but are taxable to the members. In an investor-owned corporation, in contrast, dividend income is taxable both to the corporation at the corporate rate and when received by the individual shareholder. The result is a substantial tax break to the co-op as illustrated by the hypothetical example shown in table 11.1.[9] (It should, however, be borne in mind that the Tax Reform Act of 1986 reduced corporate tax rates, and hence the extent of the tax break to co-ops.)

In this example, it is assumed that size of business, income, and operating costs are the same for the corporation and the co-op. It is also assumed that all of the co-op earnings are distributed as patronage refunds or allocated to members' accounts. The corporation shareholders' income after taxes is $274,000, a rate of return of 9.1 percent of their equity. In contrast, the after-tax rate of return for the co-op is 12.0 percent.

Sexton and Sexton contend that the preceding argument overlooks the fact that the cooperative-patron relationship is closely analogous to the stages of a vertically integrated business, and that a vertically integrated corporation gets virtually the same tax break as a co-op.[10] In a vertically integrated poultry production, processing, and marketing corporation, for example, the earnings of the parts of the corporation pass to the parent company without being taxed. However, as shown by the above example, it is the taxation of the earnings of the parent company which appears to place the corporation-shareholder relationship at a disadvantage relative to the cooperative-patron relationship.

Table 11.1   Effect of Differences in Taxation of Corporations and Cooperatives

	CORPORATION	CO-OP
Sales	$5,000,000	$5,000,000
Costs (operating and overhead)	4,500,000	4,500,000
Income	500,000	500,000
Dividends (patronage refunds)	200,000	200,000
Corporate taxes (34%)	170,000	0
Retained in business	130,000	300,000
Personal taxes (28% rate)	56,000	140,000
Owners' income after taxes	274,000	360,000
Owners' equity	3,000,000	3,000,000

123

The above example suggests why a great deal of effort is spent in maintaining the tax status of co-ops. Any co-op tax advantages, however, are offset to some extent by the inherent managerial incentive problems discussed above. Depending upon the severity of managerial problems, there could be a problem in financing co-op activities. However, most equity capital in agricultural co-ops is raised by retaining a share of member patronage refunds. Moreover, financing difficulties are offset by the federally chartered Bank for Co-Operatives, which the co-ops own and which provides a major share of the outstanding debt of co-ops.[11]

While supply co-ops raise questions of fairness in taxation, equity questions also arise in the use of co-ops for the purpose of collective bargaining. In this role (as in the case of dairy co-ops), they simply act as bargaining agents instead of replacing handlers of farm products. So long as producers are not required to join, a cooperative is unlikely to have a major effect on product prices because of the difficulties posed by free riders. In the absence of government sanctions, the free rider is likely to make cartellization ineffective.[12] Consequently, effective agricultural cartels invariably require government sanctions. Marketing orders represent a government-sanctioned method of eliminating the effects of the beneficial free rider who, when not restrained by government, acts as an impediment to anticompetitive behavior.

Marketing Orders

The enabling legislation for marketing orders was initiated under the federal Agricultural Marketing Agreement Act of 1937. Marketing orders were provided as a tool to achieve "orderly" marketing conditions and parity prices. Marketing orders, like other price support programs, were instituted at a time of strong sentiment to raise agricultural prices through restrictions on competition.

Marketing orders can be requested by producers and implemented after a hearing if two-thirds of the producers favor the proposed order (processors generally do not vote). The order defines the commodity and the market order to be regulated. Orders empower government-appointed panels of producers and middlemen to make industry-wide marketing decisions about sales volume and standards.

There are both federal and state marketing orders. While legislative provisions differ, order operation is basically the same for state and federal marketing orders. The discussion of this chapter focuses on federal orders. In federal orders, employees of the USDA assist producers of a specific commodity in developing the proposal for an order. If the order is approved by producers, the terms of the agreement are binding on all handlers. There is considerable variation in orders but the basic principle is the same: market orders provide a means to enable producers to act together to limit competition.

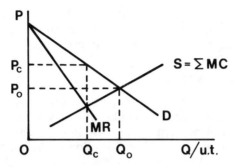

Figure 11.1. Voluntary cartels generally are ineffective because of freeriders.

Marketing Orders as a "Self-Help" Program

Marketing orders are often referred to as producer "self-help" programs. In reality, however, a marketing order, being a type of government-sanctioned and enforced producer cartel, is more aptly described as a "government-help" program. Government sanctions are used to negate the free-rider incentive that limits the effectiveness of voluntary cartels.

The free-rider incentive in voluntary cartels is shown in figure 11.1. Under competitive conditions, output OQ_o is produced and sold at the price OP_o. If producers can agree to act together and restrict output to OQ_c (where marginal revenue is equal to marginal cost), short-run profits can be increased. Such an agreement is usually unstable, however, because it is profitable for each of the producers to increase output at the cartel price (OP_c); that is, each seller has an incentive to be a free rider and to cheat on the agreement. Thus, in the case of voluntary cartellization attempts, the free-rider incentive is typically strong enough to maintain competition. A federal marketing order is an institutional arrangement which allows producers to use the police power of government to enforce compliance with restrictions on competition.

Marketing orders exist for milk, and certain fruits, vegetables, and specialty crops. While federal marketing orders for fruits and vegetables contain quantity or quality controls, price-setting, in conjunction with a government operated price support program, is reserved for milk.

Milk Marketing

Most production control programs for agricultural commodities hinge on the fact that demand is inelastic. If demand were elastic, total returns could not be increased by reducing output. In some cases, where a product is used in two or more markets, sellers may be able to increase net returns by price discrimination even if total output is not restricted. Milk is the most important farm commodity in the United States in which a two-price program is used. There are two government programs involved in milk marketing: marketing orders and price supports.

Background of Milk Marketing Orders

In 1922, the Capper-Volstead Act effectively exempted dairy co-ops from antitrust actions allowing producer organizations to restrict output and charge higher prices. During the early 1930s, many states passed laws regulating the pricing of milk. The Agricultural Marketing Agreement Act (AMAA) of 1937 and its amendments still govern the federal marketing order for milk and other products. The marketing-order system is the umbrella under which milk is marketed and sold throughout the United States today.

Classified Pricing

Classified pricing is the system of pricing fluid and manufacturing milk according to use. Under this system, different prices are charged depending upon whether the milk is used for fluid consumption or for manfacturing. The classified pricing system for milk is incredibly complex. Although classified pricing is maintained and monitored by a number of federal and state marketing orders, the practice predates the AMAA of 1937.

Grade A milk is that which meets sanitation requirements for fluid milk. About 85 percent of all milk produced in the United States is Grade A. The amount of Grade A milk greatly exceeds the demand for fluid milk at current prices. Consequently, much of this milk is sold for manufacturing uses, including cheese, ice cream, butter, and dry milk powder. Handlers pay producers different prices for Grade A milk based on the final use of the milk, i.e., depending on whether the milk is used for fluid consumption or for manufacturing purposes.

Class I milk is for fluid consumption and Class II is for manufacturing uses which have lower sanitation requirements. In some marketing orders, there is an additional classification, Class III, sold at a price below Class II but also used for processing purposes. Grade B milk is that which does not meet the sanitation requirements for Grade A milk and is not sold for fluid consumption but is used solely for manufactured products. Thus, Grade B milk competes with Grade A only in Class II and Class III uses.

Price Discrimination

Price discrimination provides one explanation for the existence of the classified pricing system of milk. Consider the situation depicted in figure 11.2. If the demand for milk for fluid consumption is less elastic than for

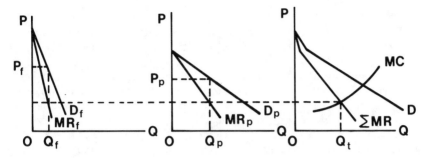

Figure 11. 2.   Price discrimination in selling milk.

processing uses and the markets can be kept separate, there is an opportunity to increase profits. The seller would attempt to allocate the product between uses in a way that would equate the marginal revenue in each market, and a higher price would be charged in the less elastic market (fluid milk).

Although milk for fluid consumption is less elastic than milk for manufacturing, price discrimination is only a crude approximation of the activities that occur under classified pricing. If marginal cost increases (as during the high-cost production season) under price discrimination, a higher price would be charged for milk (in each market). In reality, the procedure for changing price of Class I milk varies among the various state and federal orders. However, fluid milk prices are basically set and then not varied seasonally in response to changing supply and demand conditions.

Operation of the Federal Marketing Order

The marketing order is a legal instrument issued by the secretary of agriculture that regulates the terms under which processors within a specified area can purchase milk from dairy farmers. About 80 percent of the Grade A milk marketed in the United States is delivered to processing plants under federal orders.[13] Most of the remainder is marketed under state orders. Since the economic effects of state and federal orders are similar, the following discussion is mainly devoted to the operation of federal orders.

Under each order, a market administrator sets a legal minimum farm-level price for Class I milk. Milk processors then channel as much milk into fluid use as can be sold at the set price. The rest of the milk is diverted to manufacturing uses. The price of processing milk is supported through a price support system (described below). The Class I price differential varies from market to market, generally increasing with the distance from the Minnesota-Wisconsin area.

Blend Price

All producers in a given market are provided with the same average price for their output, the "blend price." In this pooling arrangement, the processor pays the farmer the same price for milk whether it is used for fluid consumption or for cheese and other manufactured products. However, each processor pays for raw milk according to its use in the order area, paying his suppliers according to the average ratio of Class I sales to all Grade A milk sold in the order area. That is, the blend price is a weighted average of the fluid and manufacturing prices. This system of market-wide pooling is used to keep producers from shifting among processors in an attempt to receive a higher blend price.

Operation of Price Support Programs

In addition to marketing orders, price supports play a key role in milk marketing. Since 1949, the federal government has supported the price of milk by guaranteeing to purchase all milk that cannot be sold at the price support level. Congress sets the level of price supports, and milk price is supported by CCC purchases of enough manufactured milk products to keep milk prices at the support level. These products, butter, cheese, and nonfat dry milk, are then disposed of outside regular market channels to school lunch and other government programs. The dairy program in this way indirectly supports the price of Class I milk by setting a floor under the market price of manufacturing milk products.

Effects of Dairy Program

Marketing orders and price supports have a number of effects in the dairy industry.[14] First, the marketing-order system in conjunction with the price support program increases milk prices to dairy producers. Moreover, the dairy program has increased the consumer price of fluid milk, resulting in a reduction in consumption of fluid milk.

Second, the price of fluid milk has been increased relative to prices of manufactured dairy products. The proportion of Grade A milk by U.S. producers not used for fluid consumption has increased dramatically and is now about one-half of Grade A production.[15] Thus, more and more higher-cost (Grade A) milk is being used for lower-value manufacturing uses. The increasing proportion of Grade A milk used for manufacturing purposes has come at the expense of Grade B production. Thus the dairy program has likely led to larger-size dairy farms, on average, because Grade A farms are larger than Grade B dairy farms.

Third, the dairy program causes an overproduction of milk. When price is increased through a price support program, the surplus problem becomes greater over time. This result occurs because both demand and supply of any product tend to become more elastic the longer the adjustment period. as shown in figure 11.3. In the case of milk production,

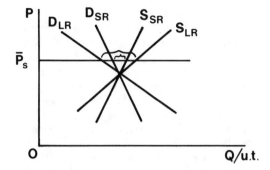

Figure 11.3. Demand and supply are affected by length of adjustment period.

expansion is a long-term process because of the time-lag from birth until a heifer enters the milking herd. Contraction following a price decrease is also likely to be slow because of the heavy investment in specialized facilities.[16]

Fourth, the dairy program creates a misallocation of resources, resulting in too many resources being used in milk production. In general, the production of Grade A milk is not restricted. Because in most orders there is no limit either on the volume of milk a dairy farmer can market at the support price or on the entry of new farms, the process of expansion will continue until the firms are making normal profits. When resources are specialized, as explained in a previous chapter, costs are affected by demand and product price. Thus, price supports lead to increased costs of specialized resources including dairy cows, equipment, land, and the managerial skills required to produce milk. In this way, potential cartel profits tend to be transformed into increased costs. The price support program not only results in higher costs, it also allows higher-cost producers to continue in operation.[17]

The dairy program has increased the proportion of total milk produced in relatively high-cost areas at the expense of production in Minnesota and Wisconsin which are usually assumed to have a comparative advantage in milk production.

Classified pricing is often justified on the basis of the cost differential in producing Grades A and B milk. Without the price differential there would undoubtedly be less Grade A milk produced. However, there is no persuasive evidence that classified pricing is necessary to maintain adequate fluid milk production in the United States.

State Orders

The North Carolina Milk Commission, operating under a state order, regulates milk marketing in that state. The commission classifies milk according to use and has the legal power to fix both maximum and minimum wholesale and retail prices. The price paid to producers is the major tool used to influence milk production in North Carolina. Under state orders, a farmer may be required to have a "base" in order to qualify for a share of the Class I price. The price paid the individual farmer varies depending upon the proportion of Class I sales of milk and the amount of base owned. The amount of base owned by a producer determines the quantity of milk eligible to share in Class I receipts of the pool. The excess over the base is paid the lower manufacturing price. The price of Class I milk in North Carolina is set about $4 per hundredweight above the Minnesota-Wisconsin price of manufacturing milk, unless that is higher than the price of milk moving into the state. The Class II price also moves with the M-W price but is usually about $4 below the Class I price.

Recent Developments

The Dairy and Tobacco Adjustment Act of 1983 provided for a milk diversion program to run from 1 January 1984 through 31 March 1985. Dairy producers were offered $10 per hundred pounds to reduce output between 5 percent and 30 percent of their previous output level. The purpose was to reduce the huge surplus of government-owned cheese, butter, and nonfat dry milk. Government stocks of dairy products were about 17 billion pounds (milk equivalent) at the beginning of 1984.[18] There was no payment limitation under the program, and several producers received in excess of $1 million.

Price support levels for milk have been substantially above the competitive level in recent years. The cost of the dairy program to the federal government was $2.7 billion in fiscal 1983, averaging $13,000 for every commercial dairy farmer. In addition to the treasury cost, restrictive import quotas are used to prevent lower-priced imports from undercutting the dairy program.[19] In recent years imports of dairy products have been curtailed by quotas to about 3 percent of U.S. manufactured dairy product consumption. As a result of these restrictions, U.S. dairy product prices were two to three times the world price in the mid-1980s. Thus the dairy program imposes a substantial cost on consumers of milk and milk products as well as on taxpayers. The beneficiaries, of course, are the dairy producers, suppliers of inputs to the dairy industry, and personnel who administer the programs.

The 1985 farm bill, in response to huge government stocks of milk products, made modest reductions in the level of price supports. It also instituted a "milk production termination program." Under this program, producers were paid to sell their cows and calves and to remain out of dairying for five years. The cows and calves had to be slaughtered or exported. This program, however, will predictably fail to solve the overproduction problem in the U.S. dairy industry since paying farmers not to produce does nothing to reduce the profitability of milk production, the crucial factor in milk output.

Marketing Orders for Fruits and Vegetables

The number of federal marketing orders for fruits, vegetables, and specialty crops has ranged around forty-five to fifty in recent years. These marketing orders typically affect the quality and quantity of product marketed.[20] Oranges and most other commodities marketed under marketing orders are subject to some form of quality control that reduces the amount available for sale. Such measures specify the minimum grades and sizes of products that may be marketed. Imports must also meet standards comparable to those specified in the marketing orders.

About half of the federal marketing orders contain quantity control provisions that permit limitation of sales in the primary (fresh) market, with the remainder moved to a secondary (processed) market. Other provisions of marketing orders may specify varieties of products that may be planted, establish standard packs and containers, and fund research, development, advertising, and promotion. Although there is considerable variation in marketing orders for fruits and vegetables, the basic principle is the same: producers act together to limit competition. There are a number of state marketing orders but the bulk of this activity is in California.

Total-Quantity Regulations

Total-quantity regulations are based on the idea that the elasticity of demand varies by use. *Market allocation* parallels federal milk orders except that quantity instead of price is set in the primary market for a number of products including walnuts, almonds, and raisins. A portion of the product is diverted from the less elastic market and members are paid by the handler on the basis of the average price received in the entire order area. The product excluded may be destroyed, exported, or diverted to a more elastic secondary market.

In the case of *producer allotments*, marketing quotas or allotments are assigned to individual producers. Producer allotments have been used for cranberries, hops, spearmint oil, and Florida celery.[21] Each year a producer is permitted to sell an amount equal to a specified percentage of his base allotment. Another possibility is to *limit production*. For example, there was a "green drop" order provision for California cling peaches to knock fruit from the trees while still small, as a way of reducing production.

Rate-of-Flow Regulations

Rate-of-flow regulations are also based on the fact that demand is less elastic in the primary market. The amount of produce shipped to market in a given period may be limited in several ways. In *reserve pool* schemes, all producers are required to place a specified portion of their crop into storage, some or all of which may later be released for unrestricted sale or for sale in a secondary market. Reserve pools are authorized in orders for tart cherries, almonds, walnuts, raisins, prunes, hops, and spearmint oil.[22] *Shipping holidays,* a minor form of volume control, can be declared, which prohibit further commercial shipments until a "temporary glut" disappears. Such holidays are typically limited to periods surrounding calendar holidays.[23]

—— In a "*prorate*" program, the total amount targeted for shipment to the primary market during a particular time period is specified and apportioned among shippers on a weekly basis. In this way, the flow per time period (c.g., week) is reduced with all shippers covered by the order sharing in the reduction. Prorate provisions, available in about a third of the federal orders, are used extensively in the citrus industry. These shipping restrictions are a close substitute for total quantity restrictions in the case of a perishable commodity. The fruit not marketed for fresh use is forced into processing uses or allowed to rot. There has been a great deal of controversy surrounding the effects of the prorate provisions of the marketing order for California navel oranges. Marketing orders face the most public criticism when crops are deliberately destroyed. In 1981, a public outcry arose when photographs of oranges rotting in parking lots appeared in the press. In defense of government-enforced destruction of 40 percent of the California navel orange crop, a USDA official was quoted in the *New York Times* as saying: "Oranges are not an essential food. People don't need oranges. They can take vitamins."[24]

Grade, Size, and Maturity Regulations

Provisions affecting quality are included in most marketing orders. These quality-control standards are enforced through mandatory federal inspection. When small-size produce is eliminated, the demand for the remaining portion of the crop is increased. Producer returns may or may not increase when there is a decrease in total quantity marketed, however, depending upon whether product demand is inelastic.

Consumers who buy lower grades and smaller sizes are affected most by eliminating the marketing of small-size products. In some cases, grade and size restrictions measurably reduce imports, further restricting the choices of domestic consumers. Marketing orders are considered as impediments to trade by foreign shippers to the United States who must meet the specifications of different orders for potatoes, tomatoes, oranges, and other products.

Advertising, Promotion, and Research

Advertising, promotion, and research provisions of marketing orders have become more important during the past decade. Handlers may be assessed to raise funds to support research, promotion, and advertising. These provisions of marketing orders differ from those previously discussed since they reduce income in the present period with the expectation of increasing it in the future. Some marketing orders also require standardization of containers and packs to promote uniformity in packaging. Advertising and promotion is undertaken on the assumption either that consumer information is incomplete or that consumer demand can be shifted through persuasion. It is difficult in practice to separate these two motives or to measure their individual impacts.

Advertising provisions of marketing orders are very similar to producer-funded advertising through "check-off" plans. A large number of state commissions are chartered to collect a levy from producers at the point of sale to the first handler. These are called check-off plans because the processor withholds or checks off a set amount per unit of product before paying the producer. Some of these plans have been defeated in the required referendum.

The object of producer-funded advertising is to increase the demand for the product. Such advertising is most likely to be effective where there is new information about the quality or the nature of a product. Demand sometimes may also be increased without changing the nature of the product through an effective advertising program (e.g., "Where's the beef?").

Factors Affecting Development and Life of Marketing Orders

Agreement by producers is more likely to be reached if the benefits are evenly spread among a small number of producers in concentrated areas or under relatively homogeneous production conditions. Producers in lower-cost regions or those with superior skills are more likely to oppose marketing orders. The prorate increases the income of the average producer at the expense not just of consumers but also of producers who could prosper under competitive conditions. Since the proportion of the commodity that can be sold in the fresh market is fixed by fiat, the lower-cost producers are prevented from capturing a larger share of the market.

The potential to increase price by diverting some of the product is greater the lower the elasticity of demand. If the elasticity of supply is also low, the expected life of a marketing order is likely to be longer than it would be in a situation where the response by producers to an increase in price is high. The revenue response for an increase in price is also greater the higher the farm value of the product. Thus it is not surprising that most marketing orders cover products of considerable value concentrated on a small number of producers in a fairly small geographic area. California crops account for a high proportion of the active federal and state marketing orders.

Effects of Marketing Orders

Consumers

Marketing orders increase the prices of fresh oranges and other products going to primary markets. Consumers are clearly adversely affected when marketing orders raise prices. This is particularly true for consumers who consumed the grades and quantities no longer offered for sale. There is a problem in determining the effect of marketing orders on quantities marketed because marketing orders stimulate production and lead to overproduction.

Handlers and Processors

Fresh produce handlers and processors have generally opposed the development and use of marketing orders for fairly obvious reasons. There is a loss of entrepreneurial freedom of action under rate-of-flow and other order provisions. There is also the possibility that the adoption of marketing orders makes the development of co-op-owned processing facilities more likely.

Producers

The prospect of higher prices leads to expanded production in the long run and the cartel profits tend to be dissipated because most orders do not effectively limit entry.[25] In the case of the navel orange order, not only are oranges diverted to juice when consumers would prefer fresh oranges, resources are diverted into growing oranges used for juice because doing so enables a grower to share in the profits from fresh ones.[26] Overproduction is a predictable result of a cartel that does not limit entry while raising prices.

Orderly Marketing

The ostensible purpose of marketing orders is to establish "orderly" marketing conditions. Although this concept is not well defined, it presumably has to do with reducing marketing risks associated with price changes. Marketing orders, however, do not necessarily stabilize prices. It would be consistent with the stabilization objective to slow down the flow of crops to market in years of high production and then remove the restrictions in years of normal or low production. In fact, prorate and other market allocation devices are used in good and bad years alike.

Even if marketing orders reduce price variation, orders would not necessarily reduce fluctuations in producer profits. If prices were constant in good years and bad, profits would plummet in bad years when producers had little to sell. Allowing prices to vary helps to stabilize profits by letting producers take advantage of higher prices in poor crop years.

It is sometimes argued that fruits and vegetables must be given special regulatory treatment because they are perishable. However, perishable goods often are subject to seasonal price fluctuations. Fresh asparagus, raspberries, hotel rooms, and oysters are highly seasonal commodities that are produced without marketing orders.[27] Trying to smooth out price fluctuations by setting a uniform price throughout the year would deprive consumers of the benefits of the months of abundance without succeeding in making the goods available during the months of scarcity.

Moreover, the orderly marketing argument implies that all agricultural products need regulation. Yet, growers of many crops similar to those now under marketing orders operate without economic regulation. Oranges grown in California are under marketing orders while those grown in Florida and Texas are not.[28]

Finally, marketing boards have resisted innovations that would make the regulated commodities more storable. The lemon committee has blocked the introduction of shrink-wrap technology that would make lemons storable for six months or longer.[29] The USDA has blocked the reconstitution of milk from dry powder that would even out seasonal fluctuations in supply. Thus, the evidence suggests that the major purpose of marketing orders is to increase price and profits, not to stabilize them.

Summary

Farmers and farm organizations have long sought ways to increase their "bargaining power." There is a widespread view that farmers would benefit from measures to decrease the role of the middleman in the marketing of farm products. Cooperatives and marketing orders are two institutional arrangements designed to increase farmers' bargaining power.

Marketing and farm supply co-ops have increased in importance since the passage of the Capper-Volstead Act in 1922. The potential for co-op activities is reduced by the inherent incentive problems. Management is not in the hands of residual claimants and co-op members acquire no rights to future co-op earnings. Since members can capture the benefits only over the time horizon of their expected membership, there is a bias toward investment decisions with short-run payoffs. A key to the success of co-ops appears to be the tax treatment of patronage refunds. Whereas dividend income in the case of investor-owned firms is taxable both to the corporation and when received by individual shareholders, patronage refunds of co-ops are not taxable to the co-op. The result is a substantial tax break to co-ops when compared with investor-owned firms.

Equity questions also arise in collective bargaining activities of co-ops involving marketing orders. A marketing order is a government sanctioned cartel-type activity that permits members of a producer group to act in concert to limit competition. Marketing orders operate under the AMAA of 1937. Federal and state marketing orders are important in the production and marketing of milk, fruits, vegetables, and specialty crops. Marketing orders empower government-appointed panels of producers and middlemen to make industry-wide marketing decisions about sales volume and standards. Oranges and most fruits and vegetables marketed under marketing orders are subject to some form of quality control. About half of these orders also contain quality control provisions. Price setting under marketing orders occurs only for milk.

About 85 percent of all milk produced in the United States is Grade A and qualifies for use as fluid milk. Under classified pricing for milk, a higher price is generated for Class I milk that is used for fluid consumption. Only about half of the Grade A milk is sold for fluid use. The remainder competes in the processing market with lower cost Grade B milk which has lower sanitation standards and cannot be used for fluid use.

Marketing orders for all products are facing increasing criticism. There appears to be no more reason for the government to foster producer cartels of milk, fruits, and vegetables than of other products. Although marketing orders are often justified on the basis of "orderly marketing," the evidence suggests that the real purpose of marketing orders is to increase producer incomes. However, marketing orders are of limited benefit to producers in the long run because short-run cartel profits attract more producers to the industry. Consumers and taxpayers ultimately pay the price of these restrictions on competition through higher product prices and higher taxes, especially for the price support activities of the dairy program.

Marketing orders are not only inconsistent with the market process in the production and marketing of domestic products. Their implementation also requires restrictions on imports to prevent domestic consumers from substituting lower-priced imports for higher-priced domestic commodities. This is particularly important in the case of cheese, butter, and other dairy products, where U.S. prices, in recent years, have been two to three times the world price.

Notes

1. Bruce L. Gardner, *The Governing of Agriculture* (Lawrence, Kan.: The Regents Press of Kansas, 1981), p. 46.

2. Walter J. Armbruster, Dennis R. Henderson, and Ronald D. Knutson, *Federal Marketing Programs in Agriculture* (Danville, Ill.: Interstate Printers and Publishers, 1983), p. 206.

3. U.S. Department of Agriculture, *Agricultural Statistics 1986* (Washington, D.C.: U.S. Government Printing Office, 1987), p. 438.

4. Leon Garoyan, "Developments in the Theory of Farmer Cooperatives: Discussion," *American Journal of Agricultural Economics* 65 (December 1983): 1098.

5. Peter Vitaliano, "Cooperative Enterprise: An Alternative Conceptual Basis for Analyzing a Complex Institution," *American Journal of Agricultural Economics* 65 (December 1983): 1078–83.

6. Charles R. Knoeber and David L. Baumer, "Understanding Retained Patronage Refunds in Agricultural Cooperatives," *American Journal of Agricultural Economics* 65 (February 1983): 30–37.

7. Vitaliano, "Cooperative Enterprise," p. 1082.

8. Gardner, *The Governing of Agriculture*, p. 47.

9. Ibid. The example reflects changes in tax rates arising from the 1986 Tax Reform Act.

10. Richard J. Sexton and Terri Erickson Sexton, "Taxing Co-ops; Current Treatment is Fair, But Not For Reason Given by Co-op Leaders," Choices 1 (1986/2), 21–25.

11. Knoeber and Baumer, "Understanding Retained Patronage Refunds," p. 30.

12. E. C. Pasour, Jr., "The Free Rider as a Basis for Government Intervention," Journal of Libertarian Studies 5 (Fall 1981): 453–64.

13. Economic Research Service, Dairy: Background for 1985 Farm Legislation, AIB Number 474 (Washington, D.C.: U.S. Department of Agriculture, 1984), p. 18.

14. James F. Thompson and W. F. Edwards, "Dairy Policy and Public Interest: The Economic Legacies," Policy Analysis, no. 57 (Washington, D.C.; The Cato Institute, 1985).

15. Economic Research Service, Dairy.

16. Ibid., p. 5.

17. Jerome Hammond and Karen Brooks, Federal Price Program for the American Dairy Industry—Issues and Alternatives (Washington, D.C.: The National Planning Association, 1985), p. 10.

18. Ibid., p. 17.

19. Ibid., p. 13.

20. Agricultural Marketing Service, A Review of Federal Marketing Orders for Fruits, Vegetables, and Specialty Crops, AER Number 477 (Washington, D.C.: U.S. Department of Agriculture, 1981).

21. Ibid., p. 26.

22. Thomas M. Lenard and M. P. Mazur, "Harvest of Waste: The Marketing Order Program," Regulation 9 (May–June 1985): 19–26.

23. Ibid., p. 28.

24. New York Times, 24 April 1983.

25. Lawrence Shepard, "Cartelization of the California-Arizona Orange Industry, 1934–1981," Journal of Law and Economics 29 (April 1986): 83–123.

26. Lenard and Mazur, "Harvest of Waste," p. 21.

27. Ibid.

28. James L. Gattuso, "The High Cost and Low Returns of Farm Marketing Orders," Backgrounder, no. 462 (Washington, D.C.: The Heritage Foundation, 1985).

29. Lenard and Mazur, "Harvest of Waste," p. 21.

12

Effects of Agricultural Commodity Programs

Farm commodity prices for milk, cotton, sugar, wheat, feed grains, tobacco, and other products have been supported through a number of different programs since the 1930s. Supply controls have taken the form of acreage restrictions and allotments, land retirement, and marketing quotas. Prices have also been supported through direct purchases of products and through the use of nonrecourse loans. Various domestic and foreign food aid programs have also been used to increase the consumption of farm products and bolster prices; these programs are described in chapters 13 and 14. The major effects of various programs were described in the discussion of the operation of these programs. This chapter summarizes the direct and indirect effects of the various commodity programs, shows why the benefits tend to be dissipated over time, and describes the major beneficiaries of these programs.

Who Are the Short-Run Beneficiaries?

Several different groups receive short-run benefits from farm price support programs but the amount of the benefit varies widely. Farmers may benefit as producers or as owners of land and other specialized resources. Those who develop, administer, and evaluate the programs may also benefit.

Owners of Specialized Resources

Owners of land, allotments, and other specialized resources are the major gainers from farm programs that increase product prices. Regardless of whether prices are supported above the competitive level by voluntary or mandatory supply controls, the benefits of price supports are largely capitalized into the values of land, production and marketing rights, and other specialized resources that are not reflected in farm income statistics. Thus, the gains go primarily to owners of specialized resources and not to farm operators as such. Moreover, when farm program benefits are capitalized into higher prices of land and other inputs, those who own more of the affected farm resources gain more.

Consider the example of land. The price of land hinges on the discounted stream of expected future returns. If there is an increase in product price so that the expected return to land increases, land prices will increase. The increase in land price means that production costs increase. It has been estimated, for example, that more than 50 percent of the value of the 1972 cotton, wheat, and feed grain programs was capitalized into higher land values.[1]

The capitalization phenomenon is even more clear-cut in the case of programs involving acreage allotments or marketing quotas. In the tobacco price support program, for example, the value of the marketing quota, which gives the producer the right to produce and sell tobacco, often has exceeded $1,000 per acre per year. In such cases, the price support program in effect increased cost of production by more than $1,000 per acre.

Although owners of land, allotments, and other specialized resources receive windfall gains when a price support program is initiated (or price support level increased), any gains received by farmers are likely to be short-lived or transitional. That is, it is the first generation of resource owners who receive most of the benefits. As benefits are capitalized into higher input prices, gains to later producers are largely negated by higher production costs (including higher land and allotment prices). Thus price support programs result in what has been called "a transitional gains trap." Once a price support program is in operation, its elimination imposes windfall losses on owners of specialized resources regardless of whether they benefited from the original windfall. In reality, at any given time owners of specialized assets, including land and allotments, often are not the same people who received the windfalls when farm programs were initiated (or when benefit levels were increased).

Owners of specialized resources lose when asset prices decrease, whatever the reason. As inflationary expectations and farm product prices decreased in the 1980s, for example, farm land prices plummeted and owners of land, capital facilities, and other farm assets incurred huge losses in real wealth. When prices of farm land and other resources decrease, those who own more resources lose more wealth. Thus it is not surprising that it is the large, highly leveraged commercial farmers who have been most affected by decreases in prices of farm assets.

Producers and Direct Payments

Producers who have more to sell stand to gain more from farm price supports. On the other hand, small farmers are affected relatively little when product prices are increased since the benefits are tied to the volume of sales. For example, farms with annual sales of less than $20,000 in 1984 received government payments that averaged less than $1,000. More generally, farmers with annual sales of less than $40,000 per year constituted 40 percent of the farms but received only about one-tenth of the direct government payments.[2] However, the short-run benefits of price support programs vary widely even for farms of given size, depending upon crops grown.

There is a $50,000 per farm ("person") annual maximum payment limitation, established in 1981, but legal loopholes limit its effectiveness. In the Payment-in-Kind (PIK) Program in 1983, for example, the PIK entitlements did not count toward the total payment ceiling of $50,000. Again, the maximum payment limitation did not apply in the 1984 milk diversion program, and average payments in Florida and California exceeded $100,000 per producer.[3] The Milk Production Termination Program under the 1985 farm bill was also exempt from payment ceilings and 112 dairy producers in California, Florida, Idaho, Texas, and Arizona received payments of more than $1 million each under the dairy termination program.[4]

The basic $50,000 per farm ("person") payment limitation does not even cover all deficiency payments. In the 1988 corn program, for example, only the first $.72 per bushel of the projected deficiency payment of $1.10 counted toward the $50,000 payment ceiling. There was an overall $250,000 payment limitation per person affecting deficiency payments, diversion payments, and marketing loans.

Under the payment limitation, "persons" are broadly defined to include individuals and other entities such as limited partnerships, corporations, and estates that are actively engaged in farming. Furthermore, under existing legislation, it is relatively easy to reorganize farming operations so that additional "persons" can receive payments. A 1987 GAO study estimated that if the current trend in reorganization continues, 31,300 additional persons could be receiving payments by 1989, increasing costs of farm programs by $2.3 billion over the 1984–86 level.[5]

Program payments of $50,000, $100,000 or $1 million per farmer are seemingly inconsistent with the objective of supporting incomes of low-income producers. Yet the establishment of a maximum payment limitation is inconsistent with the objective of increasing product price through voluntary reductions in output. Since one-third of U.S. farms produce about 90 percent of the total output, it is the output of these farmers that determine the effectiveness of the various supply-control programs. So long as participation in the cotton, wheat, and feed-grain programs is voluntary, program participation by the individual producer can only be secured by making it more profitable for the producer to participate than not to participate. Thus the lower the maximum per-farmer payment limitation is set, the smaller the incentive on the part of commercial farmers to participate in farm programs. This is a fundamental problem inherent in any price support program that is designed to increase product price by enticing producers not to produce the product in question. A high-payment limitation may have a regressive effect on incomes within the agricultural sector, but a low-payment limitation reduces the effectiveness of programs to reduce output.

Mandatory supply control is an alternative to voluntary price support programs. Once the mandatory supply control program is approved in the required producer referendum, the individual producer has no choice as to whether or not to participate. In mandatory production controls, direct government outlays are likely to be much smaller than in voluntary supply-control programs. Mandatory supply-control programs, however, are necessarily protectionist and require import controls to prevent domestic consumers from purchasing lower-priced products from foreign producers.

Farmers as Producers versus Farmers as Asset Owners

The preceding discussion suggests that it is farmers as resource owners rather than farmers as producers who are mainly affected when prices of farm assets change. Thus farmers as producers, as opposed to farmers as asset owners, gain little from farm programs. Benefits of price supports, subsidized inputs, tax preferences, and so on, are incorporated into higher asset prices. Thus the distribution of gains between producers and asset owners depends on how quickly the expected benefits or costs of program changes are incorporated into asset values. The more quickly asset values rise when program benefits are increased, the more asset owners benefit from the gain. If program benefits were immediately incorporated into asset values when a new program is announced, current producers would benefit only to the extent that they have already contracted to obtain land and other resources before the program change is made. In general, the adjustment in asset values hinges on expectations and there is no reason to expect the speed of adjustment to be the same in all markets.

Competition ensures that resource costs will rise enough so that the expected rate of return in the production of farm products will not remain higher than rates of return in other areas of productive activity regardless of how much product prices increase. Consider what happens, for example, if price supports are increased for corn. The increased profitability of higher product prices is soon reflected in increased prices of resources used in corn production. Only those renters who rent land or purchase machinery and other resources before resource prices fully adjust to higher product prices gain from increased product prices. The conclusion is that the benefits of higher product prices or lower input prices generally have little effect on farmers as producers except for these short-run transitional gains.

Labor versus Other Specialized Resources

Farm labor generally is not highly specialized in agriculture. If farm labor were completely unspecialized so that the supply of labor were completely elastic, farm programs would provide no benefit to labor resources in agriculture. However, to the extent that farmers are owners of specialized farming skills they benefit from programs designed to assist agriculture. Moreover, the effect of government farm programs on specialized labor is different in one respect from that on specialized land or capital resources. In the case of land, rights to produce, machinery, and other capital facilities, market price is determined by the properly discounted stream of expected future returns. The expected gains from government programs over time are incorporated into higher market prices of land or any other resource, however, only if property rights are well defined and the asset can be bought and sold. When corn price increases, for example, land prices increase to reflect the increased future returns to land only if there is a market in which land prices are determined by expected future supply and demand conditions. Benefits of increased future returns are capitalized or incorporated into current market prices of land and capital inputs when property rights are clearly defined and legally enforced. In the above example, expected increases in corn prices in future years are likely immediately to affect land prices when the rights to land are privately owned and can be freely exchanged.

The situation is different in the case either of specialized labor or of an entrepreneur whose services can be hired for a period of time but cannot be bought and sold. Individual liberty dictates that each person has control over the disposition of his or her own time. An employer cannot legally negotiate a binding contract to obtain the services of an employee permanently or for the life of the asset, as in the case of land, buildings, machinery, and so on. When an asset cannot be owned and freely exchanged, its value is based on its expected contribution during the contracted time period. For example, an employer receives the benefits of a more productive laborer only during the time the labor is employed by him. Moreover, there is a good market for specialized labor skills in agriculture. An outstanding dairy herd manager, for example, might capture the returns to these skills by tending his own dairy farm or by moving to other dairy employment opportunities. In this sense, the return to specialized skills is available to the farm firm in the same way that returns to allotments and other specialized resources are.

How is specialized labor or management for the dairy farmer different from specialized land? When there is an increase in milk price, the increase in price of land is based on the expected duration of the higher milk price. Thus, the gain to the farmer owning specialized land, as shown above, is transitional. The farmer's wealth increases as a result of an increase in land price, but after land prices adjust to higher milk prices, the dairy farmer, whether using or renting out the land, would expect to receive a normal rate of return on the investment in land.

Superior skill in milk production means that returns to labor and/or management are significantly lower if employed in non–dairy production activities. The farmer who has superior labor or management skills in dairying receives a higher return when milk price is increased. He receives the increased return each year as long as milk price remains higher. The increased milk price is not capitalized into higher market prices for labor or management as it is in the case of real estate, allotments, machinery, and other capital inputs because property rights for labor are not transferable. Thus the gain from an increase in product price in the case of labor is not transitory in the way that it is for private property that can be bought and sold.

Farm Operators and Farm Labor

Since increased returns are largely capitalized into higher costs, farm programs have little effect on the long-term profitability of agriculture. And, as suggested above, farm programs have little effect on the returns to farm labor because labor resources in general are not very specialized in agriculture so that the labor supply is quite elastic. When labor can flow readily between agriculture and the rest of the economy, the long-run return to labor and management in agriculture is mainly determined by opportunity cost—by the alternatives that farm people have for non-agricultural uses of their resources.[6]

Political Bureaucracy

Politicians and the political bureaucracy also benefit from price support programs. Farm state legislators use farm programs to obtain and maintain political support. Farm programs are also important to the bureaucracy which administers and evaluates the effects of these programs. As shown in chapter 7, USDA employment in 1985 was more than four times larger than in 1929 even though the number of farms decreased dramatically during this period. Thus there is a large group of people who have a vested interest in maintaining and expanding the scope of farm programs.

Indirect Effects of Price Support Programs

The direct effect of price support programs is to increase producer prices of farm products. An indirect effect (discussed above) is to increase production costs as the higher product prices are capitalized into input prices, but there are also a number of other effects.

Effect on Market Process

Farm price support programs delay economic adjustments. In the decentralized market, economic change and progress is characterized by business experimentation and a form of economic natural selection. Entrepreneurial decisions are guided by perceptions of profit opportunities, and where there are no price supports or other types of government subsidies, those enterprises that best anticipate market conditions are most likely to continue in business. In this way, market forces cause resources to be deployed from less productive to more productive firms.

Price supports of whatever kind hamper and stifle the entrepreneurial discovery process, thereby distorting the allocation of resources and the pattern of production. One can only surmise what the current pattern of production for peanuts, tobacco, milk, or other price-supported products would be today if there were no restrictions on competition. It can be safely predicted, however, that compared with current production patterns, there would be shifts in production of milk, tobacco, peanuts, and other products both between regions and between farms. Price supports thus distort the pattern of resource use. In the case of current wheat, cotton, and feed-grain programs, for example, there is the paid idling of highly productive farmland as farmers are paid to take land out of production.

Market prices provide correct signals to producers and consumers only when prices are free to change in response to changing economic conditions. Government price controls block the flow of information that prices communicate to consumers about product availability and to producers about consumers' choices. When the price of milk is raised above the market clearing price, for example, producers are induced to produce "too much" and consumers to consume "too little." The huge surplus of butter, cheese, wheat, corn, tobacco, and other products in government storage is a direct result of government price support programs. So long as prices are supported above the competitive level, surplus production will be a chronic feature of U.S. agricultural programs. Public dissatisfaction with farm programs also increases during periods when support levels for milk and other products are set considerably above market clearing levels so that huge government subsidies are required to operate the programs.

The higher prices resulting from price support programs make it more difficult for consumers, especially those in lower income groups, to buy food. Thus price support programs, ostensibly designed to increase incomes of low-income producers, not only make farm incomes less equal but also worsen the income condition of low-income consumers.

Effect on Market Stability

Price supports and marketing orders are often justified as measures to "stabilize markets." Government policies as they are implemented through the political process, however, often introduce artificial instability and uncertainty into agricultural markets. Incumbent administrations frequently manipulate short-run policies, hoping to affect upcoming elections. Prior to the 1976 election, for example, the Ford Administration raised the loan rate on wheat and tripled the tariff on sugar.[7] President Carter increased dairy price supports significantly on the eve of the 1980 election.[8] Direct payments to dairy producers under the 1983 Dairy and Tobacco Adjustment Act also coincided, fortunately for the Reagan administration, with the 1984 presidential campaign.

Every four years or so, a new farm bill is enacted by Congress. The periodic swings from relatively high to relatively low price supports tend to create instability in U.S. agriculture. The high price support levels of the 1981 farm bill, along with the inflationary monetary and fiscal policies of the late 1970s, fostered unrealistic expectations by farmers about future farm product prices, and set the stage for the financial chaos in agriculture in the 1980s. As emphasized previously, however, the primary purpose of agricultural marketing orders and price support programs generally is to increase farm incomes rather than to "stabilize markets."

Rent Seeking

Finally, price support programs divert resources from the task of production of food and fiber to the scramble to obtain and maintain government transfers. The role of recent PAC contributions by dairy co-ops at the federal level, for example, is evidence of this rent-seeking phenomenon in which groups attempt to achieve income transfers through the use of government power. Other commodity groups, farm organizations, and other narrowly focused interests also frequently attempt to achieve income transfers through the use of government power.

Short-Run versus Long-Run Effects

The short-run and long-run effects of price support programs are likely to be quite different. In the short run, an effective price support program provides windfall gains, primarily to owners of land and other specialized resources at the time the program is instituted. Competition causes prices of these inputs to increase as long as expected rates of return in agriculture are higher than those in other sectors. As suggested earlier, resource prices tend to reflect opportunity costs and the supply of labor is quite elastic. Consequently, farm incomes with or without price supports are largely determined by general economic conditions and nonfarm employment opportunities. Thus, price support programs, aside from the windfalls received when the programs are initiated or benefit levels increased, have little effect on farm incomes. The conclusion is that the effect of farm programs on farm income is transitory.

Distortions in resource use are likely to increase with the passage of time when the pattern of production is frozen so that there is little opportunity to shift production to the lowest-cost production regions. The tobacco, peanut, and dairy programs, for example, have prevented or impeded the production of tobacco, peanuts, and milk from shifting to the lowest-cost production regions within the United States.

Effect on Exports

In the short run, when price support programs increase domestic prices, there is an immediate adverse effect on exports. The longer the length of run, moreover, the greater this effect is likely to be. An increase in domestic price encourages production in competing countries. Flue-cured tobacco provides a good example of this phenomenon. The U.S. tobacco program has stimulated production in other countries, increasing competition in both domestic and foreign markets for tobacco produced in the United States. The U.S. share of total world flue-cured tobacco exports during the period from 1955 to 1959 was 60 percent. By 1985, as price was artificially increased through strict production and marketing controls, the U.S. share of flue-cured tobacco exports was reduced to only 22 percent.

Substitution in Consumption and Production

Supply and demand become more elastic the longer the adjustment period. Given an increase in price in the United States, the longer the adjustment period, the greater the response by producers of substitute products. Thus, the longer a price support program remains in effect, the greater the pressures from competing products. The substitutes may come from producers of the same product in other countries or from producers of substitute products at home or abroad. Consider the cotton price support program of the 1930s which provided a stimulus for the development of substitutes. The U.S. cotton price support program is responsible for at least some of the speed at which synthetic fibers were developed and adopted in the United States. At the same time, the higher cotton prices in the United States also encouraged cotton production in Egypt and other countries.

The cotton price support program has contributed to a dramatic reduction in the U.S. share of world cotton production. During the period 1928–1930, before price supports were instituted, U.S. annual cotton production averaged 14 million bales per year, and other countries' production averaged 12 million bales. In the 1980s, after fifty years of cotton price supports, U.S. cotton production is only about 15 million bales, while world cotton production has almost tripled to about 50 million bales. The U.S. cotton program has simultaneously throttled U.S. cotton production and encouraged production by foreign competitors by providing a price umbrella over the international market.[9]

The effect of a price increase on demand is also greater the longer the length of adjustment period. The longer the length of run, the more likely consumers are to find and adopt substitutes for a given product. As cotton price increased due to the price support program, it took time for synthetic fibers to be developed and for consumers to discover and adopt the substitutes. Cotton's share of total fiber use in the United States has been decreasing over time and is now about one-fourth.

The milk price support program, raising the price of butter, cream, and other dairy products has also encouraged the development of substitutes for these dairy products. As the price of butter has increased relative to the price of margarine over time, for example, per capita consumption of margarine has continued to increase at the expense of butter. Largely as a result, per capita consumption of butter decreased by one-third from 1965 to 1980.[10] During the same period, per capita consumption of margarine increased by about 15 percent.[11] There has also been a substitution of nondairy creamers for cream. The conclusion is that the initial benefits of price support programs are eroded by competition over time. Moreover, the longer the adjustment period, the more likely it is that substitutes will be developed and that consumers will adopt the lower priced goods.

Restrictions on Competition

Restrictions on competition are at the heart of price support programs, since all price support programs are inconsistent with the competitive market process. All impose restrictions on mutually beneficial exchange. In the case of marketing orders and quotas, for example, all producers are forced to abide by the conditions of the cartel-like organization once the restrictions on competition are instituted. Individual producers and consumers no longer have the right to engage in mutually beneficial exchange as in a free market.

The notion of individual rights is relevant in assessing the effects of such restrictions on competition if, as suggested earlier, there is no principled philosophic difference between individual economic freedoms and individual freedoms of other sorts. Government policies that force prices above or below the competitive level prevent consumers from transmitting information to producers and thus involve a type of censorship. Indeed, it may be argued that price controls "violate the right of free expression just as if the government dictated the content of the daily newspaper."[12]

Price support programs in agriculture invariably block the free flow of price information and restrict the options of consumers to buy domestically produced or imported products at the lowest prices. In the case of the milk program, for example, where prices of dairy products are held above the world market level, import restrictions must be imposed to prevent consumers from purchasing lower-priced imported products. Thus, consumers as taxpayers are hit twice by price support programs. They must pay higher prices for the products; they must also pay higher taxes to finance price support programs.

Summary

The government operates price support programs for wheat, feed grains, cotton, peanuts, tobacco, rice, milk, soybeans, wool/mohair, and honey. The programs differ in detail, are incredibly complex, and frequently change. However, the major beneficiaries of price support programs are the owners of land, allotments, and other specialized resources when the programs are initiated or when benefit levels are increased. Program benefits are capitalized into higher prices of farm land, allotments, and other specialized resources. Farmers who enter production after a price support program is initiated (or price level increased) gain little since increased costs tend to negate any benefits of the increased product price. Thus the effect of farm programs on farm incomes is transitory. The main determinant of returns to farm labor is nonfarm employment opportunities and general economic conditions.

The government payments received from farm programs are positively related to farm size: farmers producing more output receive more benefits. A $50,000 maximum payment limitation reduces the advantage of large producers to some extent, but there are numerous loopholes in the limit of payments.

The direct effect of price support programs is to increase prices of farm products to producers. Huge surpluses, fully predictable when prices are raised above the competitive market clearing level, have been a continual feature of government price support programs since the 1930s. One indirect effect of price support programs is to delay economic adjustments within farms and between production regions. Another indirect effect is to increase the resources devoted by farm groups to political activity aimed at achieving income transfers at the expense of resources used in the production of goods and services.

In the operation of price support programs, "benefits" to producers decrease the longer the length of run. Over time, supply becomes more elastic as the development of substitute products is encouraged by higher product prices. Demand for the product also becomes more elastic as consumers discover and adopt substitutes. The result is that the adverse effects on consumption become greater over time, thereby exacerbating the problem of surplus production.

All price support programs are inconsistent with the competitive market process. Mandatory production control programs prevent mutually beneficial exchange between domestic or foreign producers and domestic consumers. In addition, these programs hamper or prevent production adjustments within and between production regions. Price support programs in which producer participation is optional also distort the allocation of resources, often causing large acreages of highly fertile land to be taken out of production. Moreover, price support programs, as shown in chapter 14, are inconsistent with achieving a more open economy.

Notes

1. James D. Johnson and Sara D. Short, "Commodity Programs: Who Has Received the Benefits?" *American Journal of Agricultural Economics* 65 (December 1983): 916.

2. Economic Report of the President (Washington, D.C.: U.S. Government Printing Office, 1986), pp. 132–34.

3. Ibid., p. 144.

4. Economic Report of the President (Washington, D.C.: U.S. Government Printing Office, 1987), p. 157.

5. U.S. General Accounting Office, Farm Payments: Basic Changes Needed to Avoid Abuse of the $50,000 Payment Limit, GAO/RCED-87-176 (Washington, D.C.: U.S. Government Printing Office, 1987), p. 2.

6. D. Gale Johnson, "The Performance of Past Policies: A Critique," in Alternative Agricultural and Food Policies and the 1985 Farm Bill, ed. Gordon C. Rausser and K. R. Farrell (Berkeley, Calif.: Giannini Foundation, 1985), pp. 27–29.

7. Bruce L. Gardner, The Governing of Agriculture (Lawrence, Kan.: The Regents Press of Kansas, 1981), p. 118.

8. Dale Heien, "Future Directions for U. S. Food, Agricultural, and Trade Policy: Discussion," American Journal of Agricultural Economics 66 (May 1984): p. 232.

9. Joseph D. Coffey, "Are Government Farm Programs the Solution or the Problem?" in Farm Policy Perspectives: Setting the Stage for 1985 Agricultural Legislation, Senate Committee Print 98-174, U.S. Senate Committee on Agriculture, Nutrition, and Forestry, 98th Congress, 2nd session, April 1984, pp. 194–201.

10. U.S. Department of Agriculture, Agricultural Statistics, 1982 (Washington, D.C.: U.S. Government Printing Office, 1983), p. 341.

11. Ibid., p. 139.

12. Dwight R. Lee, "The Price Blackout," Reason 17 (October 1985): 44.

13

Subsidized Food Programs

Government-operated food assistance programs can be traced back to the 1930s. However, the scope of domestic food assistance programs has increased dramatically since 1970. While the food-stamp and school-lunch programs are the best known, there are a number of other subsidized food programs. This chapter presents a brief history of these programs and describes their major features. Inherent information and incentive problems that have plagued the implementation of the programs from the beginning are also discussed.

Brief History

The original purpose of food-stamp, school-lunch, and other subsidized food programs was to facilitate the operation of price support programs for farm products. The Federal Surplus Commodities Corporation (FSCC) of 1935, in cooperation with the AAA, purchased surplus agricultural commodities for direct distribution to the unemployed and their families. The emphasis of this program was on strengthening the demand for farm products through surplus disposal and increased domestic consumption.

Legislation Providing for Commodity Distribution Programs

The operation of the FSCC was facilitated by an amendment to the AAA of 1933 that long served as a cornerstone in funding food assistance programs: Section 32. Section 32 and two other major pieces of legislation provide the basis for commodity distribution programs today. Section 32 appropriates 30 percent of the import duties imposed on all commodities for use by the secretary of agriculture to encourage exports and the domestic consumption of "surplus" agricultural commodities. Under this program, meats, fruits, and vegetables are purchased with Section 32 funds and donated to school lunch and breakfast programs. Dairy products, rice, peanuts, wheat, and other price-supported products are also purchased and donated to schools and other nonprofit agencies under Section 416 of the 1949 Agricultural Act. Finally, Section 6 of the National School Lunch Act provides additional authorization for the purchase of agricultural commodities to be donated to schools and service institutions.[1]

The importance of *commodities* in domestic food programs has decreased over time. Although there has been little increase in the dollar value of commodities, cash expenditures for food assistance have increased dramatically since the mid-1960s. There is now an array of frequently overlapping federal food assistance programs, but the following discussion is mainly about the food-stamp and school-lunch programs.

Food Stamps

The food-stamp program of the 1930s grew out of dissatisfaction with direct food distribution which reduced regular market food purchases and afforded no choice to recipients of the commodities received. In the initial food-stamp program, low-income families were authorized to purchase orange stamps equal to their average food expenditures. For each dollar of orange stamps purchased, households received 50 cents worth of blue stamps which could be used only for those foods declared in surplus by the secretary of agriculture. The food-stamp program, initiated during the 1930s, ended during World War II, but was resumed after the war. Permanent food-stamp legislation was enacted in 1964.

In the mid-1980s, the food-stamp program was the major food assistance program in the United States, accounting for about two-thirds of all food assistance spending. The total value of the monthly food-stamp allotment is based on three factors: food costs, income, and family size. Before 1979, recipients were required to pay a portion of the value of food stamps. In 1979, the purchase requirement was eliminated and foodstamps now are provided free to recipients. In 1985, almost 20 million people received food stamps at a cost of $11.7 billion.[2] Outlays on food stamps have changed little since 1981.

The food-stamp program increases the demand for farm products. However, the increased expenditure on food is far less than the taxpayer cost of the food-stamp program since food-stamp recipients, at least to some extent, substitute food stamps for food purchases that they would otherwise make. After analyzing results from a number of studies, Professor Sylvia Lane of the University of California concludes that the food-stamp program increases the demand for food by recipient households by 5 to 10 percent.[3] But since less than 10 percent of the households received food stamps, this means that the food-stamp program expands total domestic demand for food by less than 1 percent.[4]

School-Lunch Program

The school-lunch program was also begun in connection with surplus disposal activities of the FSCC in the 1930s. Food donations to schools dropped off during World War II but a permanent program was established under the National School Lunch Act of 1946. Under the current school-lunch program, USDA commodities are provided along with a subsidy for each lunch served. From 1947 to 1981, annual federal expenditures for the school-lunch program increased from less than $100 million to $4.6 billion for cash and donated commodities.[5] Federal assistance for school-lunch, school-breakfast, and other child nutrition programs in the mid-1980s was $4 to $5 billion a year.

A significant share of school lunches are provided to students either free or at reduced prices. Of the 20 million participants in 1981, only about half paid the full price.[6] Indeed, all school lunches are subsidized to some extent, but it is very difficult to determine the extent of the subsidy when commodities from CCC stocks are used. The opportunity cost of these commodities is likely to be considerably less than the government outlays incurred in obtaining them.

The operation of the National School Lunch Program poses a number of problems and issues. First, there are producer pressures to utilize the program as a means of surplus disposal and to strengthen the demand for particular farm products. However, surplus commodities such as cheese, honey, and butter are not likely to be the foods that schools would prefer to have. Second, the minimum nutrient requirements specified by the USDA are controversial and politically sensitive. This issue was highlighted in a widely publicized cost-cutting move by the Reagan administration in 1981 to get ketchup classified as a vegetable. Third, the issue of subsidizing school lunches for children from upper- and middle-income homes has received little attention but raises an important public policy question: why should the public at large, including low-income tax payers, be taxed to provide school lunches at subsidized prices for those who can afford to pay?

Other Food-Assistance Programs

The 1964 permanent food-stamp legislation led to a tremendous expansion of subsidized food programs, not only in food-stamp and school-lunch programs, but also in food programs targeted toward child nutrition and nutrition for the elderly. Total food assistance increased from $1 billion in 1969 to about $18 billion in 1983. It has been estimated that 70 million people in the United States received food assistance of some type in 1983.[7] Outlays for food and nutrition programs have changed little since 1983.

There are now a number of food-assistance programs both for children and the elderly. There were ten food-assistance programs for children in 1983.[8] These include a feeding program for youngsters during the summer, a program for day-care and child-care centers, and a school-breakfast program. The food-assistance programs for the elderly include Meals on Wheels and Congregate Feeding For the Elderly.[9] Many of these programs for children and the elderly have no income eligibility requirements.

Providing food assistance to middle- and upper-income families poses the same public-policy question raised above in connection with the operation of the National School Lunch Program.

Food-Stamp Reform

Reform of the food-stamp program became a political issue during the Reagan administration of the early 1980s. Food-stamp abuse has a long history. The USDA estimated that 25 percent of the coupons during the period from 1939 to 1943 were misused. A 1983 GAO report found that food-stamp fraud and abuse averaged $1 billion per year.[10]

Cashing Out Food Stamps

Proposals have been made to "cash out" all programs of special assistance for one cash payment.[11] Interest in cashing out food stamps ebbs and flows over time. What would be the effects if this were done? A cash transfer system would decrease the demand for farm products when compared with direct food aid through food stamps but, as implied above, this effect likely would not be large since the food-stamp program results in only a modest increase in the demand for food. However, major farm interests are opposed to cashing out of food stamps. Moreover, budget costs could increase if cashing out caused more people to elect to participate in the program. USDA figures show that no more than 76 percent of those eligible in the course of a year elect to participate in the food-stamp program.[12]

There has been a great deal of discussion about the relative merits of food stamps versus cash income transfers from a public policy standpoint. It is sometimes argued that unrestricted income transfers are preferable to in-kind transfers which in the case of food stamps are intended to encourage people to eat more food. The individual recipient from his or her own standpoint is necessarily better off with cash than with an equivalent dollar value of food stamps, since the range of choice is expanded with an unrestricted income transfer. That is, the consumer receiving cash can, if desired, purchase the same amount of food as with the food stamp, but the unrestricted increase in income also presents additional options to that individual. Thus, the argument goes, cashing out food stamps would be an improvement according to the Pareto criterion.

Other Policy Considerations

This analysis, although valid from the viewpoint of the recipient, is flawed from a public-policy standpoint. Since the cost of subsidized food programs is borne by taxpayers, their wishes must be taken into account in determining the preferred type of assistance.[13] The taxpayer may not evaluate transfer programs in the same way that the applied welfare economist evaluates them. Taxpayers may prefer to provide food subsidies rather than income because they wish the low-income recipients to spend more income on food. Indeed, a great deal of the controversy about the food-stamp program concerns the expenditures by food-stamp recipients for nonfood items. Thus, if the objective of taxpayers in food assistance programs is to have low-income people consume more food, it is likely that taxpayers and welfare recipients will not evaluate the relative merits of food subsidies and unrestricted income transfers in the same way.

During recent years, food-assistance programs have been part of major farm legislation, providing a reason for urban congressmen to vote for farm commodity programs and for rural members of Congress to vote for welfare programs. If food stamps were cashed out, it would as a general income transfer program be administratively more appropriate in a federal department other than the USDA. Yet the removal of any food assistance program from the USDA has farm policy implications. However, it is not clear whether food assistance programs are competitive with other USDA programs or whether the transfer of some or all of these programs out of the USDA would decrease the support for other farm programs.[14]

Nutrition and Health Policies

Nutrition information and education programs are nearly as old as the USDA. The center of responsibility for these programs is the Agricultural Extension Service. Prior to 1970, the main message of the nutrition programs was to eat a variety of food from the basic food groups. The programs posed no serious threat to anyone's economic interests because they were not intended to restrict food consumption.[15] The situation changed after the McGovern Senate Select Committee on Nutrition and Human Needs published a set of dietary goals in the mid-1970s. These goals were designed to restrict the intake of fat, processed sugars, cholesterol, and salt. There was an immediate reaction by affected livestock producers, dairy farmers, sugar producers, and other agribusiness interests.

Congress authorized the USDA to be the lead agency in nutrition policy in the 1977 farm bill. In 1980, the USDA and the Department of Health, Education and Welfare (HEW—now the Department of Health and Human Services: HHS) issued dietary guidelines related to the use of fats and cholesterol, starch and fiber, sugar, sodium, and alcohol.[16]

During the Carter administration (1977–1980), there was a proposal to institute "nutrition planning." In this proposed approach, farm price support programs would have been used to further nutrition goals. "Nutrition planning" was visualized as a clear-cut technical process. In this process, the first step would be to determine what people's nutritional needs are. After these data were obtained, the levels and types of production necessary to meet those needs would be determined. The final step in nutrition planning, as visualized by Secretary of Agriculture Bergland, was to create a farm policy to "meet the nutrition and trade needs."

Nutrition planning is subject to all of the problems inherent in central planning.[17] There are many different ways for consumers to meet dietary requirements and consumers' choices are influenced by tastes, preferences, and price as well as by nutritional data. So long as consumers are free to make consumption decisions and politicians respond to short-run political concerns, nutrition planning of the type visualized is likely to have little impact on domestic farm programs. Although no serious attempt was ever made to implement "nutrition planning" during the Carter administration, it is not surprising that extension educational programs designed merely to reduce the intake of sugar, milk, beef, and other farm products were challenged by farm groups, especially by cattlemen and dairymen.

Implementation Problems

From the beginning, implementation problems have been formidable in food-assistance programs. First, there is an incentive to overprovide subsidized food services for the same reasons described in the earlier discussion of the collective decision-making process. Hence, the growth of food assistance programs irrespective of increases in consumer incomes during the past generation is predictable from public-choice theory. Furthermore, efforts by Congress, the USDA and other government employees to increase the number of food-stamp recipients are consistent with the theory of bureaucracy.[18] While early food-assistance programs were largely motivated by surplus problems incurred through government price support operations, food assistance programs have now taken on a life of their own. The major constituency of food assistance programs is no longer commercial agriculture but rather the groups advocating and benefiting generally from "poverty" programs. These groups include not only the recipients of food assistance, but also the government officials and employees who provide the funding and administration of the programs at local, state, and federal levels.

Incentive problems also arise in food-assistance programs where recipients face means tests. If a family must make less than some specified level of income in order to be eligible for food stamps, school lunches, or other food assistance, a family slightly above that income level has an incentive to change its behavior in order to qualify. Consider the example of the person choosing whether to search for a better job. Food stamps are generally available to the unemployed even if they quit work. Thus the availability of food stamps is likely to increase unemployment by reducing the cost of being unemployed.

In addition to incentive problems, there are also formidable information problems in monitoring the food-stamp, school-lunch, and any other food-assistance programs where there is a means test. Not only is there an incentive to underreport income; there is also a severe information problem in discovering whether such underreporting has occurred. In the National School Lunch Program, for example, the determination of who is eligible for free or reduced-price school lunches is based on family income as stated on the application form. The income levels necessary to qualify for free or reduced price lunches are often publicized in local newspapers so parents will know whether or not their children qualify. The perceived cost of underreporting income is likely to be low, since it would be quite difficult for the school system to verify the income reported on the application form. Thus inherent incentive and information problems have plagued implementation of food-assistance programs since the food stamp program was first begun.

Agricultural Price Supports and Food Assistance

There is a fundamental inconsistency between farm price support programs that raise product prices and food-assistance programs. Price support programs raise prices of milk, fresh fruit, sugar, peanuts, and other products at the same time low-income consumers are deemed to have too little money to provide food. Domestic consumers are legally prevented from purchasing lower-priced dairy products, for example, by import restrictions which are a necessary component of price support programs that hold domestic prices above world prices. In addition to administering the dairy program, which raises fluid milk prices, for example, the USDA has prevented reconstituted milk from being sold for less than the price of whole fluid milk. In marketing orders for fruits, lower-income consumers are harmed most by quality control provisions that restrict sales of lower grades and smaller sizes of commodities. It is ironic that billions of dollars are being spent on government programs to raise prices of milk and other commodities while, at the same time, billions of dollars are also being spent on programs to lower the price of food to low-income consumers.

Summary

Subsidized food distribution programs were initiated during the 1930s as an adjunct of price support programs. Food-stamp, school-lunch, and other subsidized food programs have increased dramatically since the late 1960s, when expenditures increased rapidly for welfare programs generally.

Farmers initially provided the major support for food assistance programs. The support for subsidized food programs is no longer restricted to beneficiaries of price support programs. Indeed, the major support for food-assistance programs now comes from urban interests and the "poverty lobby" rather than from commercial agriculture. In recent years, legislators from farm districts interested in maintaining farm price supports have traded votes with legislators from urban districts who supported food-assistance programs.

Implementation problems have plagued subsidized food programs from the beginning of the food-stamp program. There are formidable information and incentive problems inherent in food-stamp, school-lunch, and other programs having means tests. There is an information problem in determining whether an individual qualifies. There is also an economic incentive for individuals to adjust their behavior to qualify for food assistance programs. Thus it is not surprising that there have been chronic complaints about abuses in food assistance programs having income eligibility limits, especially food stamps.

Subsidized food programs pose the same problem as all other income redistribution programs. There is no objective procedure for determining how large the expenditures on these programs *should* be. The growth of food-assistance programs is consistent with the theory of public choice. The bureaucracy involved in administering the programs has an incentive to expand the scope of operations. Moreover, it is not difficult for an administrator, especially in the case of food aid to low-income people, to rationalize that what is in one's own interest is also in the public interest.

Notes

1. Kathryn Longen, *Domestic Food Programs: An Overview* (Washington, D.C.: U.S. Department of Agriculture, ESCS 81, 1980).

2. U.S. Department of Agriculture, *Agricultural Statistics 1986* (Washington, D.C.: U.S. Government Printing Office, 1987), p. 500.

3. Sylvia Lane, "Food Stamps: One Program Gramm-Rudman-Hollings Won't Get Its Teeth Into . . . But Cash Would Probably Work Better," *Choices* 1 (1986/2): 18.

4. Ibid.

5. Ronald D. Knutson, J. B. Penn, and W. T. Boehm, *Agricultural and Food Policy* (Englewood Cliffs, N.J.: Prentice-Hall, 1983), p. 309.

6. Ibid., p. 310.

7. James Bovard, "Feeding Everybody: How Federal Food Programs Grew and Grew," *Policy Review* 26 (Fall 1983): 42.

8. Ibid., p. 46.

9. Ibid.

10. Ibid., pp. 42, 47.

11. Knutson, Penn, and Boehm, *Agricultural and Food Policy*, p. 311.

12. Lane, "Food Stamps," p. 19.

13. James M. Buchanan, *Cost and Choice* (Chicago: Markham, 1969), p. 54.

14. Knutson, Penn, and Boehm, *Agricultural and Food Policy*, p. 312.

15. Ibid., p. 313.

16. Ibid., p. 314.

17. Don Lavoie, *National Economic Planning: What is Left?* (Cambridge, Mass.: Ballinger, 1985).

18. Bovard, "Feeding Everybody," p. 44.

14

International Trade and Trade Restrictions

For more than two decades after World War II, international trade of the United States was primarily viewed as a matter of rapidly expanding export markets and the acquisition of foreign assets by U.S. investors.[1] Over a relatively short time, the U.S. economy has experienced a transition to a state of considerable international interdependence with respect to the provision of goods, services, and capital. A sevenfold increase in international activity, including U.S. imports and exports and net capital transactions, occurred during the period from 1970 to 1985.[2]

International trade is highly important to U.S. agriculture as exports represent about one-fourth of the total revenue from sales of U.S. farm products. Exports are particularly important for some U.S. farm commodities. For example, about 60 percent of the wheat produced, 40 percent of the rice, soybeans, and cotton, one-third of the tobacco, and 25 percent of the corn are exported.

Both exports and imports have increased over time. In 1969, the values of agricultural exports and imports totalled $5.7 billion and $4.9 billion, respectively. By 1981, the nominal value of imports had increased to $17.2 billion but the value of exports had increased to $43.8 billion. Exports of U.S. farm products in fiscal 1986 were about $26 billion, down about $18 billion from the record high of 1981. This reduction has been attributed to a number of factors including global recession, Third World debt, a strong U.S. dollar, domestic farm programs, and rising farm productivity in other countries. While much has been written about the adverse effect of the strong dollar on farm exports, Batten and Belongia found a weak link between exchange rates and exports. The dominant factor was found to be real income in importing nations.[3]

From the mid-1970s until 1985 the value of agricultural imports was less than half the value of agricultural exports. In 1985 agricultural imports were about two-thirds as large as exports. Indeed, for several months in mid-1986, agricultural imports exceeded agricultural exports. There are two types of agricultural imports: (1) animal and vegetable products similar to those produced in the United States, and (2) products not produced here, such as coffee, bananas, and tea.

Agricultural trade is a key factor in agricultural policy, and there appears to be a direct relationship between the volume of exports of U.S. farm products and domestic price support expenditures. Exports of agricultural products increased from $6.7 billion in 1970 to $21.6 billion in 1975.[4] During the same period, government expenditures on price support programs decreased from $5.1 billion to $1.9 billion.[5] More recently, exports of agricultural products decreased from $40.5 billion in 1980 to $29 billion in 1985. As exports were declining, the cost of government price support programs increased from $4 billion to $17 billion. As exports of a product decrease, the cost of maintaining domestic price at a given level increases and political pressures intensify. Thus trade policy is highly important to U.S. agriculture.

The importance of international trade to U.S. agriculture was demonstrated during the Great Depression. The Smoot-Hawley Tariff Act of 1930 raised tariffs to the highest levels in the nation's history, 52.8 percent on an ad valorem basis. Other countries followed suit and protectionism was rampant. It was no coincidence that U.S. farm exports fell by two-thirds from 1929 to 1933. While there was a dramatic increase in the value of agricultural exports during the 1970s, from $6.7 billion in 1970 to $32.0 billion in 1979, it was only in the late 1970s that farm exports had recovered the share they represented in farm marketings sixty years earlier (about 25 percent).[6] Since U.S. agriculture is heavily dependent on exports, U.S. farmers have a strong stake in maintaining an open economy. This chapter considers the theoretical case for international trade, discusses specific types of trade barriers for agricultural products, and stresses the fundamental contradiction between a policy of liberal international trade and protectionist domestic farm programs.[7]

Comparative Advantage

Comparative advantage provides a basis for trade between individuals in different countries (as well as between individuals in the same country). To pursue comparative advantage means to sacrifice that which is less valuable for the sake of something more valuable.[8] Comparative advantage is determined by opportunity cost. The opportunity cost to Farmer Jones of using an acre of land for corn production, for example, is the value of the land in the best alternative use. Corn land can also be used to produce soybeans. If U.S. farmers become more productive in growing soybeans, the opportunity cost of land used to produce corn increases. Thus the more adept U.S. farmers become in producing soybeans (or any other product), the higher the cost of producing other products. No nation's producers can be most efficient or have a comparative advantage in the production of every good and service produced.

Consider the following example where two countries, the United States and Japan, are assumed to be able to produce two goods of similar quality.

	U.S.	JAPAN
	(PRICES PER UNIT OF GOOD)	
GRAIN	$30	¥9,000
TEXTILES	$20	¥4,500

Which country has a comparative advantage in producing textiles? In answering this question, the focus should be on opportunity cost—the real cost of producing anything is the value of what is given up in order to produce it. What is the opportunity cost of one unit of textiles? The cost of one unit of textiles in the United States insofar as prices reflect opportunity costs is ⅔ unit of grain. That is, producing and selling a unit of textile means that ⅔ of a unit of grain is sacrificed. In Japan, however, the cost of a unit of textiles is only one-half unit of grain. Therefore, Japan (in this example) has a comparative advantage in the production of textiles. This implies that the United States has a comparative advantage in the production of grain—the U.S. must sacrifice only one and one half units of textiles in producing a unit of grain whereas the Japanese must sacrifice two units. The conclusion is that each country can gain from trade by specializing in the production of goods in which it has a comparative advantage.

If trade is freely permitted, goods will tend to flow until the prices in each country are similar (except for transportation costs). Consider the simplified two-country trading situation depicted in figure 14.1. In the absence of international trade, product price is considerably higher in the U.K. than in the U.S. At the world price, Pw, the quantity exported from the United States $(Q_2 - Q_1)$ is equal to the imports by the United Kingdom $(Q_4 - Q_3)$. Trade causes the price to increase in the exporting country and to decrease in the importing country. The amount by which price changes due to trade in either country hinges on the elasticities of supply and demand. The more inelastic supply or demand, ceteris paribus, the greater the change in price for a given amount of trade.

International trade is mutually beneficial to buyer and seller, otherwise trade would not occur. Moreover, restrictions on competition or barriers to trade inevitably are harmful to parties engaging in trade. It is not the case, however, that trade makes everyone better off. If this were the case, we would not observe the chronic efforts by producer groups in all countries to erect barriers to trade. Trade barriers, as shown below, may take a number of different forms.

Barriers to Trade

Tariffs

Import restrictions are the most common form of protectionism and tariffs are a common type of import barrier. Consider the effect of a tariff

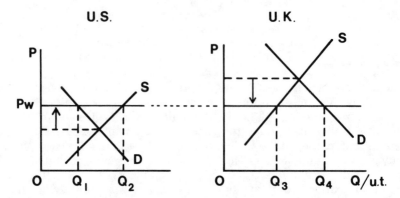

Figure 14.1. Effect of trade on exporting and importing countries.

on a domestically produced and consumed good in an importing country (figure 14.2). At the world price, Pw, the amount imported is equal to $Q_c - Q_p$ when there is free trade. If a tariff is imposed raising the price to $Pw + T$, domestic consumption decreases and domestic production increases as the tariff provides an umbrella over domestic producers, at least in the short run. In the situation depicted, domestic production increases from Q_p to Q_{pt} and domestic consumption decreases from Q_c to Q_{ct}. The effect of the tariff on imports is the sum of these two effects. Thus, after the tariff is imposed the amount imported is $Q_{ct} - Q_{pt}$. This example shows why U.S. producers of dairy products, tobacco, steel, textile products, autos, and other products frequently lobby for tariffs and other restrictions on imports.

The easier it is to make substitutions in consumption and production, the larger the effect of a tariff. If users of wheat can readily substitute other products when the price of wheat increases, an increase in the price of wheat will bring about a relatively large decrease in consumption. Generalizing this result, the effect of a tariff on domestic production and consumption is greater, the more elastic demand and supply. This conclusion can be generalized even further. If a market is distorted through tariffs, taxes, price controls, and so on, the damage is less the more inelastic are demand and supply. That is, if something is done to misallocate resources, the effect will be less the more resistant the economy is to the movement of resources.

As direct effects of the tariff, the government collects area A in tariff receipts and product price is increased to consumers (figure 14.2). Tariff receipts are equal to the quantity imported times the tariff. An indirect effect of a tariff is that resource use is distorted, as producers are induced to increase output with resources that have higher values in other uses. If the supply curve represents the opportunity cost of production (as the supply curve is typically defined), the cost of the increased output $(Q_{pt} - Q_p)$ exceeds its value by the amount of area B.[9]

Nontariff Barriers

The most inflexible nontariff barrier is the *import quota* which sets an absolute limit on the quantity of the product that may be imported. Import quotas are typically imposed at the urging of domestic producer groups. In the above example, a quota smaller than $Q_{ct} - Q_{pt}$ would increase the price in the importing country above the level $P_w + T$. An import quota will be more harmful, ceteris paribus, the more inelastic are domestic demand and supply. Other import barriers include complex packing and labeling requirements, sanitary regulations, and foreign exchange restrictions.

"Voluntary" import controls represent another means of reducing imports. In this approach, used by the U.S. government in the 1980s, agreements are worked out with foreign governments to limit the number of automobiles, quantity of textile products, quantity of beef, and so on, shipped to the United States. These restrictions on imports are "voluntary" in name only, however, since other countries are typically induced to restrict imports under the threat of quotas or other legislated import controls. The economic effects of "voluntary" controls are similar to legislated restrictions. In each case, domestic producers receive short-run benefits at the expense of domestic consumers.

Import barriers are harmful to domestic consumers, regardless of the means by which imports are restricted. What is sometimes overlooked, however, is that import controls are also harmful to domestic producers of other products. Import restrictions on Japanese autos, Hong Kong textiles, or German steel indirectly affect the exports of U.S. agricultural products. Import restrictions inevitably mean that exports are reduced since the number of dollars available to foreign buyers to purchase U.S. soybeans,

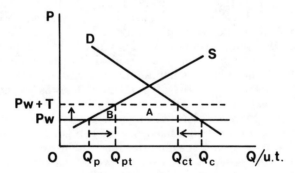

Figure 14.2. Effect of a tariff on U.S. imports.

wheat, and other products hinges on the quantity of autos, TVs, steel, and other products imported by the United States.

It is contended by some people that the critical limitation on U.S. agricultural exports isn't the availability of dollars but foreign barriers. However, the United States has little basis for criticizing other countries for protectionist trade policies affecting farm products. A recent study by the U.S. Department of Agriculture measured the levels of government intervention affecting world agricultural trade by the European Community and sixteen other countries during the period 1982–86.[10] This study found that, contrary to popular opinion, government intervention affecting U.S. agricultural trade is almost as heavy as in other industrialized countries, including the European Community. Moreover, the United States became considerably more interventionist after the 1985 farm bill was enacted.

Export Subsidies and Restrictions

The price support and production control programs instituted during the 1930s, in which domestic prices are held above world price levels, have resulted in the chronic accumulation of surplus stocks. Thus, there has been pressure over the years to subsidize exports. The effect of an export subsidy is shown in figure 14.3. In the absence of market intervention, product price through trade is increased from Pd to Pw and the quantity exported is $Q_{p1} - Q_{c1}$. However, an export subsidy gives domestic producers an artificial advantage in the export market. At the subsidized price, achieved by a fixed payment per unit of product exported (S), the quantity exported is $Q_{ps} - Q_{cs}$. The export subsidy which reduces the quantity on the domestic market also increases prices to domestic consumers. As a result of an export subsidy, domestic consumption is reduced from Q_{c1} to Q_{cs} and domestic production is increased from Q_{p1} to Q_{ps} (figure 14.3).

The seeds of export subsidies were sown in the 1920s in the proposed McNary-Haugen Bills, which would have raised domestic prices by discriminating between domestic and foreign markets and by the "dumping" of exports. "Dumping" occurs when a country sells a commodity below the "cost of production." There is a great deal of ambiguity in the concept of "dumping." The subjective nature of opportunity cost poses the same problems in determining cost of production here as in the examples discussed in chapter 8.

Exports may also be restricted through the use of export taxes or quotas. The effect of an export tax, a fixed payment to government per unit of product exported, is to reduce the price received by exporters, effectively raising the price of goods entering the world market. The export tax causes domestic producers to produce less; it causes domestic consumers to consume more. An export quota places a specific limit on the quantity

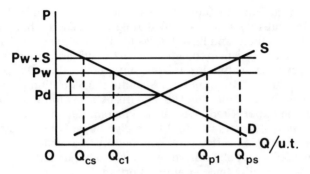

Figure 14.3. Effect of an export subsidy.

of a product that can be exported. An embargo makes it illegal to export any of the product.

Section 32

Export subsidies began with an amendment to the 1933 AAA, Section 32, that authorized the use of import tariff revenues to subsidize agricultural exports.[11] Section 32 is funded by a continuing appropriation of 30 percent of the import duties imposed on all commodities imported into the United States, both agricultural and nonagricultural. Subsidized shipments remained small until federally financed shipments for famine relief rose sharply during and immediately after World War II. Most of the Section 32 funds have been spent on the purchase and domestic donation of agricultural commodities. Export programs accounted for less than 10 percent of Section 32 expenditures between 1936 and 1976.[12]

Credit Programs including PL 480

Public Law 480 (Agricultural Trade Development and Assistance Act of 1954), commonly called the Food for Peace program, was designed to reduce the CCC stocks acquired through price support programs. Under Title I of this legislation, long-term sales to foreign buyers are made with repayment periods of up to 40 years at low interest rates. Under Title II, the United States donates commodities to countries and pays the shipping costs. For example, food was recently sent to countries in sub-Saharan Africa under Title II.[13]

The PL 480 program has led export subsidies to become strongly embedded in U.S. farm policy. During the 1950s and 1960s concessionary sales under government programs, including PL 480, often accounted for as much as one-third of export sales.[14] The gross taxpayer cost of financing such exports from 1955 to 1979 was about $40 billion.[15] PL 480 and other export subsidy programs are strongly linked to the disposal of surplus farm products, and PL 480 sales tend to decline when farm prices increase. As exports mushroomed after 1972 and farm prices increased, subsidized exports declined in relative importance. PL 480 expenditures during the 1980s typically ran from $1 billion to $2 billion per year.

The greatest credit impact on U.S. exports of farm products recently has come from the Export Credit Guarantee Program. This legislation guarantees payment to U.S. lenders should a foreign buyer fail to repay any loan used to purchase U.S. agricultural commodities. From 1982 to 1986, the USDA provided about $22 billion in export credit guarantees.[16]

Current laws require that certain proportions of U.S. exports be carried in U.S.-flag ships when taxpayer money is used to fund the exports, as in PL 480 shipments. Shipment in U.S.-flag ships is sometimes also specified for other reasons, as in the Soviet grain agreement. Shipping in U.S.-flag ships is generally more costly, which increases the cost of U.S. commodities to foreign buyers.

There has been a great deal of controversy about the impact in the recipient countries of PL 480 and other programs that encourage exports. The increase in supply reduces prices received by local farmers, which leads to decreases in output and may aggravate rather than alleviate hunger problems in the recipient countries.

New Agricultural Export Subsidies

Another program that reduces export prices, the export enhancement program, was initiated in 1985. This program, using CCC stocks as in-kind payment to exporters, is targeted to markets taken over by competing nations using "unfair trade practices." It enables exporters to sell to foreign buyers at low prices.

In addition, in an effort to dispose of government stocks of farm products, the 1985 farm bill instituted a new kind of export subsidy, the "marketing loan." Marketing loans permit prices of commodities placed under loan to fall below loan rates by enabling farmers to buy back their government-purchased crops at prices below those paid to them by the CCC. The use of generic commodity certificates in lieu of cash payments also allows market prices to fall below loan rates (chapter 9). Thus marketing loans and generic PIK certificates represent other examples of the use of the U.S. Treasury to drive down prices in international markets.[17]

Target-Price System as Export Subsidy

The target-price system of price supports for cotton, wheat, feed grains, and rice may also operate as an export subsidy, as shown in figure 14.4. In panel 1, there is a decrease in supply from SS to S_1S_1 because of the requirement that producers must take land out of production in order to

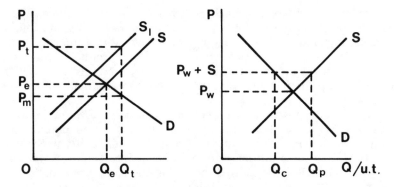

Figure 14.4. Target-price system as export subsidy.

participate in price support programs of this kind. When the target price is set at OP_t (panel 1), production is likely to be increased above the free-market level and market price will probably be lower than it would be in the absence of the program. In the situation depicted, output under the target-price approach is increased from OQ_e to OQ_t and market price is reduced from OP_e to OP_m. This, in effect, is tantamount to the conventional type of export subsidy. In the market situation shown in panel 2 (figure 14.4) there would be no exports under free-market conditions, but an export subsidy results in exports of $OQ_p - OQ_c$. The price reduction associated with the target-price system of price supports has the same effect (from the perspective of other countries) as an export subsidy, unless the loan rate is set high enough so that producers have no artificial advantage in the export market. The conclusion is that if price supports lead to larger production and lower market prices, the program effects are similar to those of a direct export subsidy.

GATT, Protectionism, and Agricultural Price Supports

The General Agreement on Tariffs and Trade (GATT) is a multilateral treaty among more than eighty governments, dating from 1947. The purpose of GATT is to liberalize and expand trade through negotiated reductions in trade barriers. A number of GATT negotiating conferences or "rounds" have been held and several of these have been important to U.S. agriculture.[18] In late 1986, Gatt agenda-setting talks began in Uruguay to set guidelines for the eighth general meeting since World War II. Agricultural export subsidies were considered to be an important topic for negotiation. The GATT principles generally prohibit quantitative restrictions and subsidies (including export subsidies) but there are important exceptions to these general principles in agriculture trade.

There is a fundamental inconsistency between domestic price supports and free trade.[19] The conflict between domestic farm programs and free trade was apparent when GATT was established. At that time, the United States insisted on special treatment for agricultural products. Thus it is no coincidence that agricultural and other "primary products" are not bound by the GATT principles that generally prohibit import quotas and export subsidies.

Domestic farm programs also frequently contradict U.S. foreign-policy objectives. Marketing loans for rice (which subsidize exports), for example, have damaged the market for Thailand, a major ally in Southeast Asia. Such subsidies not only are harmful to U.S. taxpayers and other exporting countries, they also benefit the main importers such as the Soviet Union. "Recently we've subsidized the Soviet Union in grain sales, and it now will be true that one can buy grain cheaper in Moscow than in Chicago."[20]

Import Restrictions Under GATT

The GATT exemption for agricultural products was made necessary by section 22 of the AAA of 1933 which requires that the government impose quantity restrictions whenever imports would "materially interfere" with the operation of any U.S. farm program.[21] It is not difficult to see why such protection is required for dairy, sugar, peanuts, tobacco, and other products where domestic prices are held above world price levels. Without rigid import controls for price-supported products, consumers would substitute lower-priced imports for domestically produced products.

The GATT principles that permit special exemption for farm products also specify limits on how far countries can go in limiting imports. Import quotas are not to be used to reduce imports by a greater proportion than that by which domestic production is restricted. For, example, if imports would amount to 20 percent of domestic production in the absence of restrictions on imports, an import quota should not reduce the ratio of imports to domestic production to less that 20 percent. This principle has been "grossly violated" by the United States for a number of products.[22] In the case of sugar and beef, for example, import quotas exist even though no attempt is made to reduce domestic production.

Section 8E of the AMAA provides that grade, size, quality, or maturity regulations established for fruits, vegetables, or nuts under a marketing order shall apply equally to imported products. This restriction on competition, necessary to the operation of marketing orders, is also an important impediment to trade preventing consumers from purchasing lower-priced imports.

There are some import restrictions affecting foreign producers that are similar to those imposed on domestic producers. For instance, it is U.S. policy that imported products must meet the same standards for safety, sanitation, and disease as U.S. produced products.[23] The plants in which imported beef is slaughtered, for example, must meet the same standards as those for beef produced in the United States. Foreign plants are inspected periodically and imported beef is checked for residues of banned chemicals or drugs when it enters the United States.

Export Subsidies Under GATT

GATT principles permit export subsidies for agricultural products so long as they are not applied "in a manner which results in [their] having more than an equitable share of world export trade in that product."[24] As described above, the United States has spent billions of dollars under PL 480 and other credit programs, and the target price and deficiency payments system is similar in effect to an export subsidy. These programs along with import controls on farm products have permitted prices received by U.S. farmers significantly to exceed prices in international markets, insulating U.S. producers from world market prices. Such policies, which provide U.S. producers with an artificial advantage, inevitably evoke complaints by foreign producers.

The conclusion is that U.S. trade policies have long been used with price support programs to hold domestic agricultural prices above international market prices. Import controls and export subsidies are likely to bring retaliation from importing countries in the form of tariffs, quotas, or other trade barriers. These policies also cause other nations to be skeptical of the professed U.S. desire to achieve a more open economy. The unwillingness of the United States to subject its domestic farm programs to the discipline of international trade resulted in the GATT exemptions for agriculture. These exceptions, designed to make it possible for the United States to hold its domestic prices above world market levels, are now being used by other countries for the same reason. Appeals to Japan and other countries to open their markets are not credible so long as these protectionist policies are maintained.[25]

What are the policy implications for the United States? Agricultural resources would be used most productively if all countries acted together in reducing trade barriers for farm products. Even if current GATT negotiations fail, however, the elimination or phasing out of U.S. agricultural subsidies and trade barriers would be superior to the current subsidy contest between nations.[26] The United States stands to gain from reducing trade barriers, regardless of whether other countries do so.

International Trade and the Elasticity of Demand for Farm Products

The U.S. farm price support programs were originally developed on the assumption that the affected products were inelastic with respect to domestic demand. World demand for wheat, tobacco, and other products is more elastic than domestic demand because of the greater availability of substitutes. However, demand for U.S. farm products has become more elastic (or less inelastic) during the past decade as exports of farm products have increased. If the overall demand for a farm product were elastic at the farm level, a program to restrict output would reduce total receipts. Indeed, it may well be that for most of the U.S. commodities exported today, "an increase in price actually leads to a reduction in total income to agriculture rather than an increase."[27]

U.S. farmers reacted strongly to the export boom of the mid-1970s for farm products. More land was brought back into production, more machinery and equipment were purchased, and prices of farm land were bid up to unprecedented levels. When a global recession occurred in 1981, many recent entrants into agriculture and farmers who expanded rapidly in highly leveraged operations during the 1970s suffered cash-flow problems. The increase in exports of U.S. farm commodities has likely increased the instability of markets for agricultural products since a host of factors including weather, trade policies, exchange rates, and consumer income affect export demand.

Summary

Comparative advantage provides a basis for trade between countries. Despite the general beneficial nature of trade, trade does not benefit everyone. Thus we observe groups attempting to limit trade through tariffs, quotas, and other measures. Exports of farm products were drastically reduced by the protectionist legislation of the 1930s and it was only in the late 1970s that farm exports recovered the share of farm marketings which prevailed fifty years earlier—about 25 percent. After increasing rapidly throughout the 1970s and peaking in 1981, agricultural exports decreased throughout the early 1980s.

As the proportion of farm products exported has increased over time, the demand for many farm products has become more elastic. Thus with the increased importance of trade, protectionist farm programs may have become counterproductive to farmers, even in the short run.

Price support programs create surpluses and pressures to subsidize exports of farm products. During the past thirty years, concessionary sales under PL 480 and other government programs often accounted for a substantial proportion of export sales. Subsidized exports decreased in importance following the export boom for farm products in the early 1970s, but protectionist pressures led to new export subsidy programs for agricultural products in the 1985 farm bill.

In expanding opportunities for exports of farm products, the U.S. government must reduce (not increase) trade restrictions and work to reduce trade barriers in other countries. Foreign buyers must have dollars to purchase U.S. farm products. Consequently, "voluntary" import restrictions and other trade barriers for autos, steel, and so on are likely to prove especially damaging to the agricultural sector. It is inconsistent to attempt simultaneously to reduce imports and increase exports.

There is a fundamental inconsistency between domestic price supports and free trade. When prices are raised above the competitive level, imports must be restricted to prevent consumers from purchasing lower-priced imports. The price support programs instituted during the 1930s were accompanied by legislation to restrict imports and to increase exports of farm products. These measures evoke protectionist measures by other countries. The harmful effects of protectionist policies are well known. Protectionism prevents farmers, other workers, and consumers throughout the world from reaping the benefits that occur when individuals are permitted to engage in those activities in which they are most productive.

Notes

1. Jack L. Hervey, "The Internationalization of Uncle Sam," Federal Reserve Bank of Chicago, *Economic Perspectives* 10 (May–June 1986): 3–14.

2. Ibid, p. 4.

3. Dallas S. Batten and Michael T. Belongia, "The Recent Decline in Agricultural Exports: Is the Exchange Rate the Culprit?" *Federal Reserve Bank of St. Louis Review* 66 (October 1984): 5–14.

4. U.S. Department of Agriculture, *Agricultural Statistics, 1982* (Washington, D.C.: U.S. Government Printing Office, 1983), p. 525.

5. Clifton B. Luttrell, *Down on the Farm with Uncle Sam* (Los Angeles, Calif.: International Institute for Economic Research, 1983), p. 17.

6. Clifton B. Luttrell, "Rising Farm Exports and International Trade Policies," *Federal Reserve Bank of St. Louis Review* 61 (July 1979): 3–10.

7. An enlightening discussion of comparative advantage, exchange rates, balance of trade versus balance of payments, and the harmful effects of protectionism may be found in Phil Gramm, "The Truth About Trade," *Intercollegiate Review* 23 (Fall 1987): 45–48.

8. Paul Heyne, *The Economic Way of Thinking* (Chicago: Science Research Associates, 1987), p. 131.

9. Imports may be subsidized rather than taxed. An import subsidy would have effects just opposite to those of a tariff. An import subsidy would lead to a decrease in domestic production and an increase in domestic consumption. Thus, domestic producers and taxpayers bear the cost of the subsidy. The cost to the government would be the quantity imported times the subsidy.

10. U.S. Department of Agriculture, *Estimates of Producer and Consumer Subsidy Equivalents, Government Intervention in Agriculture, 1982–86,* (Washington, D.C.: U.S. Government Printing Office, 1988).

11. Ronald Knutson, J. B. Penn, and W. T. Boehm, *Agricultural and Food Policy* (Englewood Cliffs, N.J.: Prentice-Hall, 1983), p. 305.

12. Kathryn Longen, *Domestic Food Programs: An Overview* (Washington, D.C.: U.S. Government Printing Office, 1981), p. 24.

13. W. Gene Wilson, "Government Policies: Will They Increase Farm Exports?" *Federal Reserve Bank of Atlanta Economic Review* 72 (January–February 1987): 21–31.

14. Knutson, Penn, and Boehm, *Agricultural and Food Policy*, p. 145.

15. Luttrell, *Down on the Farm with Uncle Sam*, p. 6.

16. Wilson, "Government Policies," p. 22.

17. Joseph V. Kennedy, "Generic Commodity Certificates: How They Affect Markets and the Federal Budget," *Choices* (1987/3): 14–17.

18. Knutson, Penn, and Boehm, *Agricultural and Food Policy*, pp. 137–38.

19. E. C. Pasour, Jr., "On Free Trade's Price: U.S. Farmers Can't Have Free Access to World Markets and Price Supports, Too," *Choices* 1 (1986/2): 33–35.

20. Thomas Gale Moore, "Farm Policy: Justifications, Failures and the Need for Reform," *Federal Reserve Bank of St. Louis Review* 69, no. 8 (October 1987): 8.

21. D. Gale Johnson, "Domestic Agriculture Policy in an International Environment: Effects of Other Countries' Policies on the United States," *American Journal of Agricultural Economics* 66 (December 1984): 736.

22. Ibid.

23. Knutson, Penn, and Boehm, *Agricultural and Food Policy*, p. 142.

24. Kenneth W. Dam, *The GATT: Law and International Economic Organization* (Chicago: University of Chicago Press, 1970), p. 142.

25. Thomas Grennes, "Helping U.S. Farmers Sell More Overseas," Heritage Foundation, *Backgrounder*, 27 February 1985.

26. Fred Sanderson, "Food, Fiber, and Foreign Trade," *Resources* 84 (Summer, 1986): 6.

27. G. Edward Schuh, "U.S. Agriculture in the World Economy," in *Farm and Food Policy: Critical Issues for Southern Agriculture*, ed. M. D. Hammig and H. M. Harris, Jr. (Proceedings of a Symposium, Clemson University, June 2–3, 1983), p. 65.

15

Crop Insurance, Market Stabilization, and Risk Management

Farming is a risky business due to weather, insects, disease, price variability, and so on. Public policies to stabilize markets and to reduce risk in agriculture have been rationalized on the grounds that these forces of nature, being difficult or impossible to control, warrant a sharing of risk by the public at large. The rationale favoring government intervention to stabilize agricultural markets and to reduce risk appears to be quite strong, at least when actual markets are compared with "perfectly competitive" markets. It is important, however, to compare agricultural markets with a realistic alternative, with stabilization policies as government programs actually operate under real world conditions. It is also important to compare the current agricultural sector including stabilization policies with the *same* sector excluding such policies, rather than to compare the current sector, including stabilization policies, with the agricultural world that existed prior to the advent of the New Deal farm programs.

This chapter demonstrates that the case for government programs to stabilize markets and reduce risk is far less strong than is often assumed. First, the results of a recent analysis of crop insurance throughout the world are described. The major federally subsidized crop insurance programs in the United States over the past half century are then briefly described and their effects analyzed. The results in the United States are shown to be similar to experiences with crop insurance throughout the world. Emphasis is placed on the problems inherent in government programs to stabilize markets or to reduce risk.

Crop Insurance: An Expensive Disappointment

Crop Insurance Worldwide

Experience in highly developed and less developed countries demonstrates that there are many problems with crop insurance programs.[1] First, crop insurance is plagued with "moral-hazard" problems. All insurance programs face moral hazards. A moral-hazard problem exists when individuals are encouraged to engage in high risk activities because they are protected from the consequences of their actions. That is, insured individuals may deliberately suffer a loss or avoid adequate precautions to collect insurance benefits. For example, farmers faced with bad prices may collect benefits by setting fire to a field or by neglecting to protect the crop from pests. Or program administrators in subsidized insurance programs may fail to take precautions because they do not bear the full cost of their actions.

Second, administrative costs of crop insurance have generally been higher than for other types of insurance.[2] One reason is the number of field inspections required to contain moral-hazard problems. Operating costs for a government crop insurance program may also be high because the program's payroll is bloated by political patronage.

Third, indemnity claims in most crop insurance programs have been high in relation to premium income, especially when there is not a lot of diversification among types of crops or production regions.[3] Farming tends to be risky relative to many other businesses, so losses are higher. Moreover, a small program covering a small number of crops in a few areas is particularly vulnerable if disaster strikes. As a result of these problems, premiums have to be high for a crop insurance program to be self-financing. Consequently, most crop insurance programs have been subsidized by the government. Yet even with subsidized insurance, many farmers have chosen not to participate. A recent study of crop insurance in a number of different countries throughout the world concluded that "most crop insurance programs have not been successful" and that crop insurance generally has been an expensive disappointment.[4] Let us now consider the experience of crop insurance in the United States.

Federal Crop Insurance Corporation (FCIC)

The U.S. government became involved in crop insurance after several private sector attempts to provide multiple-peril crop insurance failed.[5] A political decision was made in the New Deal era to provide subsidized crop insurance. The first national program began in 1938. The objective of the Federal Crop Insurance Corporation (FCIC), a wholly owned government corporation, was to improve the economic stability of agriculture. Millions of farmers had been adversely affected by the droughts of the 1930s, and the purpose of the program was to insure against such catastrophes. The FCIC insured selected crops against major causes of crop losses including weather, insects, and plant diseases. The FCIC in the beginning was authorized to set premiums at rates sufficient to cover crop losses but not to cover administrative expenses.[6] Thus the government has subsidized federal crop insurance from its inception. Low participation and underwriting losses despite good weather caused Congress to cancel the program in 1943.[7] It was revived the following year and operated from 1944 to 1979.

Initially, crop insurance was limited to wheat and cotton, but coverage was broadened over time. However, through the 1970s coverage continued to be available only on a limited number of crops and in only about half of the counties in the United States. Prior to 1980, FCIC contracts covered less than 5 percent of the total value of crops grown in the United States and farmer participation averaged only 10 to 20 percent.[8] Thus crop insurance had little effect on farm production.

Disaster Payments Program (DPP)

A Disaster Payments Program (DPP), introduced in the Agricultural and Consumer Protection Act of 1973, operated from 1974 to 1980. Under this program which operated without premiums, direct payments were made to producers suffering losses from natural forces in the production of feed grains, wheat, cotton, and rice. Compensation was made for losses incurred from the inability to plant due to drought or flood and for abnormally low yields resulting from weather, insects, and pests. The basic objective of the DPP was to cover the producers' out-of-pocket losses.[9] The DPP amounted to free insurance for farmers at a treasury cost which averaged about half a billion dollars a year.

The moral-hazard problem was especially acute in the DPP. The "prevented plantings" payments provide a striking example. When farmers received compensation for losses from the inability to plant crops due to drought or flood, the insureds' behavior was affected by the existence of the program. That is, the DPP made it less rewarding for farmers to avoid risks of crop failure, which made it more likely that a loss would be incurred. Hence, in one sense the DPP was a disaster subsidy program.

The DPP also created a moral-hazard problem in farming of "fragile lands," defined as those especially subject to erosion by wind or water which rapidly deplete the land. Some counties in arid areas of Texas, California, and New Mexico had such risky production conditions that FCIC insurance was not available. However, these areas were included in the DPP, and farming practices changed noticeably between 1974 and 1978 as acreages of grains increased and claims for disaster payments soared. Thus, the DPP discouraged soil conservation by subsidizing crop production on marginal lands in the Southwest and Western Great Plains. Federally subsidized irrigation programs also have harmful ecological effects since wildlife and government water projects usually do not mix well.[10] The DPP was dropped in 1981 after a comprehensive all-risk insurance program was authorized by Congress in 1980. When the DPP was eliminated, however, crop insurance was provided on fragile lands where FCIC insurance had not been available.

Federal Crop Insurance Act (FCIA) of 1980

The Federal Crop Insurance Act (FCIA) of 1980 created "all-risk" crop insurance, replacing the old federal crop insurance program and the disaster payments program. This program is administered by the secretary of agriculture through the FCIC. In 1986, the program covered about 40 crops in about 3000 counties in all regions of the United States. However, program participation has been far below what FCIC envisioned it would be. In 1985, FCIC insured less than 20 percent of the acres it considered potentially insurable compared with a 1981 projected goal of 65 percent.[11]

Under all-risk crop insurance, farmers have a choice of three levels of yield protection (50, 65, and 75 percent of average county yield) and three levels of price protection.[12] Premiums are based on expected average losses on a county basis. The government pays 30 percent of the premium for the 50- and 65-percent coverage levels and a smaller subsidy at the 75-percent yield level. Thus, the political price paid for ending the DPP was the introduction of an expanded set of crop insurance programs that include explicit 30-percent subsidies of insurance premiums. Moreover, the premiums are set to cover only the expected indemnity payments and not the operating costs of the FCIA. However, the FCIC has had financial difficulties and has incurred substantial losses in every year of the expanded program. For fiscal years 1982 through 1985, claim payments exceeded premium income by $849 million.[13]

Emergency Loans

In addition to crop insurance, emergency loans are provided to farmers in areas experiencing tornadoes, floods, hurricanes, or other natural disasters. These loans, with an interest subsidy of 50 to 75 percent, are made through the Small Business Administration and the FmHA. Eligibility is dependent on the presidential designation of a county as a disaster area. Such designations are affected both by the extent of crop loss and by political factors (e.g., an upcoming election).

Economic Implications

Insurance involving the substitution of a small known cost for the possibility of a large loss is a key means of coping with risk in many areas of life. Some agricultural risks, such as losses due to hail, are better suited for an actuarially sound insurance program than others. Hail losses are not affected by management decisions and occur frequently enough to induce farmers to purchase hail insurance. In contrast, the large variability in annual losses and incentive problems make the provision of drought insurance by private companies more difficult.[14]

Gardner and Cramer estimate that it would take a large subsidy—probably more than 50 percent of premiums charged—to get a majority of U.S. farmers enrolled in crop insurance.[15] A lack of participation in insurance at levels high enough to cover costs is sometimes taken as evidence of market failure and, consequently, as a justification for subsidized crop insurance. This conclusion follows if one measures real-world markets against the norm of perfect competition where all risks would be fully insured. In the real world, however, where risk reduction is achievable only at a cost, it is economic to shift risk only when the expected gains exceed the costs. Thus the absence of insurance in a given area of economic activity does not imply market failure. It may merely be evidence of an unwillingness to participate in an insurance program when premium levels are set high enough to cover the full cost of providing the insurance.[16] There is no known way to determine whether crop insurance is economic in the absence of a market test.

It is commonly held that past private crop insurance programs were unsuccessful because the insurance firms were unable to cope either with moral-hazard problems or with geographically widespread disasters. Thus, it is argued, the current crop insurance program is justified. As suggested above, however, it is not economic to insure against all risks. If farmers are willing to buy insurance, private firms will likely provide it. However, if crop insurance is not provided privately and is provided by the government, there is no good reason why farmers should pay less than its actuarial value. Under current conditions, the subsidized crop insurance program is an effective barrier to the provision of crop insurance by private firms. Moreover, the subsidized crop insurance program appears to be better explained by political than by economic factors, and as described below, other private-sector innovation in risk management is now quite often discouraged or forbidden.

Market Stabilization and Risk Management

The public interest is often given as the justification for crop insurance and other programs to decrease risk or to stabilize farm prices and income. That is, it is argued that crop insurance and price supports are not transfers to farmers but benefit the public at large. It is important, however, to judge the effects of programs on the basis of outcomes rather than objectives.

If government is to stabilize individual commodity markets, the planners must overcome the same kinds of problems faced in attempting to stabilize the entire economy. The stabilization idea is based, at least to some extent, on the "genie" concept of government, which assumes that government wants to, knows how to, and is able to coordinate economic activity. In reality, information and incentive problems are always present in the collective-choice process. Stabilization policies, whether of individual markets or the entire economy, are not administered by impartial and omniscient experts but through a political process in which decision makers act in light of their own interests and incentives.[17]

How Government Policies Increase Market Instability

Consider some of the ways in which government actions destabilize the agricultural sector. First, inflationary monetary and fiscal policies have had a destabilizing effect on U.S. agriculture. Monetary disturbances affect relative prices, particularly interest rates, a key factor in investment decisions. High interest rates are especially important in agriculture, which is characterized by a high ratio of capital investment per unit of labor. Many farm bankruptcies in the early 1980s involved highly-leveraged operations involving money borrowed at the historically high interest rates of the late 1970s. Anticipated inflation is the product of government's monetary and fiscal policies and the primary cause of high interest rates. Thus, the government's inflationary monetary and fiscal policies of the late 1970s created major problems in the farm sector.

Second, government actions are often ineffective or counterproductive in market stabilization. During the Carter administration, for example, CCC storage was supplemented by a Farmer Owned Reserve (FOR) program ostensibly to stabilize the market. The FOR, as explained in Chapter 10, was a complex system of incentives and subsidies to encourage farmers to store grain when prices are low and to encourage them to release it when prices are high. Subsequent study of the price patterns of that time, compared to the pre-FOR period, however, "showed no significant improvement in stability" due to the program.[18]

In 1983, the PIK program—the largest acreage cutback program in the history of U.S. price support programs—greatly intensified the effects of weather-induced reductions in output. Similarly, the Dairy and Tobacco Adjustment Act of 1983 paid dairy farmers for reducing milk production in an attempt to alleviate the dairy surplus problem. This program ignored the fact that the surplus of dairy products is caused by high price supports dictated by political rather than economic considerations. There have been many other examples in the operation of farm programs where short-run political considerations have dominated stabilization concerns (see chapter 5). There is also a great deal of uncertainty about future benefit levels of federal farm programs. High price supports that are later lowered in response to pressures to decrease government expenditures may foster unrealistic expectations by farm investors. Indeed, USDA economist John Lee concludes that the single greatest source of uncertainty for many farmers (and other agribusiness firms) is not weather or international markets, but federal farm programs.[19]

Third, government-subsidized and government-sponsored credit programs create an incentive to expand the size of farm operations through borrowing. (Government credit programs in agriculture are described in the following chapter). Moreover, when the cost of capital is decreased, farmers are induced to substitute capital for labor. "Too much" credit is more likely to be extended when credit is subsidized and when lenders do not bear the full consequences of their actions. It is likely that easy government credit was an important factor contributing to the increase in farm bankruptcies in the early and mid-1980s.[20]

Fourth, agriculture is heavily dependent on international trade and consequently is greatly affected by government policies that disrupt trade. The suspension of grain sales to Russia by President Carter in 1980, for example, increased uncertainty in domestic grain markets. Moreover, it is not only the measures directly affecting agricultural exports that are important. Import restrictions on autos, steel, textiles, and other products, as described in the previous chapter, are especially damaging to U.S. agriculture.

Since much of the instability of U.S. commodity markets during the 1970s and 1980s can be traced to government policies, government can make an important contribution to the stability of agricultural markets. That contribution, however, does not hinge on the provision of price supports, subsidized crop insurance, and other government programs designed explicitly for agriculture. As suggested above, farm programs may increase rather than decrease instability. Instead, government can make its greatest contribution to the stability of U.S. agriculture by reducing trade restrictions, and perhaps most important, by adopting noninflationary monetary and fiscal policies. That is, government policies should not introduce artificial instability into agricultural markets.

When the inherent information and incentive problems are taken into account, government might make its greatest contribution to agricultural stability by attempting to do less.[21] That is, if government policies are destabilizing, a reduction in the scope of government programs may increase market stability.

Ways to Reduce Risk and Stabilize Income

Government can also create a climate to facilitate rather than impede the development of institutions dealing with weather, market, and political risks. The current government-subsidized crop insurance program, as suggested above, is an effective barrier to the provision of crop insurance by private firms and exacerbates the moral-hazard problem. Therefore an important first step in developing institutions to reduce risk is to phase out subsidized crop insurance.

Futures Markets. A second component of an improved risk-management policy is to encourage private-sector alternatives to government programs. Producers will insure against risk so long as the expected benefits exceed the cost of providing the insurance coverage. The futures market is an effective way of generating and transmitting information about expectations of future market conditions. It also provides an important means of shifting risk in the production of crop and livestock products in those markets for which futures markets exist.

Trading in futures for agricultural products is now limited to about one year. There have been proposals to extend trading in selected futures contracts two or three years into the future to enable the private sector to take a longer view.[22] In such an approach, it is suggested that a government agency might buy and sell futures contracts in order to keep prices close to market clearing levels based on expected supply and demand conditions.[23] There would presumably be no government stockpile of commodities since the program would operate through the purchase and

sale of futures contracts. This type of program, according to its proponents, would provide buyers and sellers with a mechanism "to put current supply and demand conditions into perspective with expectations
about the future" so that producers and processors would be able to
eliminate price risks up to three years in advance.[24]

Theoretically, this mechanism would provide a relatively stable environment in which producers and processors of farm products could
hedge production and storage decisions over a much longer period than
currently can be done. Unfortunately, however, this approach involving a
government trading agency is also rooted in the "genie" concept of government. Any program of this type faces information and incentive problems similar to those endemic to all other actions by public agencies. The
fundamental problem is that the political process is short-run oriented. It
is unrealistic to expect government officials to ignore political considerations in making decisions affecting storage. Consequently, problems are
likely to arise when a government agency trades in futures markets similar to those that arise when the government attempts to stabilize markets
directly through storage operations. Even if government officials have the
necessary information and know what "should be done," their actions are
likely to be dominated by short-run political considerations. In view of
the inherent incentive and information problems associated with government intervention in commodity markets, it may well be that government
can make the greatest contribution in the case of futures markets simply
by providing a stable legal framework for private traders.

In any comparison of government and private-sector stabilization programs, the basic question is whether government is better able than the
private sector to coordinate and implement production, marketing, and
storage decisions. There are good reasons to expect that risk-taking entrepreneurs placing their own money on the line will, on average, make
better decisions than individuals in public agencies who do not fully bear
the consequences of their decisions. For example, when wheat and corn
stocks were drawn down in the early 1970s following the huge exports of
U.S. farm products, U.S. consumers were left vulnerable to large price
increases when there was a corn crop shortfall in 1974.[25] The management decision was made primarily by the CCC which sold off its long-
held inventories when prices first began to rise during the grain sales to
Russia during 1972 and 1973. Since the managers of CCC stocks are not
residual claimants, it is predictable that the management of government-
owned stocks would be more short-run oriented than decisions by managers of privately owned stocks.

Option Markets. Option markets are a private-sector device providing a
potentially attractive substitute for current government programs in insur-
ing against risk in agricultural markets. Agricultural options are contracts
that give farmers the right to sell (or buy) commodities at a predetermined
price during some future period. For example, a corn farmer at planting
might purchase a put option giving the grower the right to sell a corn
futures contract at harvest at a specified price. If market price of corn at

harvest exceeds the specified price, the option would not be exercised, and the farmer would receive the benefits from the higher market price. If corn price at harvest were below the option price, on the other hand, the farmer could exercise the option. The purchaser of a put option which entitles the purchaser to sell a commodity at a specified price is thus insured against a decrease in price. The put option, like the conventional futures market hedge, provides security against price decreases. However, unlike the conventional hedge, the put option allows a farmer to reap the benefit of an increase in price. Of course, this method of reducing risk involves a cost. The farmer incurs the cost of the option, regardless of whether the option is exercised.

There were no markets for put options in agricultural products from the New Deal era until 1984. The absence of option markets in agriculture was not due to market failure, however, but rather to a congressional ban on agricultural commodity options in 1936 following allegations of market manipulation. The 1982 Futures Trading Act lifted the 1936 ban and authorized a three-year pilot program; actual trading of agricultural commodity options began in late 1984.[26]

Options markets would have a number of advantages over current farm programs.[27] First, the trading of options facilitates rather than hinders the operations of markets. Options markets provide information to producers and consumers based on the underlying supply and demand conditions.

Second, unlike traditional price support programs which are financed by taxpayers, farmers pay for price protection in options markets. Moreover, the farmer may chose the level of price protection desired. Of course, the cost is higher the more protection obtained.

There are also some drawbacks to the use of options markets.[28] From the standpoint of the farmer, price protection through options markets is costly—when compared with conventional price support programs financed by taxpayers. As in the case of futures markets, option markets may not offer price protection for sufficiently long periods of time. Currently, agricultural option contracts extend for only approximately six months.

Agricultural options are traded for only a few commodities and are unlikely ever to be traded for some farm products where the demand would be too small to create a market. Similarly, the size of option contract (e.g., 5,000 bushels of soybeans) may be too large for many small farmers to use. In spite of these practical difficulties, options markets for agricultural products are one way to stabilize markets for farm products without cost to taxpayers. However, current taxpayer-financed farm programs significantly reduce the demand for futures and option market contracts.[29]

Summary

Farmers face a multitude of risks from weather, disease, pests, and changing market conditions. Countries around the world have instituted multiple-risk crop insurance programs to deal with these problems. The record shows that most crop insurance programs have not been successful. Crop insurance programs are plagued by moral-hazard problems, high administrative costs, and high indemnity claims in relation to premiums. Premiums on an actuarially sound basis must be high to make crop insurance programs self-financing.

A host of government programs, including product price supports and crop insurance, have been instituted to reduce risk and to stabilize agricultural markets in the United States during the period since the 1930s. Federally subsidized crop insurance, available on a limited basis until 1980, is now available in all regions of the United States.

In the real world, where risk reduction is achievable only at a cost, it is economic to shift risk only when the costs exceed the gains. Moral-hazard problems are inherent in the current heavily subsidized all-risk crop insurance programs. This program is also an effective barrier to the provision of crop insurance by private firms. The optimal amount of insurance can be determined only through a market test. Regardless of how crop insurance is provided, insurance premiums should reflect the actuarial cost.

There is a strong a priori case for decentralized competitive markets as the most effective means of coping with changing economic conditions.[30] Government attempts to stabilize the overall level of economic activity in the United States during the past twenty years suggest that government policies as they are implemented through the political process often introduce artificial instability into agricultural (and other) markets. There is an important lesson for agriculture: government might make its greatest contribution to economic stability by attempting to do less. Noninflationary monetary and fiscal policies and a more open economy are likely to be more beneficial to agriculture in the long run than stabilization policies designed specifically for agriculture.

Government can also encourage the development of institutions and mechanisms that help farmers to cope with uncertainties caused by weather and market conditions. Futures and options markets for agricultural products have the potential to provide more price protection than is currently available through price support programs—and at a considerable reduction in cost to the taxpayer. These market alternatives to government programs, however, do not guarantee farm incomes.

Notes

1. Peter Hazell, Carlos Pomareda, and Alberto Valdes, *Crop Insurance for Agricultural Development: Issues and Experience* (Baltimore: Johns Hopkins University Press, 1986).
2. Ibid., p. 294.
3. Ibid.
4. Ibid.
5. Bruce L. Gardner and Randall L. Kramer, "Experience with Crop Insurance Programs in the United States," in *Crop Insurance for Agricultural Development:*

Issues and Experience, ed. Peter Hazell, Carlos Pomaredo, and Alberto Valdes (Baltimore: Johns Hopkins University Press, 1986), p. 222.

6. Harold Halcrow, *Agricultural Policy Analysis* (New York: McGraw-Hill, 1984), p. 242.

7. Ibid.

8. Ronald D. Knutson, J. B. Penn, and W. T. Boehm, *Agricultural and Food Policy* (Englewood Cliffs, N.J.: Prentice-Hall, 1983), p. 235.

9. Ibid.

10. Renee Wyman and John Baden, "The Garrison File: Profile of a Pork Barrel," *Reason* 16 (January 1985): 33–38.

11. U.S. General Accounting Office, *Crop Insurance: Federal Crop Insurance Needs to Improve Decision Making*, GAO/RCED-87-77 (Washington, D.C.: U.S. Government Printing Office, 1987), p. 42.

12. Knutson, Penn, and Boehm, *Agricultural and Food Policy*, p. 236.

13. U.S. General Accounting Office, *Crop Insurance*, p. 2.

14. Bruce L. Gardner, R. E. Just, R. A. Kramer, and R. D. Pope, "Agricultural Policy and Risk," in *Risk Management in Agriculture*, ed. Peter J. Barry (Ames: Iowa State University Press, 1984), p. 246.

15. Gardner and Kramer, "Experience with Crop Insurance Programs," p. 222.

16. Harold Demsetz, "Information and Efficiency: Another Viewpoint," *Journal of Law and Economics* 12 (April 1969): 1–21.

17. Paul Heyne, *The Economic Way of Thinking*, 4th ed. (Chicago: Science Research Associates, 1984), p. 447.

18. Bruce Gardner, "Agriculture's Revealing—and Painful—Lesson for Industrial Policy," Heritage Foundation, *Backgrounder*, no. 320, 3 January 1984.

19. John E. Lee, "Observations on the Setting for Agricultural Policy," *Farm and Food Policy: Critical Issues for Southern Agriculture*, ed. M. D. Hammig and H. M. Harris, Jr. (Proceedings of a Symposium, Clemson University, 2–3 June 1983), p. 258.

20. Michael T. Belongia, *Agriculture: An Eighth District Perspective* (St. Louis: Federal Reserve Bank of St. Louis, Spring 1984).

21. Heyne, *Economic Way of Thinking*, p. 448.

22. J. Bruce Bullock, "Future Directions for Agricultural Policy," *American Journal of Agricultural Economics* (May 1984): 234–39.

23. H. S. Houthakker, *Economic Policy of the Farm Sector* (Washington, D.C.: American Enterprise Institute, 1967).

24. Bruce Bullock, "What is the 1985 Farm Problem?" *Policy Analysis*, no. 55 (Washington, D.C.: The Cato Institute, 1985), p. 14.

25. Gardner, "Agriculture's Revealing and Painful Lesson," p. 9.

26. David E. Kenyon, *Farmer's Guide to Trading Agricultural Commodity Options*, USDA AIB Number 463 (Washington, D.C.: U.S. Government Printing Office, 1984).

27. Kandice H. Kahl, "Agricultural Options: An Alternative to Federal Farm Programs," The Heritage Foundation, *Backgrounder*, no. 414, 7 March 1985.

28. Ibid.

29. "The principal reason that a private-sector mechanism for hedging risks has not been developed is government's heavy involvement in agricultural affairs." Thomas Gale Moore, "Farm Policy: Justifications, Failures and the Need for Reform," *Federal Reserve Bank of St. Louis Review* 69, no. 8 (October 1987): 6.

30. F. A. Hayek, *Individualism and Economic Order* (Chicago: University of Chicago Press, 1948).

16

Subsidized Credit in U.S. Agriculture

It has long been held by farm spokesmen that the credit needs for agriculture are not adequately met by conventional financial institutions.[1] In this view, private lending procedures, sources of funds, and loan terms are not well suited to the "needs" of agriculture. Government began to make direct loans to farmers and ranchers to meet short-term credit "requirements" in the 1920s. During the 1930s, the establishment of the Farm Credit System (FCS) was completed and the Farmers Home Administration (FmHA), the Rural Electrification Administration (REA), and the Commodity Credit Corporation (CCC) were created.

There are a number of different types of government lending programs, and it is difficult to get a complete picture of federally assisted borrowing. Direct loans are made by the CCC, FmHA, and REA. In some cases, there is also government-guaranteed lending where private loans are guaranteed by these agencies. In addition to direct loans and loan guarantees, there is federally assisted borrowing in agriculture through the Farm Credit System, a government-sponsored enterprise. In this case, and others described below, the anticipated outlays of the official federal budget do not accurately portray the full extent of federal credit activity in agriculture. Some of these problems are discussed following a description of the major government credit agencies and programs in U.S. agriculture.

The Farm Credit System (FCS)[2]

The FCS was established and chartered by the federal government to perform specific credit functions but is now privately owned. In the mid-1980s, the Farm Credit System held about one-third of the nation's farm debt.

The roots of the FCS predate the New Deal era. They reach back to the Federal Land Bank Act of 1916. The Federal Intermediate Credit Banks were formed in 1923 and the Production Credit Associations and Banks for Cooperatives were added in 1933.[3] The Farm Credit System began as a government-sponsored effort to provide a cooperative system through which farmers could provide their own credit. The original loan from the federal government was repaid and, within the rules it operated under, the

FCS was self-supporting prior to 1985 when the federal government came to the rescue of the financially troubled system. Legislation was passed to assist the FCS in 1985, 1986, and 1987. However, there was an implicit subsidy involved in the operation of the FCS even before direct federal assistance was provided for in 1985.

Government sponsorship of the various components of the FCS provided a number of direct benefits to them which amounted to an implicit subsidy to users of credit extended by the FCS (when compared with commercial banks). Earnings of the FCS banks that operate as cooperatives are exempt from state, federal, and local income taxes. Interest income derived from FCS securities is also exempt from state and local income taxes. In addition, after 1985, the FCS had a line of credit at the Treasury if deemed necessary. The FCS also enjoys other advantages relative to commercial banks as a result of its federal "agency status."[4] Despite the absence of federal guarantees prior to 1985, the FCS generally was able to borrow at interest rates only slightly higher than the interest rates paid by the U.S. Treasury on comparable issues of federal debt because of the perceived special relationship between this government-sponsored enterprise and the federal government.

The following description of the components of the FCS describes the structure as it operated prior to the Agricultural Credit Act of 1987. This act involves some mandatory mergers together with other possible restructuring of the system, as explained below.

The FCS is divided into twelve Farm Credit Districts covering the United States and Puerto Rico. Each district includes a Federal Land Bank (FLB) and its affiliated Federal Land Bank Associations (FLBAs), a Federal Intermediate Credit Bank (FICB) and its affiliated Production Credit Associations (PCAs), and a Bank for Cooperatives (BC). In addition, there is a Central Bank for Cooperatives in Denver, Colorado. Each of the thirty-seven banks and more than nine hundred local associations is organized as a cooperative.

The credit policies of the FCS are supervised, administered, and coordinated by the Farm Credit Administration (FCA), an agency of the executive branch of the U.S. government. The FCA was an arm of the USDA from 1939 to 1953 but is now a separate agency. The three enterprises regulated by the FCA, the Banks for Cooperatives, Federal Intermediate Credit Banks, and Federal Land Banks, borrow by issuing consolidated farm credit bonds and notes rather than securities under their separate names. The FCS obtains funds through the sale of securities to investors on the national money markets.

Federal Land Banks

Each FLB is authorized to make long term loans secured by a first mortgage on real estate for maturities ranging from five to forty years, although most of the loans are made for periods of twenty-five to thirty years. Loans are made to farmers and ranchers, corporations producing farm products, farm-related business, and rural homeowners. The loans can be used to acquire farms, land, equipment, and livestock or to refinance existing debt. Federal land banks account for more than 40 percent of all outstanding farm real-estate debt.[5] The loans are made through some five hundred local land bank associations (FLBAs). These local FLBAs serve as the local contact for FLB loans.

Federal Intermediate Credit Banks (FICBs) and Production Credit Associations (PCAs)

The primary activity of the FICBs is to provide funds to approximately 400 PCAs. The FICBs can also discount the notes of farmers and fishermen held by other financial institutions making agricultural loans. The PCAs make short-term and intermediate-term loans. The loans can be used for a wide range of activities in farming and farm-related businesses including the production of farm products, the production and harvesting of aquatic products, and the purchase or repair of rural homes. PCAs make loans of up to seven years in agriculture and loans of up to fifteen years to commercial fishermen.[6] About 17 percent of all non-real-estate farm debt outstanding in 1985 (excluding CCC loans) was held by PCAs.[7] The FLBAs and PCAs share facilities and staff at the local level.

Banks for Cooperatives (BCs)

The Banks for Cooperatives make long-term and short-term loans directly to cooperatives of farmers and commercial fishermen. Long-term loans are made for constructing or remodeling facilities, or for purchasing land, buildings, or equipment. There are thirteen BCs, one in each of the twelve farm credit districts and a central bank in Denver. Although private individuals cannot borrow money from the BC, these banks, by financing agricultural co-ops, play a large role in agricultural credit.

Funding the FCS

Borrower stock requirements are being changed under the Agricultural Credit Act of 1987. Prior to that legislation each borrower was required to purchase stock in the association at a level equal to 5–10 percent of the loan.[8] The stock is retired in the final loan payment. The local FLBAs and PCAs in turn buy stock in the respective district bank. Prior to the federal bailout under the 1987 Act (see following section), these stock purchases by borrowers along with retained earnings provided the source of capitalization of the FCS.

Independence of FCS and the 1985 Federal Bailout

In 1968, the last loan made by the government to finance the FCS was repaid and the system became wholly owned by its user borrowers. Yet even before the federal rescue of the system, the FCS as a government-sponsored enterprise (GSE) enjoyed benefits not available to private lenders, as explained above. Moreover, the FCS was not completely independent, as shown during the credit crunch of the mid-1980s. The FCS lost some $2.7 billion in 1985 through mortgage and loan defaults—more than any other financial institution in U.S. history.

Congress responded with a federal bailout, the Farm Credit Amendments Act of 1985. There were three main parts to the act.[9] First, it set up a new body, the Farm Credit Corporation of America (FCCA), to reorganize operations and handle troubled loans. This corporation was supposed to purchase bad loans at market value, restructure the loans, and assess FCS members to cover the costs. Second, it gave the FCA more enforcement authority as the regulator of the FCS. Third, it gave the secretary of the treasury the discretion to provide financial assistance to the FCS.

A subsequent law, the Farm Credit Amendments Act of 1986, was intended to provide the system with an opportunity to work through its financial difficulties without direct financial assistance by the federal government. However, a 1987 GAO study concluded that these amendments would "not substantially delay the need for federal assistance."[10] Congress responded by enacting a multi-billion dollar package of federal assistance to the FCS in late 1987. The legislation guaranteed the value of existing borrower stock, mandated the restructuring of loans when the cost is less than that of foreclosure, established a process for restructuring the system, and among other things, established a secondary market for farm real estate loans.[11]

The Agricultural Credit Act of 1987 provides for up to $4 billion in federal financial assistance to institutions within the FCS.[12] In addition to the recapitalization of the FCS, the act provides for restructuring the FCS and mandates the merger of the FLB and FICB in each Farm Credit District. It also provides for the existing twelve Farm Credit Districts to be consolidated into no fewer than 6 districts, the potential merger of FLBAs and PCAs with similar territories, and a possible merger of the BCs into a single nationwide BC. The bailout legislation was designed to reduce operating costs but it is likely to increase the overall cost of operation because the FCS is required to devote more resources to deal with financially distressed borrowers.[13] As the structure and operation of the system changes, the role of the FCS as an agricultural lender appears destined to change over time. And there is much uncertainty (in mid-1988) as to the effect of recent legislation on the system's long-term viability in agricultural lending.

Farmers Home Administration (FmHA)

The FmHA is a direct lending arm of the USDA which makes loans for purchasing and operating farms, improving rural housing, and developing rural community facilities. The FmHA was created by the Farmers Home Administration Act of 1946. However, the roots of the FmHA go back to the Resettlement Administration of the New Deal in 1933. The FmHA was formed to implement all direct lending, loan insurance, and grant programs for low-income farmers. It is commonly held that the major purpose of the FmHA is to "provide credit to farmers who are unable to get adequate credit from other sources at reasonable rates."[14] Thus, the FmHA is designed to be a "lender of last resort."

The role of the FmHA has been broadened a number of times since 1948, both to enlarge its credit programs for farmers and to provide credit for a variety of rural development programs. In 1949, loans became available to finance housing for farmers. In 1961, nonfarm rural residents also became eligible for FmHA loans. In 1968, coverage was extended to low-income rural housing. However, the greatest increase in FmHA coverage occurred in 1972 when loans for community facilities including fire departments, hospitals, and recreational facilities were greatly expanded. In 1982, about half of the FmHA loans and grants were for farmer programs.[15] The remainder were for rural housing programs, community programs, and business and industry programs.

Major FmHA Programs for Farmers

Farm ownership loans are long-term loans for farmers "lacking other sources of credit." These loans enable farmers to buy, improve, or refinance farm real estate. Borrowers must refinance through conventional lenders "when sufficiently qualified."[16] In 1985, about 10 percent of all outstanding farm real estate debt in the United States was held by the FmHA—almost as much as was held by all commercial banks.[17]

Farm operating loans available to farmers and ranchers "lacking other sources of production financing" usually range from one to seven years. These loans are typically secured by chattel mortgages on feed, growing crops, livestock, or machinery. In 1985, 19 percent of all outstanding farm non-real-estate debt (excluding CCC loans) was held by the FmHA.[18]

So-called limited resource loans are made for the same purposes as farm ownership and operating loans but to owners or tenants who "need a lower interest rate to have a reasonable chance of success."[19] The farmer in this case borrows at the lower interest rate "until able to pay the regular lending rate."[20]

"Emergency loans" are available to help farmers recover from actual-production and physical losses inflicted by natural disasters. In order for a farm to qualify for an emergency loan, the county in which it is located must be designated a disaster area. Eligible applicants unable to receive "suitable" credit elsewhere may receive subsidized loss loans.[21]

The interest rate on FmHA loans of different types is well below the cost of government borrowing. Thus there is an explicit subsidy when contrasted with the cost of credit obtained from commercial lending agencies. The interest rate charged in the rental housing program in 1985, for example, was only 1 percent.[22]

FmHA as a Lender of Last Resort

The FmHA today cannot be characterized as a lender of last resort to farmers. Since lending authorizations of the FmHA have been broadened over time, as indicated above, subsidized loans are available for almost any purpose if the borrower lives outside a major metropolitan area. Loans and grants are available not only for farm operations but also for a host of other programs including rural labor housing, community facilities, watershed protection, flood prevention, waste programs, and recreational facilities.

FmHA Loans: The Situation in the Mid-1980s.

The FmHA faces the dilemma of avoiding troubled loans while providing credit to high-risk farmers. Thus the high degree of financial stress by FmHA borrowers in the mid-1980s should not be surprising. In 1985, only 15 percent of the FmHA borrowers had a positive cash flow and the average borrowers had a yearly negative cash flow of about $56,000.[23] The seriousness of financial stress is indicated by the fact that the average FmHA borrower had a debt-to-asset ratio of 83 percent. Indeed, more than half of the borrowers, having debt-asset ratios of over 70 percent, were either technically insolvent or had extreme financial problems.[24]

The nature of FmHA lending activity is changing under the Food Security Act of 1985. Unless there is a change in policy, the FmHA is scheduled to phase out of direct lending activity by 1991 and to become a guarantor of farm operating and ownership loans.[25]

CCC Loans

The Commodity Credit Corporation extends credit through price support programs to any eligible farmer. The demand for CCC price support loans, and hence CCC credit, varies greatly from year to year depending upon the level of production and the difference between loan rates and market prices. For example, CCC loan debt outstanding was $5.0 billion in 1980 but was $16.9 billion in 1985.[26] Credit obtained through CCC loans represents a double break for borrowers. First, the amount of money a farmer can obtain as a nonrecourse loan on a given amount of collateral in the form of wheat, corn, or other commodity exceeds the amount that could be obtained from private lending sources. Second, there is also a direct interest subsidy when the farmer obtains a nonrecourse loan. If the borrower elects to repay the loan, the interest rate paid is below the market rate. (In 1985, CCC commodity loans averaged 9.5 percent, some 4.5 percent below the private loan rate).[27] If the borrower defaults, ownership of the commodity passes to the CCC, fully satisfying the loan obligation including the accumulated interest. Thus, whether or not the loan is repaid, there is an interest subsidy to the farmer-borrower. Since the benefits vary with volume of production, large farmers get more benefits from subsidized credit programs.

The Rural Electrification Administration (REA)

The Rural Electrification Administration was designed to be a lending agency responsible for electrification and telephone service to rural areas. However, REA's original mission is now largely complete. Over 99 percent of farms have electric service and over 95 percent of farms have telephones. Current REA programs have gone far beyond their original goal of providing electricity and telephone service to rural areas.[28]

REA programs have expanded to include subsidized lending to electric cooperatives serving high-income urban and suburban areas throughout the United States. REA loans have also been used to provide electric service to exclusive recreation areas, including Aspen, Colorado and Hilton Head Island, South Carolina.[29]

The REA makes both direct loans and loan guarantees. REA loans have been heavily subsidized since interest rates increased dramatically during the late 1970s. In 1985, for example, the cost of long-term treasury borrowing was over 11 percent, but REA's lending rate was only 5 percent. The present value of the subsidy of REA direct loan obligations in 1985 was more than three-quarters of a billion dollars.[30] This is a measure of the additional payments that the REA would have had to pay had the loans been purely private. The evidence suggests that this interest rate subsidy persists for political rather than economic reasons.

Economic Analysis of Subsidized Credit Programs

The CCC, FCS, FmHA, and REA may be viewed as federally assisted borrowing or subsidized credit programs. In this section, the general effects of subsidized or cheap credit are examined, focusing on the direct and indirect effects of federally assisted borrowing, whatever the type.

Government-Assisted versus Private Credit in U.S. Agriculture

The objective of federal credit programs is quite different from that of profit-seeking private credit institutions. The purpose of federal credit programs is to offer terms and conditions to selected borrowers that are more favorable than those otherwise available from private lenders. When compared with fully private loans, government-assisted credit may include lower interest rates or loan guarantees, less stringent credit risk thresholds in making credit available, or more generous repayment schedules.[31] Moreover, as is also the case with other government activities, a federal credit program has no standard measure of performance, such as profit, in assessing success. Thus a large increase in federal outlays on agricultural credit programs during the farm financial stress of the 1980s is not surprising.

Problems arise, however, when a lending agency only deals with one sector of the economy, whether the credit institution is public or private. In recent years many private commercial banks in farm areas have also been in trouble. A problem is likely to arise when a bank at a given location is not able to diversify its risk outside of its geographic area and outside of agriculture. This problem of inability to diversify risks is inherent in federal agricultural credit institutions. It is also a problem with commercial banks located in predominantly agricultural areas, such as those in the Corn Belt, which cannot diversify their risks by making loans in nonagricultural areas because of restrictions on branch banking.

The potential significance of portfolio diversification is illustrated by the situation in California, which allows statewide branching. Agricultural lenders there fared much better than agricultural banks in other areas during the 1980s because large banks, which account for most of the lending in agriculture, hold less than 5 percent of their portfolios in agricultural production loans.[32] The conclusion is that nationwide banks would be able to diversify their risks much more effectively than banks restricted to a given geographical area. A bank that makes loans in different regions does not have its fate tied to the economy of one region. Moreover, under interstate banking a bank in a farming region would not have all its loans dependent on the state of the farm economy.[33] Thus restrictions on interstate banking have played an important role in recent farm credit woes.

Outlays versus Opportunity Cost of Credit Programs

The federal budget is based on expected outlays and receipts for various government programs. However, government outlays for agricultural credit activities understate the opportunity cost of these activities for a number of reasons. First, outlays for direct and guaranteed loan programs are either excluded or presented in net terms after repayments and sales of assets are considered. Government loan guarantees are excluded, because a guaranteed loan commitment, by itself, does not affect budget outlays, since it is only a contingent liability. However, by assuming this liability, the government induces lenders to invest in loans and, thereby, redirects capital as effectively as through direct loans.[34] Second, outlays in the federal budget do not reflect the implicit subsidies received by borrowers through interest rates lower than those charged by private lenders.

The difference between official budget outlays and "program levels" of agricultural credit activities has been estimated by the office of Budget and Program Analysis of the USDA. The "program level" is an estimate of the total financial value of a particular activity. The estimated FmHA budget outlay for 1986, for example, was $8.0 billion, while the estimated

FmHA "program level" including value of loans, guaranteed loans, interest subsidies, and other costs was $11.3 billion. Similarly, the 1986 estimated REA budget outlay was only $1.0 million but the program level was $2.2 billion.[35] Thus the budget outlays greatly understate the economic impact of these programs.

A Government-Sponsored Enterprise: The FCS

Lending activities of the FCS, a government sponsored enterprise, are not included in the federal budget. However, the FCS effectively redirects credit by stimulating larger amounts of credit through direct lending to agriculture. The FCS debt instruments compete directly with U.S. treasury securities and thus raise the government's cost of borrowing. Therefore, it is appropriate to include the FCS when discussing the effects of federally assisted credit programs in agriculture.

The Federal Financing Bank and Off-Budget Spending

The Federal Financing Bank (FFB), administered by the Treasury Department, began operation in 1974 and has played a leading role in financial federal credit activities. "The FFB performs three functions: (1) it purchases guaranteed loan assets from Federal agencies; (2) it disburses loans directly to borrowers when the loans are guaranteed by a federal agency; and (3) it buys debt of federal agencies that are otherwise authorized to borrow from the public."[36]

The FFB thus acts as a source of funds for agencies obtaining loans that would otherwise have to borrow from the public. Use of the FFB by federal agencies leads to lower debt financing costs than if the agencies were to borrow individually in the credit market. Interest rates are higher when individual agencies borrow because of relative illiquidity and smaller size of issue.[37]

Prior to the Gramm-Rudman-Hollings (GRH) legislation of 1985, outlays of the first two types of FFB transactions (see above) were "off budget." That is, they were excluded from the unified budget totals of the U.S. government. The primary beneficiaries of the off-budget spending through the FFB were the FmHA and REA. FFB transactions are no longer off budget because under GRH legislation, outlays of the FFB are now attributed to the agencies using the FFB.[38]

Effects of Easy Credit Policies in U.S. Agriculture

Subsidized credit is in effect an income redistribution program. Consequently, as emphasized in chapter 6, economic theory cannot be used to justify subsidized credit programs, which benefit some farmers at the expense of other farmers and taxpayers generally. Economic theory is useful, however, in analyzing the information and incentive problems that are inherent in publicly funded credit programs. Easy-credit policies in agriculture also lead to a number of indirect and unintended effects.

Information Problems

What is the "optimal" amount of credit in agriculture? Unlike with private banks, there is no standard measure of performance to assess the success of federal credit programs. In the absence of a market test, there is no reliable procedure to determine how credit should be allocated, either within agriculture or between agriculture and other sectors of the economy. The lack of a measurement tool makes it impossible to determine how effectively credit is being used in federally assisted agricultural credit programs. A number of arguments have been used to justify cheap credit in agriculture. A recent analysis of the most widely used arguments made in defense of cheap agricultural credit concluded that the arguments were either unsound, counter to economic logic, or not supported by the evidence.[39]

Incentive Problems

Incentive problems arise in subsidized credit programs as they do in all other situations where resources are allocated through the collective-choice process. In the case of the FmHA's so-called limited resource loans, for example, credit is to be extended when farmers "need a lower interest rate to have a reasonable chance of success."[40] However, there is no defensible criterion by which FmHA officials can determine which farmers "need" a lower interest rate.

There is also a moral-hazard problem in all cases where the FmHA acts as a "lender of last resort." If subsidized credit is available for farmers who cannot obtain credit elsewhere, the farmer has an incentive to demonstrate that credit cannot be obtained from commercial sources. Similarly, holders of FmHA farm ownership loans are legally supposed to refinance when sufficiently qualified to obtain credit from conventional sources. However, FmHA borrowers have an incentive, regardless of their economic condition, to demonstrate that they are not sufficiently qualified.

Politicians are likely to be motivated by political considerations in making decisions about subsidized credit programs. During the late 1970s and early 1980s, there was a shift in policy toward "easier credit" for farmers in financial difficulty. In response to the American Agriculture Movement's disorderly lobbying, for example, the Emergency Agriculture Act of 1978 supplemented the long-standing FmHA emergency loan programs with a new $6 billion program of "economic emergency" loans. These loans were made to farmers already in financial trouble who could not obtain credit from commercial sources.[41] Such loans simply postponed the failure of some farms until the next round of depressed farm product prices in 1981–82. Credit programs of this type substitute the politically influenced judgment of lending officials for market profit-and-loss signals.

The 1984 FmHA debt deferral and adjustment program is another example where political considerations appear to have influenced a farm credit program. The program, initiated in the heat of the 1984 presidential election campaign, allowed the FmHA to grant its farmer borrowers deferrals on the repayment of up to 25 percent of the borrower's indebtedness. It also permitted the FmHA to guarantee 90 percent of a problem farm loan held by other lenders provided the lender reduced the principal amount of the debt or the interest rate charged on the indebtedness by specified amounts.

A change in FmHA rules, especially foreclosure, is politically sensitive. Secretary Bergland imposed a moratorium on farm foreclosures during much of the Carter presidency. Secretary Block of the Reagan administration lifted the moratorium after the 1980 election, but it was reimposed again in 1982 under political pressure. Without a firm foreclosure policy, government lending agencies are likely to get dragged into more and more hopeless economic ventures. This problem is inherent in lending activities when political judgment is substituted for the discipline of the marketplace. When credit is only available from those who hope to profit from lending, there is much less likelihood of overexpansion of landholding or capital facilities.

Indirect Effects (Resource Allocation)

Subsidized credit programs enable farmers to obtain additional credit at interest rates lower than could be obtained from commercial banks for loans of comparable risk (figure 16.1). The short-run effects of credit subsidies on interest rates paid by farmers obtaining the loans are obvious. The indirect effects, however, are not so obvious. First, subsidized credit affects which producers remain in production. When allocated on the basis of its opportunity cost, credit is used by those producers who best accommodate consumer demand. If credit is subsidized, some less productive producers are kept in production beyond the level dictated by market forces. The increased output also results in lower product prices. Thus farmers not receiving subsidized credit are harmed since their product prices are reduced. The result is that less productive farmers are benefited at the expense of the more productive, thereby reducing overall productivity.[42]

Second, easy credit has led to the substitution of machinery and other capital inputs for labor in agriculture, resulting in more highly mechanized farms. Lower interest rates also have encouraged farmers to buy more land. In view of widespread public concerns about farm size and capital requirements in commercial agriculture, it is ironic that government-operated and government-sanctioned credit programs have contributed to the trends toward larger and more highly mechanized farms.

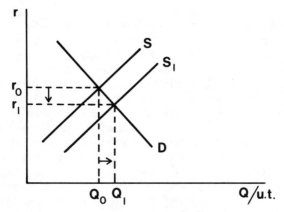

Figure 16.1. The direct effect of subsidized credit programs in U.S. agriculture.

Third, when credit use in agriculture is subsidized, less credit is available to other sectors of the economy. Consequently, nonagricultural credit users are harmed by subsidized agricultural credit because interest rates to them are increased.

Summary

The FCS, FmHA, CCC, and REA are the major credit agencies for U.S. agriculture that are operated or supervised by the federal government. The FCS, which includes the FLBs, the FICBs (and PCAs), and the Bank for Cooperatives, provides credit for farmers, ranchers, and agricultural cooperatives. The FCS, being privately owned, does not have direct access to the FFB and historically has relied on private credit markets for funds. However, the FCS as a government-sponsored enterprise enjoys special legal advantages that enable it to borrow at rates only slightly higher than those of the Treasury. Moreover, legislation was passed to assist the financially troubled FCS in 1985, 1986, and 1987. This federal bailout legislation not only provided $4 billion in financial assistance, it also mandated a complete restructuring of the FCS.

The FmHA and the CCC are the primary federal agencies providing explicit credit subsidies through direct loans to agricultural borrowers. The FmHA under the 1985 farm bill is in transition from direct lender to guarantor of loans. However, loan guarantees are no less important than direct loans in redirecting lending activity. Moreover, it is difficult to determine the extent of federal credit programs in agriculture. Outlays in the official budget greatly understate the magnitude of federally assisted borrowing because guaranteed and direct loan programs are presented in net terms.

The alleged "need" for subsidized credit to farmers is based on the argument that private lenders will not supply credit on terms and in amounts required by farmers. However, the fact that a farmer cannot obtain credit from a private lender at usual terms does not imply that subsidized credit is warranted. It is likely that the would-be borrower does not meet the creditworthiness standards of the private sector and is denied credit because the loan is viewed as potentially unprofitable.[43]

The immediate effect of subsidizing credit is to reduce interest rates and increase the amount of credit used in agriculture. The reduction in interest rates has contributed to increased production and to the trends toward larger and more highly mechanized farms. Subsidized credit is harmful to nonusers of subsidized credit in agriculture because it increases output and decreases product prices. It is also harmful to potential borrowers, either in or out of agriculture, who do not receive assistance because less credit is available to them and because interest rates they must pay are increased.

Finally, subsidized credit poses the same problems as all other intervention affecting market prices. The market process allocates capital on the basis of its expected productivity and profits. In federal credit programs, in contrast, there is no standard measure of performance. In the absence of a profit benchmark, there is no objective procedure to determine how much credit *should be used* in agriculture. Incentive as well as information problems arise when credit decisions are made through the collective-choice process. Where the FmHA operates as a lender of last resort, for example, moral-hazard problems arise since borrowers have an incentive to demonstrate that they "lack other sources of credit." Political decision makers have an incentive to respond. In contrast, when credit is made available on the basis of profit and loss expectations by private lending agencies, farmers are less likely to overexpand land and capital facilities.

Government regulations that adversely affect the ability of agricultural credit institutions to diversify portfolios are also harmful. Problems arise when lending institutions only deal with one sector of the economy, whether the credit agencies are public or private. Government restrictions on nationwide banking reduce diversification in bank loan portfolios, thereby increasing risk and the likelihood of bank failure.

Notes

1. W. Gifford Hoag, *The Farm Credit System: A History of Financial Help* (Danville, Ill.: Interstate Printers and Publishers, 1976).

2. The following description of FCS structure and activities that existed prior to federal bailout legislation in the mid-1980s draws upon D. F. Neuman, "Organization of the Farm Credit System," *Tar Heel Economist* (February 1984): 2.

3. N. Omri Rawlings, *Introduction to Agribusiness* (Englewood Cliffs, N.J.: Prentice-Hall, 1980), p. 90.

4. David A. Lins and Peter J. Barry, "Agency Status for the Cooperative Farm Credit System," *American Journal of Agricultural Economics* 66 (December 1984): 601–6.

5. Emanuel Melichar, *Agricultural Finance Databook* (Washington, D.C.: Board of Governors of the Federal Reserve System, 1986), p. 19.

6. Office of Management and Budget, *Special Analyses, Budget of the United States Government, Fiscal Year 1986* (Washington, D.C.: U.S. Government Printing Office, 1985), p. F-27.

7. Melichar, *Agricultural Finance Databook*, p. 21.

8. New capital plans under the 1987 Act must require minimum stock purchases of $1,000 or two percent of the loan, whichever is less.

9. Office of Management and Budget, *Special Analyses: Budget of the United States Government, 1987* (Washington, D.C.: U.S. Government Printing Office, 1986), p. F-28.

10. U.S. General Accounting Office, *Farm Credit: Actions Needed on Major Management Issues*, GGD-87-51 (Washington, D.C.: U.S. Government Printing Office, 1987), p. 11.

11. Farm Credit Administration, *Economic Perspectives: Agricultural Credit Outlook* (Washington, D.C.: Farm Credit Administration, 1988), p. 19.

12. Gary L. Benjamin, "The Agricultural Credit Act of 1987," *Agricultural Letter,* no. 1729 (Chicago: The Federal Reserve Bank of Chicago, 11 March 1988).

13. Farm Credit Administration, *Economic Perspectives*, p. 22.

14. Rawlings, *Introduction to Agribusiness*, p. 93.

15. U.S. Department of Agriculture, *A Brief History of Farmers Home Administration* (Washington, D.C.: U.S. Government Printing Office, 1983), p. 19.

16. Ibid., p. 14.

17. Melichar, *Agricultural Finance Databook*, p. 19.

18. Ibid., p. 21.

19. U. S. Department of Agriculture, *A Brief History*, p. 15.

20. Ibid.

21. Ibid.

22. Office of Management and Budget, *Special Analyses 1986*, p. F-33.

23. General Accounting Office, *Farmers Home Administration: Financial and General Characteristics of Farmer Loan Program Borrowers*, GAO/RCED-86-62BR (Washington, D.C.: U.S. Government Printing Office, 1986), p. 2.

24. Ibid.

25. Farm Credit Administration, *Economic Perspectives*, p. 18.

26. Melichar, *Agricultural Finance Databook*, p. 21.

27. Office of Management and Budget, *Special Analyses 1986*, p. F-33.

28. Office of Management and Budget, *Special Analyses: Budget of the United States Government, 1988* (Washington, D.C.: U.S. Government Printing Office, 1987), p. F-16.

29. Ibid.

30. Office of Management and Budget, *Special Analyses 1986*, p. F-34.

31. Office of Management and Budget, *Special Analyses 1985*, p. F-4.

32. Lindley H. Clark, Jr. "Interstate Banks Could Ease Farm Credit Woes," *Wall Street Journal*, 20 January 1987, p. 35.

33. Michael Becker, Steve Horwitz, and Robert O'Quinn, "Interstate Banking: Toward a Competitive Financial System," *Issue Alert*, no. 18 (Washington, D.C.: Citizens for a Sound Economy Foundation, 1987), p. 9.

34. Office of Management and Budget, *Special Analyses 1986*, p. F-5.

35. U.S. Department of Agriculture, 1987 Budget Summary, p. 2.

36. Office of Management and Budget, Special Analyses 1987, p. F-41.

37. Office of Management and Budget, Special Analyses 1986, p. F-40.

38. Ibid., p. F-42.

39. Dale W. Adams, "Are the Arguments for Cheap Agricultural Credit Sound?" in Undermining Rural Development with Cheap Credit, ed. Dale W. Adams, Douglas H. Graham, and J. D. Von Pische (Boulder, Colo.: Westview Press, 1984), p. 75.

40. U.S. Department of Agriculture, A Brief History, p. 15.

41. This example is taken from Bruce L. Gardner, Agriculture's Revealing—and Painful—Lesson for Industrial Policy (Washington, D.C.: The Heritage Foundation, 1984), p. 7; and Bruce L. Gardner, "Bringing a Free Market to the Farm," in Agenda '83: A Mandate for Leadership Report, ed. Richard N. Holwill (Washington, D.C.: The Heritage Foundation, 1983), pp. 29–40.

42. E. C. Pasour, Jr., "The Farm Credit Crisis," The Freeman 38 (March 1988): 108–13.

43. Clifton B. Luttrell, The High Cost of Farm Welfare (Washington, D.C.: The Cato Institute, 1989), p. 84.

17

Conservation and Protection of Natural Resources

The conservation movement in the United States was begun in 1908 when President Theodore Roosevelt called together a conference of state governors. The conventional wisdom at that time was that natural resources were being used too rapidly and that political controls should be instituted to conserve resources for future generations. The conservation movement led to large quantities of forest, mineral, park, and other lands being kept under public ownership. It also led to the creation of several new government agencies including the Forest Service, the Grazing Service, and the Fish and Wildlife Service.

Soil conservation efforts received a major impetus with the creation of the Soil Conservation Service (SCS) in 1935 in the New Deal era. The SCS was augmented in 1937 by a system of conservation districts that now governs the soil and water conservation policies in most counties of the United States through locally elected boards. The SCS provides technical assistance to landowners and operators for soil conservation plans and projects. It also provides subsidies to reclaim, conserve, and develop lands as in the construction of terraces. The SCS provides technical assistance to the FmHA in making soil and water conservation loans and also assists other government agencies in developing conservation plans.

This chapter analyzes the meaning of the concept "conservation," and describes why private ownership promotes wise stewardship of natural resources. The rationale for government soil and land conservation programs is discussed along with the problems inherent in achieving optimal levels of resource use through the collective-choice process. The economic problems involved in the conservation and efficient use of water resources, while not discussed in this chapter, are similar to those for land resources.[1] The "new resource economics" approach to natural resource problems that is used in this chapter involves a blend of the economics of property rights, public choice, and entrepreneurship.[2]

What is Conservation?

Conservation is frequently taken to mean *not consuming*. During the decade of the 1970s, for example, "energy conservation," as the term was used, typically referred to measures to reduce energy consumption. Conservation in the sense of not consuming and preserving resources for future generations, however, provides no guidance as to the proper rate of resource use over time. The relevant conservation problem for petroleum, timber, copper, soil, or any other resource concerns the optimal rate of use.

Conservation involves capital investment and the conservation problem is one of choosing among alternative patterns of resource use over time. Sound conservation practices can be determined only by comparing the properly discounted costs and benefits that hinge on future conditions. Setting the most profitable rate of resource use is an entrepreneurial decision and is necessarily based on a subjective assessment of uncertain future conditions. Whether it is economic to "conserve energy" by insulating the walls of a house, for example, depends upon heating costs over time and insulation costs—both of which are uncertain. Let us turn now to the relationship between the institutional arrangement and resource conservation.

Conservation and the Market

There are two methods of organizing the use of natural resources: the market and central direction. The history of past "resource crises" contains an important lesson in analyzing today's resource problems. First, consider the importance of private property as a social institution.

Common Property versus Private Property

The nature of ownership is no less important for natural resources than for other assets. The problem associated with the use of "common property resources" was aptly described by Aristotle more than 2000 years ago: "What is common to many is taken least care of, for all men have greater regard for what is their own than for what they possess in common with others."[3] Private ownership, in sharp contrast to ownership in common, encourages resource owners to conserve for the future because current market values of marketable property reflect expected future income.

So long as property is transferable, a current resource owner will have a strong incentive to take the preferences of future generations into account even though the current owner does not expect to personally reap the future harvest.

Suppose a 60 year-old tree farmer is contemplating whether or not to plant Douglas fir trees which will not reach optimal cutting size for another 50 years. When ownership is transferable, the market value of the farmer's land will increase in anticipation of the future harvest as the trees grow and the expected day of harvest moves closer. Thus, the farmer will be able to capture his contribution at any time, even though the actual harvest may not take place until well after his death.[4]

The conclusion is that the private property system is highly important in motivating current resource owners to take the interests of future generations into account.

The Market and Resource Crises

The price system is a way of rationing scarce resources both at a given point in time and over time. It is in the owner's interest to use a resource in a way that will maximize wealth or the present value of the resource, whether the resource is petroleum, timber, or land. A key argument of many conservationists is that market price signals typically cause natural resources to be used too rapidly. However, forecasts of "doom and gloom" have existed for as long as civilization has existed. Yet these forecasts have been wrong and there is no persuasive evidence that current resource problems are different from those of the past.[5] Indeed history provides a great deal of hope that market forces have the power to eliminate resource crises today as in the past.

Historically perceived economic crises relating to the use of whale oil, petroleum, timber, and other resources were solved by freely functioning markets with individuals acting in their own self-interest. The lesson from the past is that if the operation of market forces is not suspended by government edict, crises will be short lived as people react to higher prices both by substitution in consumption and by making technological changes. In a market economy, approaching resource scarcities trigger price increases that provide the motivation for actions that mitigate the effect of these scarcities.[6] The actions may involve increased exploration, recycling, or development of substitutes.

Throughout history, people have assumed a fixed amount of particular natural resources such as whale oil, petroleum, and coal to predict doom. In a fundamental sense, however, natural resources are not fixed in amount but are functions of capital accumulation, science, and technology. The quantity or supply of petroleum, for example, hinges on price. As price increases, it becomes profitable to dig deeper wells, to make petroleum and petroleum substitutes from coal, grain, and so on.

It is often argued that extraction of mineral resources has been too fast and that conservation programs should be legally mandated. A study analyzing prices of fourteen depletable natural resources—aluminum, bauxite, coal, copper, crude petroleum, gold, iron ore, lead, lime, magnesium, nickel, silver, tin, and zinc—from 1900 through 1975 does not support this argument.[7] In studying price changes over time, it was found that mandated conservation programs would not have paid off. For none of the fourteen depletable resources analyzed would conservation from 1900 through 1975 have been a superior economic alternative to selling the resource in 1900 and investing the proceeds at the AAA corporate bond rate.[8] During the period analyzed, enforced long-term conservation of mineral resources would thus have been bad public policy both for the people forgoing consumption at the time and also for later generations that obtained the use of the resources. These results do not suggest that conservation is unwise. Rather they suggest that market prices are likely to take into account expectations about future economic conditions more accurately than can be done through central direction.

Time Preference

It is sometimes suggested that a high rate of time preference is likely to cause resource owners to use resources too quickly.[9] Time preference refers to the value placed on consumption in the near future relative to the more distant future. If a decision maker's rate of time preference (RTP) is high, the individual is willing to forgo a relatively large amount of future income in order to obtain income in the present time period. Thus, the higher the RTP, the less likely is an individual to save, and if an individual's RTP increases, that person will save less and consume more in the present time period.

It is often assumed that the conservation of soil and other depletable resources is socially beneficial even though judged uneconomic by the resource owner. That is, the resource owner might exploit the resource in the sense of disinvesting where the cost of conservation is less than the value of resources saved. As an example, assume that the value of a forest is increasing at 15 percent per year and that the market interest rate is 10 percent. In this case, it appears desirable to let the trees grow since the return from an additional year's growth is more than the opportunity cost of capital. Would the tree owner with a high RTP cut the trees in order to obtain income now? Not necessarily. The owner might either borrow, using the timber as collateral, or sell the timber at the discounted value of its expected future yield and let the new owner harvest the trees at the "proper time." Thus under competitive conditions, a high RTP by a resource owner need not imply uneconomic exploitation or disinvestment.

Where the landowner is not able to borrow money (or sell the forest land) on the basis of the timber's future value, the problem is not the landowner's high RTP but rather a difference in expectations concerning the present value of the timber stand. High transactions costs could also make a loan unprofitable. In the real world, where future prices are always uncertain, there is no reason to expect people to have similar expectations about timber prices or other production risks. Thus, a high rate of time preference by resource owners does not imply that resources will be used too quickly.

Soil Erosion

Although the preceding discussion suggests that freely functioning markets with people acting in their own self-interest will conserve resources and eliminate resource "crises," public concern about soil erosion increased during the late 1970s and early 1980s. The concern was about whether farming practices were exhausting soil resources, making future food supplies uncertain. Is the soil conservation problem unique in the sense that the market does not work to properly husband soil resources? Consider the evidence.

A Growing Problem?

There was relatively little information about the extent and severity of the soil erosion problem prior to 1977 when the SCS completed a national resource inventory of soil and water conservation problems. The 1977 survey revealed that erosion is not uniformly distributed and occurs at relatively low rates on most agricultural land. As one might expect, most erosion occurs on row-crop land. However, the survey found more than three-fourths of cropland with only slight erosion.[10] Indeed, nearly 70 percent of the "excess erosion" (erosion greater than 5 tons per acre) was found to occur on less than 8.6 percent of the cropland.[11]

Nobel laureate T. W. Schultz, on the basis of a comparison of soil erosion survey results from 1934 and 1977, concludes that soil resources in the U.S. have improved over time.[12] There has been an increase in crop yields and a decrease in row crops. Acreages of corn and cotton have declined and are now produced on soils not as prone to erosion.[13] Thus there is a considerable amount of evidence that the severity of soil erosion has been greatly exaggerated.

Moreover, not all soil erosion *can* be stopped.[14] Even if there were no agriculture, there would still be erosion. Thus the practical problem is to achieve the optimal level of soil erosion. As shown below, it is difficult, because of information and incentive problems, to determine when there is a soil erosion problem that warrants government action.

Possible Reasons for the Problem

It is often assumed that there is a general soil erosion problem, and this problem is attributed to three factors. First, there is alleged to be a lack of knowledge by farmers concerning the effects of soil erosion. In this view, present rates of erosion will force up future production costs to unacceptably high levels. Second, it is held that farmers renting land overexploit soil resources. As more and more land is rented, it is argued, those who lease land pay less attention to conservation practices. Third, it is contended that runoff creates externality problems associated with land use.

What is the evidence on these points? First, the success of U.S. agriculture over time is evidence that farmers are knowledgeable and competent entrepreneurs.[15] The increasing productivity of cropland per acre in the U.S. suggests that farmers do not lose their entrepreneurial ability in investment decisions about soil resources. Moreover, a recent task force of the American Agricultural Economics Association, after reviewing the

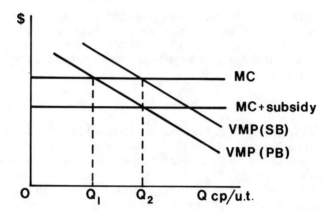

Figure 17.1. The externality rationale for subsidized conservation practices.

evidence, was not convinced that present rates of erosion will force up future production costs of farm products.[16] Soil is only one ingredient in production and some loss of soil productivity can be compensated for by increases in nonsoil inputs. The costs of nonsoil inputs relative to the potential costs of yield loss and erosion control measures are the key variables in determining the "optimal" level of soil conservation.

Second, even in the case of land rented out, landowners have a large stake in maintaining soil resources since the value of farmland for agricultural uses is determined by its productivity. Thus there appears to be little evidence supporting the first two of the alleged reasons for misuse of soil resources.

Government efforts to reduce soil erosion have been justified mainly on the basis of the third factor, externalities. A spillover or externality problem arises when property rights are not clearly defined and effectively enforced. In the case of soil erosion, the argument is made that farmers do not use sufficient conservation practices. In the situation depicted in figure 17.1, for example, farmers on the basis of private costs and benefits would purchase the quantity OQ_1 of terracing and other conservation practices. If there are benefits of these practices to society over and above those to the individual farmer, as indicated by *VMP (SB)*, the farmer would invest too little in conservation practices. In this case, the socially optimal level of conservation practices presumably is OQ_2 instead of OQ_1. Thus, the argument goes, conservation practices should be subsidized to reduce the cost, thereby inducing the decision maker to invest in the "optimum" level of conservation expenditures.

There undoubtedly are spillover effects associated with soil erosion. Soil carried as suspended sediment may harm fish and other aquatic life and reduce the aesthetic value of water for recreational uses. Suspended sediment also decreases the value of water for residential and industrial uses.[17] Gully erosion on land owned by farmer Jones that spills over and damages farmer Smith's land is another common type of externality in agriculture. A spillover occurs, as in water erosion, when an action (or lack of action) by one person infringes on the property rights of another. The presence of a spillover effect, however, does not imply that there is a spillover problem warranting action through the collective-choice process.

In the traditional approach to soil erosion (and other externalities), the presence of a spillover effect is considered to be evidence of a spillover problem. That is, a difference between private and social cost is simply postulated. In determining whether government intervention is warranted, however, soil conservation under market arrangements must be compared with government solutions as soil conservation agencies operate under real-world conditions.[18] When an attempt is made to determine and mandate an optimal level of soil conservation, a similar problem arises to that in any other government program.

Implementation Problems in Soil Conservation Programs

A national soil conservation program is likely to be a model of inefficiency.[19] Soil erosion that is economically important occurs on particular farms in specific locations, and a small percentage of the total amount of land in crops, pasture, range, and forests is affected.[20] Yet the SCS provides funds and services to *all* parts of U.S. agriculture. Why does the SCS spend funds in counties with few (if any) erosion problems? These decisions are basically dictated by political rather than economic considerations. Members of Congress have an incentive to provide jobs and federal spending in their own legislative districts, regardless of whether such expenditures are economic. John B. Crowell, Jr., Assistant Secretary of the USDA, presented evidence on this point in a letter to the Editor of the *Wall Street Journal*:

> Congress appropriates almost $1 billion a year for conservation activities. . . . In the past these funds have not sufficiently reached the areas with the most serious erosion. . . . In 1983 the Administration initiated a five-year program to target an increased share of total conservation and financial assistance . . . to areas most needing erosion control. Despite the fact that targeting clearly was controlling erosion . . . on more acres with the same Federal dollars, Congress this year ordered that from 1985 on, no increase in targeting . . . should be attempted. . . . Congress felt heat . . . from constituents in non-targeted areas who were fearful that "their" traditional conservation funding was in jeopardy.[21]

The key public policy issue in soil conservation, even in areas where erosion appears to be a serious problem, is not how many tons of soil are lost annually. The basic issue concerns the relative merits of market versus nonmarket approaches in protecting soil quality. The problem of political or nonmarket "failure" due to information and incentive problems is no less important in government programs to reduce soil erosion than in other decisions made through the collective-choice process.

The information problems that arise in attempts to mandate optimal soil conservation practices are formidable. Since conservation is an investment, it should be judged by criteria similar to those used in judging other investments. Profitable soil management and conservation practices, however, can be determined only by comparing the costs and benefits. Moreover, since these costs and benefits occur over time, there is a great deal of uncertainty about their magnitudes, and there is no reason to expect the evaluation of a particular conservation measure by an outside observer to correspond to that of the landowner. Thus attempts to determine and mandate optimal levels of soil conservation face the same problems as other attempts to second-guess real-world decision makers.[22]

Conservation programs are often inconsistent with other government programs. Price support programs and subsidized crop insurance give farmers an incentive to cultivate fragile lands. Farmers are paid to create new cropland from forests and swamps while other farm programs simultaneously pay farmers to idle cropland that was already productive.[23] The use of agricultural lime which increases output and places downward pressure on product prices already considered too low is subsidized for conservation reasons. The conclusion is that there are formidable nonmarket or "government failure" problems which should be taken into account in any analysis of the relative merits of market versus government approaches to soil conservation.

Soil Conservation Provisions of the 1985 Farm Bill

The 1985 farm bill contains a conservation reserve program. This program provides 50-percent cost-sharing plus annual rental payments for ten-year contracts to retire highly erodible land and plant it in grass or trees.

There are also so-called "swampbuster," "sodbuster," and conservation compliance provisions in the bill affecting farm program benefits for those cultivating highly erodible land. Sodbusters are defined as those who begin cultivating highly erodible land. Swampbusters are those who begin to cultivate wetland. The penalties for noncompliance are quite severe. Sodbusters and swampbusters cannot receive farm program benefits including price supports, CCC storage loans, federal crop insurance, or FmHA loans.

This 1985 farm bill represents a dramatic increase in mandated federal supervision of farmer production practices. The "conservation compliance" provision requires that all farmers farming "highly erodible" land (eight times the "tolerable rate" of erosion) must have a SCS approved conservation plan in place by 1990 for fields on their farms having "highly erodible" land to avoid loss of farm program benefits. This erosion rate sounds high but, according to an SCS estimate, more than one-half of the land currently farmed in North Carolina meets that standard and, consequently, will need a conservation plan by 1990.[24] When one considers the formidable task of implementing and monitoring the "swampbuster," "sodbuster," and conservation reserve programs, and of developing conservation plans for farmers throughout the United States, the soil and water provisions of the 1985 farm bill can be viewed as an employment boon to the SCS and ASCS. It has been estimated that the number of SCS employees delivering technical assistance at the field level would need to be increased by more than 50 percent to implement the new conservation programs.[25]

Moreover, the soil conservation section of the 1985 farm bill is no panacea in achieving the most appropriate soil conservation practices. The conservation-reserve, "sodbuster," "swampbuster," and "conservation compliance" features of this legislation are subject to the implementation problems emphasized above that affect all national soil conservation programs.

Preservation of Agricultural Land

During the late 1970s, a National Agricultural Lands Study (NALS) found that agricultural land markets were not working properly and that the conversion of cropland to nonfarm uses posed a major threat to future agricultural production in the United States.[26] Two reasons are commonly cited for protecting agricultural land beyond the level dictated by market forces. First, it is alleged that agricultural land must be protected to ensure future production of sufficient food and fiber.[27] However, there appears to be little or no basis for this argument. Indeed, there is a great deal of evidence that land markets are unique in their ability to allocate land to agriculture, housing, business, recreation, and other uses. Luttrell shows that the amount of cropland in the United States has varied over time according to the relative demands for farm products. Indeed, the acreage of cropland harvested in the United States from 1970 to 1980 increased dramatically in response to product price increases.[28]

Second, the theory of externalities is another possible justification for preserving agricultural land. It is contended that agricultural land should be protected to provide "visual amenities," to insure more "orderly" development, and to provide local economic benefits that derive from a viable agricultural industry. However, most economists place little weight on these factors. It seems just as likely that measures to arbitrarily restrict the conversion of agricultural land to other uses will hold land in lower valued uses and impede "orderly" economic progress. Moreover, the disamenities associated with livestock production, pesticide use, and so on may more than offset any visual amenities associated with agricultural production.

The theoretical case for restricting the conversion of agricultural land to

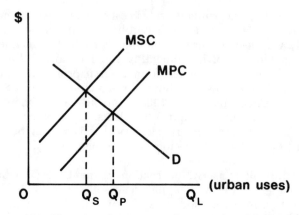

Figure 17.2. The externality argument for protecting agricultural land.

urban uses is depicted in figure 17.2. If the cost and benefits of land for urban uses were as depicted, too much land would be converted from agricultural to urban uses (OQ_p rather than OQ_s). The fact that MSC (marginal social cost) is higher than MPC (marginal private cost) suggests that there are externalities; that is, there are costs of using agricultural land for nonfarm uses that are not included in costs paid by developers. The difference between marginal private costs and marginal social costs in this example, however, is merely asserted. It has not been demonstrated that a nonmarket method of land allocation is preferable to the market process. If the pattern of land use cannot be improved by government measures to protect agricultural land, there is no basis for contending that "marginal social cost exceeds marginal private cost." Despite the lack of empirical or theoretical justification for public policies to reduce the conversion of agricultural land, several different policies have been widely adopted to "protect" agricultural land.

Every state in the nation has at least one program, either at the state or local level, to preserve land in agriculture. Some states, such as Maryland and Pennsylvania, currently utilize over five different preservation tools.[29] Several of the techniques are discussed below.

Agricultural Use-Value Taxation

With the exception of Kansas, every state has now enacted agricultural use-value taxation for farm and forest lands, often at the behest of USDA and land grant colleges. "In nearly every state that passed the legislation, research describing its virtues was carried out by the extension service and experiment station network. . . . Conducted first by the Department of Agriculture and then by the Extension Service in each state, the research was influential in getting the legislation through."[30]

This legislation permits qualifying agricultural and forest lands to be assessed for property tax purposes on the basis of present use rather than market value. This approach faces theoretical as well as practical problems of effectiveness. From a theoretical standpoint, there is a problem of determining the use-value of land in agriculture. The market value of any marketable asset is based on expected future income. Future income from farmland, however, is highly uncertain as is the appropriate discount rate. Thus the estimation of agricultural use values must be based on highly subjective assessments of future economic conditions.[31]

Purchase of Development Rights and Agricultural Districts

Another possible way to keep more land in agricultural uses is for farmers to retain the title to land while local or state governments purchase only the rights to develop land for nonfarm purposes.[32] The creation of agricultural districts is still another method that is being used to maintain land in agriculture. New York's Agricultural Districts Law, enacted in 1971, granted tax relief and discouraged the conversion of agricultural land through restrictions on eminent domain and local government ordinances that affect agriculture. Zoning ordinances remain the most common means of implementing land-use plans in the urban fringe, and zoning has been imposed in attempts to preserve open space, to "manage growth," and so on.

Responding to farm versus nonfarm conflicts over noises, odors, and dusts associated with farming, most of the states have also enacted nuisance suit legislation. For example, the North Carolina General Assembly enacted the Agricultural Nuisance Suit Law in 1979. This legislation provides that an agricultural operation will not become a nuisance because of changed conditions if it has been in operation for more than one year and if it is properly managed. However, protection is not provided where water pollution occurs.

Evaluation

Use-value taxation and agricultural districts have had little effect in restricting the conversion of agricultural land to nonagricultural uses. The potential economic gain to the landowner from converting land to nonagricultural uses in rapidly urbanizing areas is likely to swamp any tax advantages of keeping land in agriculture through use-value taxation or agricultural districts. The purchase of development rights is a potentially more effective way to keep land in agriculture but involves a relatively high cost to taxpayers. Moreover, as suggested below, government measures designed to control land use, even if effective in doing so, may impede rather than promote the most productive pattern of land use. The effectiveness of nuisance-suit legislation as a means of coping with spillover problems will not be known until it is tested in the courts.

The Market versus Central Direction
in Land-Use Decisions

Most of the research concerned with preserving agricultural land has focused on the relative effectiveness of different programs, whether the goal is to decrease erosion or to maintain land in agriculture. The problem in determining the "optimal" amount of land in agriculture (or the "optimal" amount of soil erosion) has largely been ignored, as has the more basic question of whether land-use controls to protect and conserve agricultural land are beneficial.

Information Problems

The basic problem is to secure the most economic use of land resources utilizing the knowledge of all affected members of society. The market process is unique in its ability to allocate land to different uses, taking into account factors affecting demand and supply. Market prices coordinate and transmit widely dispersed information more effectively than is possible through any other known method. The information that influences choices by buyers and sellers of land is decentralized and cannot be objectively determined, except as revealed by the actions of market participants.[33] Thus, there is inevitably a loss of valuable information when price signals of the land market are overridden by administrative land-use controls.

The importance of price signals in coordinating and transmitting information has been largely ignored in the land-use planning literature. In proposals to institute "comprehensive" land-use planning, for example, land classification is often suggested as a means of land allocation. A proposed land policy program for North Carolina recommended that all land in the state be classified on a county-by-county basis into one of five different classes: developed, transition, community, rural, and conservation.[34] Preservation of "prime" agricultural land is often a major focus of efforts to plan land use through central direction. Although prime agricultural land is productive in agriculture, it is often even more productive in other uses. The land classification approach fails to take into account that, aside from the land market, there is no objective procedure to weigh the merits of competing uses of land—of determining which parcels of land should be in agriculture and which in other uses both now and in the future.

Incentive Problems

Although political land-use planning is presumably based on widespread citizen participation, any land-use plan must be carried out by government officials. Decisions are reached through a political process that is short-run oriented and dominated by special-interest groups with narrow interests. Thus low-income and other groups that participate least effectively in the political process are likely to be most disadvantaged by political land use controls.[35]

There is also a problem in obtaining an objective evaluation of legal measures affecting land use. The evaluation is costly and in most cases must be financed by the government. However, government monitoring of land-use control activities relies on the cooperation of those whose interests are markedly affected by any reforms or changes that might be implied. Thus, the nature of the evaluation system is likely to affect the findings. How likely is it, for example, that a study by SCS personnel will conclude that there is a reduced need for public expenditures on conservation measures?

Summary

Conservation is a capital investment problem and sound conservation practices can be determined only by comparing costs and benefits over time. Historically, economic crises relating to whale oil, petroleum, timber, and other products were solved through freely functioning markets with people acting in their own self-interest. Approaching resource scarcities trigger price increases, which motivate actions by consumers and producers that mitigate the effects of these scarcities. The conclusion is that resource scarcities are likely to be handled best in decentralized markets, where decision makers have the most information and where economic actors bear the consequences of their own decisions.

In recent years, there has been a great deal of discussion about two land policy issues. First, it is said that there is a serious and worsening problem of soil erosion. Second, it is argued that too much land is being converted from agriculture to urban uses. In the latter case, none of the commonly cited reasons to "protect" agricultural land will withstand careful scrutiny. Moreover, increasing productivity of cropland over time suggests that the problem of soil erosion has been exaggerated. Indeed, there is evidence that the soil erosion of cropland has declined and that the quality of soil resources in the United States has improved over time. Thus, an assessment of the evidence suggests that neither of the above allegations are correct.

Despite the evidence that the soil erosion problem has not worsened, there was a significant increase in federal supervision of farmer conservation practices under the 1985 farm bill. Farmers found to be in violation of these new program requirements will lose all farm program benefits. The increased federal supervision of farming practices on "highly erodible land" will dramatically increase both numbers of SCS personnel and outlays on conservation programs.

The case for government measures to reduce soil erosion and to protect agricultural land rests on two basic assumptions. First, it assumes that spillover or externality problems are important in a significant number of land use decisions. Second, it assumes that the problem of "political failure" in political land use controls to correct for spillover problems will be less than the "market failure" problems the political controls are designed to correct.

When transactions costs, incentive costs, and information costs are taken into account, there is little if any basis for thinking that an increased role of government in protecting land and soil resources is warranted. There is no persuasive evidence that land conservation problems are unique. If this is correct, freely functioning land markets will eliminate loss of farmland, soil erosion, and other "crises" affecting agricultural land, just as the market has eliminated resource crises in the past.

Notes

1. Water and power subsidies that reduce the cost of irrigation of agricultural crops are important in a number of western states. The inconsistency of Department of Interior irrigation subsidies that increase farm output with USDA programs to reduce farm production are further described in chapter 20. An examination of existing water rights institutions, an analysis of the role of government in distorting water use in the West through federal water projects, and proposals for institutional reform may be found in Terry L. Anderson, ed., *Water Rights* (San Francisco: Pacific Institute for Public Policy Research, 1983).

2. Terry L. Anderson, "The New Resource Economics: Old Ideas and New Applications," *American Journal of Agricultural Economics* 64 (December 1982): 928–34.

3. Citation from James Gwartney, "Private Property, Freedom and the West," *Intercollegiate Review* 20 (Spring–Summer 1985): 42.

4. Ibid., p. 44.

5. Charles Maurice and C. W. Smithson, *The Doomsday Myth: 10,000 Years of Economic Crises* (Stanford, Calif.: Hoover Institution Press, 1984).

6. Dwight R. Lee and R. F. McNown, *Economics in Our Time*, 2nd. ed. (Chicago: Science Research Associates, 1983), pp. 145–47.

7. G. Anders, W. P. Gramm, and S. C. Maurice, *Does Resource Conservation Pay?* (Los Angeles, Calif.: International Institute for Economic Research, 1978).

8. Ibid., p. 24.

9. E. C. Pasour, Jr., "Conservation, 'X-Efficiency' and Efficient Use of Natural Resources," *Journal of Libertarian Studies* 4 (1979): 371–90.

10. Leo V. Mayer, "Farm Exports and Soil Conservation," *Proceedings of the Academy of Political Science* 34 (1982): 99–111.

11. Sandra S. Batie, "Resource Policy in the Future: Glimpses of the 1985 Farm Bill," in *Farm and Food Policy: Critical Issues of Southern Agriculture*, ed. M. D. Hamning and H. M. Harris, Jr. (Proceedings of a symposium, Clemson University, June 2–3, 1983), p. 95.

12. T. W. Schultz, "Dynamics of Erosion in the United States: A Critical View," in *The Vanishing Farmlands Crisis*, ed. John Baden (Lawrence, Kan.: Regents Press of Kansas, 1984).

13. Ibid., pp. 49–50.

16. Ibid., p. 45.

15. Ibid., p. 54.

16. Pierre Crosson, et al., *Soil Erosion and Soil Conservation Policy in the United States*, Occasional Paper No. 2 (American Agricultural Economics Association, 1986), p. 54.

17. Ibid., p. 38.

18. E. C. Pasour, Jr., "Agricultural Land Protection: Is Government Intervention Warranted?" *The Cato Journal* 2 (Winter 1982): 739–58.

19. Schultz, "Dynamics of Erosion," p. 54.

20. Crosson, et al., *Soil Erosion*, p. 57.

21. *Wall Street Journal*, 12 October 1984.

22. Pasour, "Agricultural Land Protection," p. 752.

23. Bruce L. Gardner, *The Governing of Agriculture* (Lawrence, Kan.: Regents Press of Kansas, 1981), p. 113.

24. John Hudson, "If Rule Broken, All USDA Benefits at Stake," *Southeast Farm Press*, 27 May 1987, p. 18.

25. Joe Williamson, "Washington Perspective," ibid., 28 January 1987, p. 2.

26. National Agricultural Lands Study (NALS), *Where Have the Farmlands Gone?* (Washington, D.C.: Government Printing Office, 1979).

27. Clifton B. Luttrell, "Our 'Shrinking' Farmland: Potential Crisis?" in *The Vanishing Farmland Crisis*, ed. John Baden (Lawrence, Kan.: University Press of Kansas, 1984), p. 32.

28. Ibid., p. 34

29. JoAnn Kwong, "Private Property Rights and the Economics of Agricultural Land Preservation," Ph.D. thesis, University of Michigan, 1986.

30. John Brigham, "The Politics of Tax Preference," in *Property Tax Preferences for Agricultural Land*, eds. Neal A. Roberts and H. James Brown (Montclair, N.J.: Allanheld, Osmun, 1980), p. 109.

31. E. C. Pasour, Jr., "Estimating Agricultural Use Values in New York State: Comment," *Land Economics* 55 (1979): 405–7.

32. Kwong, "Private Property Rights," p. 198.

33. F. A. Hayek, *Individualism and Economic Order* (Chicago: University of Chicago Press, 1948), p. 81.

34. Land Policy Council, *A Land Resources Program for North Carolina* (Raleigh, N.C.: Land Policy Council, 1976), p. 4.1.

35. David Ervin et al., *Land Use Control: Evaluating Economic and Political Effects* (Cambridge, Mass.: Ballinger, 1977).

18

Agricultural Research
and Extension Activities

Agricultural research today often evokes mixed emotions. On the one hand, publicly and privately funded agricultural research has both reduced the price and greatly expanded the range and scope of fresh, frozen, and processed food products available to the American consumer. Everyone benefits from this increase in choice of food products throughout the year. During the past twenty years, however, increasing concerns have been voiced about the effects of agricultural research and the application of new technology on agricultural labor, family farms, and the environment. Despite the dissatisfaction with some aspects of agricultural research, publicly funded research and extension activities in U.S. agriculture continue to be viewed by many people as a model to be followed in other sectors of the U.S. economy and in other countries throughout the world.[1]

The view that the level of public investment in agricultural research and educational activities in the United States is too low is well established in the agricultural economics literature. This conclusion is based on cost-benefit studies suggesting that the return to past investments has been quite high. In addition to a discussion of limitations in the evidence supporting this underinvestment hypothesis, a number of other issues and questions are investigated in this chapter. The following questions are specifically addressed. When did the federal and state research activities in U.S. agriculture begin? Who are the beneficiaries of new technology? What is the rationale for publicly funded research and extension activities? Is the theory of bureaucracy applicable in agricultural research and educational programs? If so, what are the implications of public choice theory in publicly funded agricultural research and extension activities?

The Beginning

The publicly financed research and educational activities in agriculture were begun more than a hundred years ago. A few states instituted agricultural experiment stations in the early nineteenth century, but it was in 1862 that the USDA was created as an information agency for farmers.[2] Also in 1862, Congress passed the Morrill Act to encourage the establishment of an agricultural and mechanical college in each state. The Act provided for a grant of thirty-thousand acres of land to each of the several states for each representative and senator in Congress. The proceeds were to be used for the endowment and support of at least one land-grant college in each state. Although the development of these institutions would probably have occurred even if there had been no Morrill Act, the rate of development quite likely would have been slower.[3]

A second step in the creation of the nationwide system of agricultural education and research agencies was the Hatch Act passed by Congress in 1887. This Act initiated the system of state agricultural experiment stations that are associated with the land-grant colleges and universities in most states. The Smith-Lever Act of 1914 offered aid to the states in developing a nationwide system of publicly supported agricultural extension activities. Finally, the Smith-Hughes Act of 1917 provided federal support for the teaching of vocational agriculture in high schools.

Change in Scope of USDA Activities Over Time

From 1862 to 1932, the USDA was mainly a scientific and statistical agency. Agricultural research was conducted on crops, soils, and animals with the primary objective of discovering cost-reducing methods of producing and marketing farm products. The extension and educational activities were designed to disseminate the latest research findings from the experiment stations to farmers.

From the beginning, publicly funded agricultural research received support from three types of political supporters: "public interest" advocates who wished to improve agriculture through science, agricultural scientists, and farmers.[4] The first two groups were instrumental in founding the agricultural research institutions described above.

The nature of the activities of the USDA changed dramatically during the New Deal era. During that era, a host of previously discussed action programs were initiated including programs involving product price supports, soil conservation, rural electrification, subsidized credit, crop insurance, food assistance to low-income families, and so on. Despite the growth of these action programs over time, publicly funded research and extension programs (with an annual outlay of about $1 billion) continue to play an important role in U.S. agriculture.

Who Are the Beneficiaries?

The primary focus of agricultural research and extension activities continues to be agricultural productivity. Farmers in the U.S. Midwest, for example, planted the world's first hybrid wheat in 1984 with yields 25 to 30 percent higher than yields of varieties previously available.[5] The effect

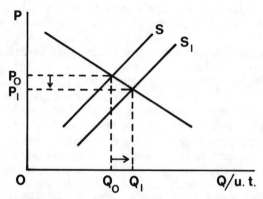

Figure 18.1. The effects of technological advances in U.S. agriculture.

of a technological innovation of this type is to shift supply, resulting in an increase in output and a decrease in price (figure 18.1). Consumers, benefiting from lower food and fiber prices, are the main beneficiaries of increases in agricultural technology. The effect of new technology on product prices hinges on the responsiveness of consumers and producers to price changes. The more inelastic is demand and the more elastic is supply, the more consumers will benefit from a given increase in technology.

The effect of a technological innovation is not the same for all producers. Producers who adopt a cost-reducing innovation first—the innovators—stand to gain. For the innovators, costs are lower and output higher (figure 18.2), but neither total output nor price is appreciably

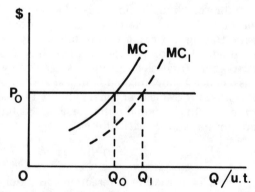

Figure 18.2. Technology reduces costs and increases profits to innovators (before product price decreases).

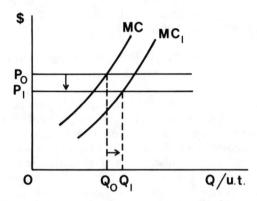

Figure 18.3. Effect of technology on producer after innovation is widely adopted.

affected. Thus the profits of innovators are increased. The situation is quite different, however, after a technological innovation is widely adopted and product price decreases, due to an increase in supply (figure 18.1). Competitive forces lead producers to increase output enough so that the expected rate of return is no higher than it was before the cost-reducing innovation. The individual producer following these adjustments faces not only lower costs but also lower product prices (figure 18.3). Output per firm may or may not increase depending upon whether the number of firms changes. If the number of firms does not increase, a technological innovation leads to an increase in output per firm.

The price decrease following the widespread adoption of new technology tends to eliminate the cost advantage of the new technology to the firm. The producer who does not adopt the new technology faces the same cost but lower product price and is worse off because of the new technology. Some technology is appropriate only for large-scale producers. Thus an increase in technology affects producers differently, depending upon time of adoption, nature of the innovation, and so on.

There is an inconsistency between research to increase agricultural productivity and supply-control programs administered by the USDA. On the one hand, the USDA funds research to develop new technology and increase output of crops and livestock through varietal and breeding programs, development of better cultural and husbandry practices, and so on. At the same time, acreage allotments and land set-aside programs are being used to decrease output. In the dairy program, for example, where government purchases are used to support milk prices, cost-reducing research in milk production makes it more expensive for the government to support the price of milk at any particular level. In the case of price support programs based on acreage allotments or marketing quotas, the greater the increase in technology, the more acreage or output must be reduced to achieve a given level of prices.

Rationale for Public Funding of Research and Education

It is estimated that the magnitudes of private and public research in agriculture are about the same. A great deal of agricultural research is privately financed by agribusiness firms including farm equipment manufacturers, feed companies, fertilizer and farm chemical companies, and seed companies. There are also private companies providing farm planning, price information, and other extension type services to U.S. farmers. In view of the large amount of research and educational services provided by private firms, what is the justification for public funding of research and educational activities in U.S. agriculture?

Public Goods

Public funding of research and education in U.S. agriculture is usually justified on the basis that these goods and services are "public goods."[6] It may be recalled from chapter 3 that public goods have two distinguishing characteristics, nonrivalness and nonexcludability. First, the fact that Farmer Jones makes use of a new cultural practice—no till, for example—does not prevent Farmer Smith from also doing so. In contrast, a private good such as fertilizer that is used by Farmer Jones cannot also be used by Farmer Smith. Much of the information arising from agricultural research is largely consistent with the nonrivalness aspect of a public good. In general, the use of information by one person does not preclude other people from using the same information.

Second, if the firm providing a good or service cannot exclude nonpayers, market provision is not likely to be feasible. The extent to which exclusion is feasible depends to some extent upon whether it is basic science, applied science, or the development of technology and its extension to information users. Basic research is often published in scientific journals that are accessible to everyone. In this and other cases where much of the gain from research is captured by other firms and consumers rather than by the innovating firm, private-sector research may not induce enough research investment.[7]

However, this justification for public investment in "social overhead capital" in agriculture where investment benefits accrue to a wide variety of individuals who do not themselves incur the cost of making the investment can be used as an argument for government intervention in a virtually unlimited range of activities. Raising children to be honest, for example, is an investment made by parents, but "credit card companies, self service stores, and the Internal Revenue Service are among the beneficiaries."[8] Yet most people would not conclude that the separation of costs and benefits necessarily implies a role for government in this case. In assessing the appropriate role of the public sector in subsidizing new knowledge on which technology is based on agriculture, it is important to take a comparative-institutions approach. In this and other situations where there may be a divergence between those who bear the costs and those who reap the benefits, the outcome of the market allocation of resources to these activities must be compared with the results when resources are allocated through the governmental process.

Furthermore, the public-goods rationale is less and less valid as one moves from basic science to the development and extension of new technology. Developers of new technology in agriculture can often appropriate the returns from goods and services through patents, copyrights, and fees. A new plant variety or a new machine can be patented. Printed information can be copyrighted. Admission fees can be charged for information provided through lectures, demonstrations, and so on. The conclusion is that much agricultural research and education does not meet the nonexcludability condition of the public-goods model. That is, it is often possible to exclude nonusers by charging for the types of goods and services commonly provided by agricultural research and extension specialists. Moreover, even in the case of research that meets the public-goods criterion, the potential gains from public sector investment must be weighed against distortions of resources through the political process (as shown in the following section). Thus, public-goods theory alone is not sufficient to justify governmental financing of research and education in agriculture.

Spillovers and Research Funding

The fact that new technology developed by researchers in one state often has beneficial spillover effects in other states is also cited as a justification for public funding of research. A new variety of corn developed by the North Carolina Agricultural Research Service, for example, may be useful to farmers in nearby states. Thus it is sometimes contended that when research is funded at the state level, research expenditures are too low because of this beneficial spillover effect. The argument is that since the beneficial spillover effects are not properly taken into account at the state level, the level of investment in state-funded research is "too low," and this is taken as a justification for increased funding of agricultural research at the federal level.

However, the conclusion that spillover effects of this kind warrant a shift of research funding from the state to the federal level does not necessarily follow. First, as suggested above, the benefits of new machinery, new varieties, and so on developed at the state level can often be appropriated through patents and copyrights. Second, the argument that federal funding is warranted where there are beneficial spillovers also ignores the fact that centralization of decision making at the federal level *creates* inefficiencies and spillovers due to nonmarket failure.

In reality, agricultural research appropriations at the federal level appear to be influenced more by political considerations than by public goods or externality theory. For example, legislators are often motivated by the pork barrel—the desire to place buildings, jobs, and research missions within their own states. Thus 44 percent of all research construction authorized between 1958 and 1977 occurred in states of sitting members of the Senate appropriations subcommittee on agriculture.[9] Senate pork-barreling is graphically described by Hadwiger:

> Senate pork-barreling has been a mixed blessing for agricultural research. The pork-barrel impulse has been useful in gaining support for new activities. . . . But the demand for state laboratories has obliged the federal Agricultural Research Service to operate a "traveling circus" opening new locations in current Senate constituencies, while closing some in states whose senators are no longer members of the subcommittee.[10]

Thus the existence of spillovers associated with state funding of research does not imply that publicly funded research in agriculture should be further centralized at the federal level. Indeed, significant bureaucratic inefficiencies are inherent in the current system of funding agricultural research.

Complementarity of Research and Higher Education

Public-sector investment in agricultural research is also rationalized on the basis of its complementarity with higher education.[11] There frequently is a productive interaction between research and education in the agricultural sciences in land-grant colleges and universities. Moreover, effective graduate education in these institutions means that both students and faculty are engaged in research.[12]

On the other hand, these benefits must be weighed against the problems associated with the current system of government-operated higher education. For example, Edwin Mills suggests that substantial benefits from privatization of state-owned and operated educational institutions would be generated by greater competition, greater freedom of choice among educational institutions, and by removal of distortions, such as excessive enrollments, induced by underpricing higher education.[13]

The relative weight of these arguments, one defending and the other critical of the status quo, is difficult to assess. How important, for example, are the information and incentive problems of the political process in analyzing the funding of agricultural research and educational activities? The following section explores some of the problems with rate-of-return estimates on publicly funded research in agriculture, and further demonstrates why it is difficult or impossible to get a definitive answer to the question of the "optimal" funding system of agricultural research and educational activities.

The Theory of Bureaucracy and Agricultural Research

The theory of bureaucracy holds that there is a tendency for services provided through the public sector to be oversupplied. The head of a research bureau of the USDA or of a state agricultural experiment station is faced with incentive and information problems similar to those of other decision makers in the collective-choice process. The agricultural bureaucrat cannot acquire the information on individual preferences and production opportunities required to determine the overall level or the pattern of research expenditure that would be in the public interest.[14] Thus because of limits on information, even the most selfless research or extension decision maker must choose some feasible, lower-level goal such as budget maximization. There are also incentive problems due to the separation of power and responsibility (see chapter 4). In the collective-choice process determining publicly funded research and extension activities, budgets tend to be treated as common-pool resources which no one owns. Thus there are strong a priori reasons to expect that public financing will lead to an oversupply of research and extension services in agriculture just as in other areas.

Vernon Ruttan suggests that agricultural research is not consistent with the theory of bureaucratic productivity.[15] Citing a number of studies that suggest that the rate of return on publicly funded agricultural research typically falls in the 30 to 60 percent range, Ruttan contends that there is underinvestment rather than overinvestment in publicly funded agricultural research. On the basis of the results of these rate-of-return studies, he concludes: "There is little doubt that a level of expenditure that would push rates of return to below 20 percent would be in the public interest."[16]

There are a number of reasons to be skeptical both of the finding that rates of return on public funding of agricultural research and educational activities are extraordinarily high and of Ruttan's policy conclusions. First, as suggested above, the returns to a large part of agricultural research can be appropriated by the developer through patents, copyrights, and other means.[17] If agricultural research and educational activities are largely private goods, one would expect entry of new firms producing these services until the expected rate of return is similar to returns from other investments of comparable risk. Consequently, in the absence of significant barriers to entry, estimates of abnormally high returns to publicly funded research and extension activities should be viewed as suspect.

Second, rate-of-return estimates on publicly funded research in agriculture are not comparable with rates of return on private investments because of tax considerations.[18] State and federal research agencies pay no taxes. Therefore, rates of return in the private sector are naturally lower because of taxes. In a study investigating the magnitude of this effect on 1,000 private firms, adjusting the rates of return for taxes raised the average rate of return from 10.8 percent to about 20 percent.[19] Thus if a correction is made for taxes paid in the private sector, the rates of return on publicly funded research appear less imposing.

Third, the rate-of-return estimates on publicly funded agricultural research fail to consider the misallocation of resources resulting from taxation. These estimates implicitly assume that one dollar of government expenditure has an opportunity cost of one dollar. Taxation to finance publicly funded research, however, causes distortions in product and input markets so that the opportunity cost of one dollar of public expenditure is more than a dollar—and is often referred to as a "deadweight loss."[20] These resource misallocation costs "have been estimated to range between 20 and 50 cents per additional tax dollar collected."[21] Consequently, rate-of-return estimates on publicly funded research that fail to take this misallocation of resources into account have a strong upward bias.

Fourth, there is a problem of specifying the appropriate costs and benefits to be used in rate of return studies. All rate-of-return studies are based on *ex post* data. Current investment decisions, however, are based on *ex ante* data, and a high *ex post* return does not imply a high *ex ante* return. Thus, the fact that the rate of return is high on the development of a new tobacco harvester, for example, does not imply that the rate of return on future research in tobacco mechanization will be high. Underinvestment in a choice context implies that the *ex ante* internal rate of return is high relative to the opportunity cost of capital. Of course, a high *ex ante* return in a world of uncertainty does not imply a high *ex post* return. Moreover, the economic analyst has no way to measure the *ex ante* costs and returns that influence collective-choice decisions. What is the cost of spending, say, an additional billion dollars on agricultural research? It is the *opportunity cost* of these funds in the best alternative use, whether that use is for prisons, roads, defense, welfare, or for increased private spending and lower taxes.

Although the market rate of interest in many cases provides a good indication of the opportunity cost of capital, its usefulness in investment decisions is limited when the alternatives being considered include nonmarket activities. Consider the problems of determining the opportunity cost in spending an additional $1 billion on agricultural research if, say, national defense is the sacrificed alternative. The expected benefits from additional defense expenditures are highly subjective and there is no reason to expect different observers to make the same assessment of these benefits. A similar problem arises in evaluating the benefits of expenditures for prisons, income transfers, and so on in which the benefits are often not reflected in market prices. Yet it cannot be said that there is underinvestment in publicly funded agricultural research unless the rate of return is higher than it would be on these spending alternatives.

Undesirable spillovers associated with changes in agricultural technology present still another problem in specifying the costs and benefits of agricultural research. New agricultural technology has had enormous consequences, "most of them unintended."[22] The potential problems in the use of chemical pesticides were dramatized by Rachel Carson's *Silent Spring* in 1962.[23] Carson imagined a farm on which human and nonhuman life had been blighted by deadly chemicals resulting in a "silent springtime." The influence of environmental groups on pesticide decisions in commercial agriculture has increased dramatically since that time. However, it was not until 1977 that the USDA announced a goal of reducing reliance upon chemicals by increasing research on strategies that use a combination of biological, chemical, and other controls.[24] The uncertainties, lack of information, and lack of consensus about the risks associated with pesticides use pose formidable problems to the economic analyst in estimating rates of return to agricultural research for improved pest control.

Uncertainty over the results of uses of biotechnology in agriculture also complicates rate-of-return estimates for agricultural research. Biotechnology is the application of living organisms to improve economically important processes. Frost-inhibiting bacteria, soil-dwelling microbes with insecticidal properties, growth hormones, and plant and animal vaccines using live, biologically novel organisms are examples of the application of recombinant DNA techniques in the development of products for agriculture. Proposals for release of genetically engineered microbes, plants, and animals in the open raise questions about the potential effects on human health and the environment since the dimension of the risk is unknown.[25]

Agricultural research, including developments in biotechnology such as the use of bovine growth hormone to boost milk production, may also affect the structure of U.S. agriculture. An alleged spillover effect of publicly supported agricultural research was highlighted in Jim Hightower's book *Hard Tomatoes, Hard Times*, published in 1972.[26] Hightower argued that agricultural colleges in focusing on the problems of large agribusiness firms had abandoned their function of serving family farmers.[27] Is agricultural research antithetical to the family farm? If so, how important is this? It is impossible to identify, let alone measure, all of the indirect spillover effects associated with labor-saving technology, new herbicides, new pesticides, biotechnology developments, and other fruits of agricultural research. Yet these effects are relevant in any realistic measurement of the costs and benefits associated with expenditures on agricultural research.

In view of the problems in isolating and measuring the costs and benefits associated with publicly financed investments, "policymakers must estimate the prudent level of investment without exact quantitative evidence of rates of return," weighing the costs of diverting resources from other productive uses.[28] Moreover, there may be little or no relationship between the objectively defined costs and benefits by any particular economic analyst and the evaluations that public officials (or the public at large) place on various alternatives. Collective-choice decisions inevitably are based on subjective considerations by members of the legislative process. Consequently, the problem of identifying inefficiency on the part of decision makers in the collective-choice process appears to be quite similar to that of identifying inefficiency on the part of private entrepreneurs (chapter 2). In view of these considerations, there are ample reasons for skepticism both about the high rate-of-return estimates, and the conclusion that there is underinvestment of publicly funded agricultural research.

Summary

There is a long history of publicly funded research and extension activities in U.S. agriculture. The effect of these activities is to increase technology, which increases supply and places downward pressure on prices of farm products. Increases in technology do not have the same effect on all farmers. Innovators gain from increases in technology because their costs are reduced before the innovation has a significant effect on product price. After a technological innovation is widely adopted and product price decreases, consumers receive most of the benefits of new technology. Expenditures that increase technology are inconsistent with farm price supports since increases in product supply make it more difficult to support prices at any given price level.

About half of the expenditure on agricultural research is privately funded. Public funded research is often justified on the basis of public goods and externality theory. However, most agricultural research and extension activities involving new varieties, new machinery, books, and demonstrations and fees, do not conform to the public-goods model since developers of new technology of these types can generally appropriate the returns through patents, copyrights, and user fees.

Despite the fact that agricultural research and educational activities appear to be mainly private rather than public goods, it is widely held that there is underinvestment of publicly funded research activities in U.S. agriculture. This proposition is based on empirical estimates of rates of return that are quite high. However, the high estimated rates of return from publicly funded research and educational activities in agriculture do not necessarily imply underfunding.

There are a number of reasons to be skeptical of the apparently high rates of return. First, the rates of return are not comparable with rates of return in the private sector because of tax considerations. Second, the estimates fail to consider the misallocation of resources resulting from taxation. Third, there is a problem of specifying the appropriate costs and returns when there is no market measure of opportunity cost, as in the case of national defense, prisons, and so on. Fourth, the cost of undesirable spillovers associated with new technology are not taken into account. Finally, since the returns from much of the agricultural research and educational activities can be appropriated through fees, patents, copyrights, and so on, rates of return are unlikely to be significantly higher than those in the private sector.

In analyzing the merits of public versus private funding of agricultural research, it is important to compare private with public financing, as each system operates under real-world conditions taking into account information and incentive problems. Private firms have incentives to invest the amount that yields the greatest net return, but governments do not face comparable incentives or constraints.[29] In comparisons of public and private investment, it is no less important to consider pork-barreling and other non–market failure problems associated with publicly funded research than it is to consider the "market failure" problems associated with privately funded agricultural research and educational activities. When these "government failure" problems are taken into account, it will be found that governments usually can best encourage research investment by defining and enforcing property rights so that privately funded research can be profitably undertaken.[30] The analysis in this chapter demonstrates that even in basic agricultural research, where much of the gain is captured by other firms and consumers rather than the innovating firm, it is important to take into account problems inherent in collective decision making. When this is done, the appropriate amount of agricultural research and the desirable amount of public support for these investment activities appear to be unresolved issues.

Notes

1. Bruce Gardner, "Agriculture's Revealing—and Painful—Lesson for Industrial Policy," *Backgrounder*, no. 320 (Washington, D.C.: The Heritage Foundation, 1984).

2. Don F. Hadwiger, *The Politics of Agricultural Research* (Lincoln: University of Nebraska Press, 1982), p. 15.

3. Murray R. Benedict, *Farm Policies of the United States 1790–1950* (New York: Twentieth Century Fund, 1953), p. 84.

4. Hadwiger, *The Politics of Agricultural Research*, pp. 15–16.

5. Dennis T. Avery, "The Dilemma of Rising Farm Productivity," Senior Agricultural Analyst, Bureau of Intelligence and Research, U.S. Department of State, lecture before the Agribusiness Roundtable, 10 September 1984.

6. David N. Hyman, *Public Finance: A Contemporary Application of Theory to Policy*, 2nd ed. (Chicago: Dryden Press, 1987), Chap. 4.

7. Vernon W. Ruttan, *Agricultural Research Policy* (Minneapolis: University of Minnesota Press, 1982), p. 182.

8. Thomas Sowell, *Knowledge and Decisions* (New York: Basic Books, 1980), p. 37.

9. Hadwiger, *The Politics of Agricultural Research*, p. 120.

10. Ibid., pp. 121–23.

11. Ruttan, *Agricultural Research Policy*, p. 182.

12. Ibid.

13. Edwin S. Mills, *The Burden of Government* (Stanford, Calif.: Hoover Institution Press, 1986), p. 161.

14. William A. Niskanen, Jr., *Bureaucracy and Representative Government* (Chicago: Aldine-Atherton, 1971), p. 39.

15. Vernon W. Ruttan, "Bureaucratic Productivity: The Case of Agricultural Research," *Public Choice* 35 (1980): 529–47.

16. Ibid., p. 531.

17. E. C. Pasour, Jr. and Marc A. Johnson, "Bureaucratic Productivity: The Case of Agricultural Research Revisited," *Public Choice* 39 (1982): 301–17.

18. Glenn Fox, "Is the United States Really Underinvesting in Agricultural Research?" *American Journal of Agricultural Economics* 67 (November 1985): 806–12.

19. Ibid., p. 809.

20. Ibid.

21. *Economic Report of the President* (Washington, D.C.: U.S. Government Printing Office, 1988), p. 188.

22. Don F. Hadwiger, "U.S. Agricultural Research: Utopians, Utilitarians, Copians," *Food Policy*, August 1984, p. 199.

23. Rachel Carson, *Silent Spring* (Boston: Houghton Mifflin, 1962).

24. Hadwiger, *The Politics of Agricultural Research*, p. 167.

25. Susan Offutt and Fred Kuchler, "Biotechnology: Is Safety All That Matters?" *Choices* 2 (1987/4): 12–15.

26. Jim Hightower, *Hard Tomatoes, Hard Times: The Failure of the Land Grant College Complex* (Washington, D.C.: Agribusiness Accountability Project, 1972).

27. Hadwiger, *The Politics of Agricultural Research*, p. 107.

28. *Economic Report of the President*, p. 183.

29. Ibid., p. 182.

30. Ibid.

19

Taxation in Agriculture

Federal tax laws historically have extended special treatment to individuals engaged in agricultural production. Prior to the Tax Reform Act (TRA) of 1986, the tax benefits available to farm operators were also available to nonfarm investors who qualify as farmers for income tax purposes. Consequently, farming often has been used as a tax shelter by nonfarmers because of the incentive to invest in farming by people in higher marginal tax brackets. As a result, farm "losses" for tax purposes exceeded farm "profits" reported on tax returns for several years prior to the TRA of 1986. The 1986 tax legislation, as shown below, curtailed tax shelters and significantly reduced the attractiveness of investments in agriculture to nonfarm investors.

The special tax treatment of farmers raises a number of questions. What are the major tax advantages in agriculture? How are these advantages related to the system of progressive tax rates? What are the implications of tax preferences for agriculture? These questions are addressed following a discussion of "progressive" income taxes and the importance of marginal tax rates in decisions made by tax payers.

Marginal Tax Rates and the Progressive Income Tax

Taxation affects personal decisions related to work yielding taxable income, and hence it also affects individual productivity. Moreover, it is the marginal tax rate that is important in individual decisions affecting resource use. The marginal tax rate (MTR) can be expressed as follows:[1]

$$MTR = \frac{\text{Change in tax liability}}{\text{Change in taxable income}}$$

For an increase in income, the marginal tax rate reveals how much of the additional income must be paid in taxes and how much will be retained by the wage owner. For example, if an individual's marginal tax bracket is 28 percent and the worker earns $100 additional taxable income, $28 of this income must be paid in taxes.

Much of the attractiveness of U.S. agriculture as a tax shelter over the years has been due to the fact that the structure of federal income tax rates in the United States is *progressive*. A progressive tax is one which takes a larger percentage of income as taxable income increases. Under a progressive income tax structure, the marginal tax rate increases as income increases. The maximum marginal federal income tax rate in the United States under the 1986 tax law is 33 percent.

The importance of economic incentives in individual behavior is sometimes heavily discounted, even by economists. The income-expenditure or Keynesian approach, for example, stresses the importance of maintaining a high level of aggregate demand. In the Keynesian approach, increased government spending will lead to economic growth, regardless of tax rates. In this view, taxes are "merely a transfer" and tax rates can be varied with little affect on production.

The recent supply-side school of thought, in contrast, stresses the disincentive effects of taxes. This emphasis on the importance of economic incentives and disincentives is not new but is rooted in the ideas of Adam Smith and other classical economists. Taxes affect incentives in a number of different ways. First, as the marginal tax rate increases, the opportunity cost of leisure decreases. Consider the North Carolina worker in (say) the 33-percent federal income tax bracket. If an additional $100 is earned, $37.69 must be paid in federal and state income taxes. Thus, for one who itemizes deductions, the maximum state and federal income tax rate for North Carolina residents is 37.7 percent since state income taxes are deductible from federal taxable income and the maximum North Carolina rate is 7 percent. In contrast, the worker in the 15-percent federal tax bracket must pay $20.95 for federal and state income taxes if he or she itemizes deductions and earns $100 additional income. Thus as tax rates increase, people can be expected to substitute leisure for work by taking longer vacations, doing less overtime work, taking earlier retirement, and so on.

Second, high marginal tax rates not only discourage work, they also cause people to work on jobs where they are less productive. An individual in the 38-percent tax bracket, for example, must earn $1,000 additional income to have $620 after taxes. Thus a lawyer or teacher may be induced to paint the house, repair the automobile, or perform other tasks where he or she is less productive. In this way, progressive income taxes result in a pattern of labor use that is not consistent with the law of comparative advantage.

Third, high tax rates increase the incentive of individuals to evade taxes. In the United States, Great Britain, Sweden, and Italy, for example, increasing tax rates during the late 1970s led to a growing underground economy where exchanges were "off the books" and not included as taxable income. There is no accurate way to determine the precise magnitude of the underground economy since the transactions are not reported.

However, a 1979 study estimated that unreported transactions in the United States totalled a staggering $700 billion in 1978.[2]

Finally, high marginal tax rates mean that more and more valuable resources are devoted to the tax shelter industry. Thousands of tax lawyers, accountants, and financial planners in the United States are employed in assisting physicians, lawyers, teachers, and other taxpayers in finding ways to reduce their taxes.

The 1986 TRA significantly reduced the progressivity of the federal income tax. Three tax rates, 15, 28, and 33 percent, replaced a tax structure having 15 tax brackets with a top rate of 50 percent. The number of corporate income tax brackets was reduced from five to three and the maximum rate was lowered from 46 to 34 percent. Although simplification of the tax system was supposedly a primary goal, the 1986 legislation significantly increased the complexity of federal income taxes in a number of ways. Let us now consider the federal tax policies affecting agriculture.

The Federal Income Tax and Agriculture

The individual income tax, as suggested above, is designed to impose a progressive tax on an individual's net income each year. In order to tax net income, there must be rules for determining both gross income and offsets against gross income.[3] While cash receipts from the sale of farm products are easy to measure, making offsets to obtain net or taxable income becomes complicated, especially where production involves more than one time period, as is often the case in agriculture. The most important tax advantages for agriculture are cash accounting and the deductibility of certain capital expenditures.

Accrual versus Cash Accounting

The use of accrual accounting is generally required in calculating net income in the ordinary course of business. Under accrual accounting, income from the sale of specific commodities is matched with the expenses of producing those commodities. This matching of income and expenses requires that records be kept on expenses, production, inventories, and sales for each year. Under this system of record keeping, all sales in a given year are treated as income regardless of whether payment is actually received during that year. Expenses related to goods sold, whether paid or not, are taken as offsets against income in the year of sale. Under accrual accounting, unsold goods and purchased inputs are inventoried and included with income from sales of farm products in determining farm profits for tax purposes.

Under cash accounting, income from the sale of farm products is taxed in the year payment is received. Moreover, with the exception of livestock purchased for resale (the cost of feeder cattle purchased one year and sold the following year, for example, cannot be deducted until the year of sale), expenses generally can be deducted from taxable income in the year the expenses are paid rather than the year in which the goods are sold. Under the 1986 TRA, the deductibility of prepaid expenses of most variable inputs, such as feed, seed, and fertilizer, is limited to half of nonprepaid farm expenses until the inputs are actually used. Inventories of unsold goods are ignored under cash accounting but the costs related to these goods are deducted when the costs are paid.

How does the cash method of accounting differ from the accrual method? In the accrual method, there is an attempt to match expenses with income from sales in the year that the sales occur. Outlays on fertilizer and other inputs bought in the fall for use in the following spring, for example, are effectively matched against income from sales of the crop on which the inputs are used under accrual accounting. Under the accrual method, farm business expenses are deductible in the tax year in which the farmer becomes liable for them. Thus, the fertilizer in the above example would be deductible when purchased but must be inventoried so that the cost of the fertilizer, in effect, is matched against income from sale of products that the fertilizer is used to produce. In the cash accounting system, in contrast, the fertilizer expense is deducted in the year bought, regardless of when it is used. As a result, expenses of production are matched with income from sales of those products under cash accounting only in cases where expenses are paid and payment is received for the resulting products during the same year. For example, expenses are matched with income if all costs of producing corn are paid and the entire crop is sold within a tax period. In farming, however, the payment received in one year often results from production in an earlier year (e.g., stored corn may be sold) and the expenses paid in one year frequently relate to production in a future year. When compared with producers operating under the accrual system, this mismatching of income and expenses in different tax years reduces the tax liabilities of farmers since it is always beneficial to receive a benefit sooner rather than later. Stated differently, cash accounting causes taxable income to be lower in present value than the economic income accrued.[4]

Farmers are permitted to use cash accounting rather than accrual accounting presumably because of the complex record-keeping requirements required in accrual accounting. The ability to use cash rather than accrual methods is justified on the grounds that the more complicated accrual bookkeeping methods would impose a substantial burden on many family farmers. The use of cash accounting by corporations engaged in farming is limited to those with gross receipts of $1,000,000 or less per year (or to those corporations organized as S corporations). However, corporations engaged in certain types of farming activities are exempt from this restriction on cash accounting.

Thus nurseries (including sod farms), and agricultural firms involved in the growing or harvesting of trees (except fruit and nut trees) may elect to use cash accounting. Prior to tax legislation enacted in 1987, corporations that met the qualifications to be defined as a "family farm" or a "closely held corporation" were permitted to use cash accounting, no matter how large their gross receipts were in any year.[5]

Consequently, it is not only farmers with simple bookkeeping systems who have benefited from the use of cash accounting. Tyson Foods, a corporate "family farm" poultry producer with sales of $1.1 billion in 1985, was permitted to use cash accounting prior to the 1987 Revenue Act. Hudson Foods Inc. and Perdue Farms Inc. were also considered family farms for tax purposes and received huge tax benefits from cash accounting.[6] The 1987 Revenue Act requires that "family farming corporations" must use the accrual method if their annual gross receipts for any year after 1985 exceeds $25 million.[7]

Expensing versus Depreciation

Operating expenses incurred by farmers and other businesses are generally tax deductible as an offset to earned income. However, a capital expenditure as an offset to income generally must be depreciated. That is, the expenditure on a capital asset must be apportioned over the asset's life rather than deducting the total expenditure in the year the asset is purchased. However, income tax laws prior to the 1986 legislation allowed businesses (including farmers) to expense (deduct) up to $5,000 of newly acquired depreciable property. The TRA of 1986 increased the amount to $10,000. On the other hand, the act abolished the investment tax credit which served to reduce the taxpayer's tax liability in the purchase of qualifying depreciable farm property.

The 1986 TRA generally increased the depreciation life for capital assets but increased early years' depreciation allowances by changing the depreciation method applicable to most farm machinery and buildings. Depreciation periods continue to be quite short relative to the expected life for most types of farm property. For example, farm machinery and equipment items have a seven-year recovery period; single-purpose agricultural buildings (hog houses, milking parlors, and greenhouses) have a ten-year recovery period. That is, these assets can be fully depreciated over seven- or ten-year periods. There are tax benefits if costs of depreciable assets are written off before the property stops contributing to farm income.

In addition to favorable depreciation rules, expenditures incurred in the production of some farm products can be expensed or fully deducted in the year of purchase. Examples include: (1) costs of lime, fertilizer, and other materials that enrich the land for more than one year; (2) soil and water conservation expenditures on USDA-approved conservation projects. Currently, costs of growing plants taking two years or longer to reach the productive stage must be capitalized and either depreciated or subtracted from the sale price to determine the taxable gain when the property reaches the productive stage. Farmers eligible to use cash accounting can still deduct preproduction expenses for these enterprises if they use the straight-line depreciation method on all farm assets put into use in the year the deduction is taken.

There is a tax benefit from being able to deduct the entire amount of a capital expenditure in the year of purchase rather than merely deducting the amount of depreciation, since the benefit from a cost deducted now is greater than if deducted later. Moreover, the reduction in taxes because of expensing for a given amount of capital expenditure will be greater, the higher the marginal tax rate.

Gains on the Sale of Capital Assets

A change in value of a capital asset is not treated as income for tax purposes until the asset is sold. That is, only when a capital asset is sold is its increase (or decrease) in value recognized for income tax purposes. Prior to the Tax Reform Act of 1986, long-term capital gains were taxed at lower rates than ordinary income, with a maximum rate of 20 percent. Under the 1986 act, capital gains are taxed at the same rates as ordinary income. This increase in taxes on capital gains significantly reduces the benefits of agriculture as a tax shelter. Repeal of the capital gains exclusion significantly increases the tax burden from sales of farmland, timber, and raised assets such as breeding cattle.

The Estate Tax

The federal estate tax is a progressive tax on wealth transferred because of death. The tax is computed on the value of the property owned by the deceased, and the tax is generally due nine months after death. There are exceptions to both of these rules in agriculture. First, the estate tax may often be calculated on the basis of "agricultural use value" rather than on market value. In addition, qualifying farms and other small businesses are given an extended time to pay the tax during which time interest on estate taxes due accrues at a rate well below market rates.

Corporate Farming

Federal law generally does not place direct restrictions on the corporate form of ownership in farming. However, farm corporations are not eligible to borrow from the FmHA. Moreover, income earned by corporations and distributed to shareholders is taxed twice. Corporate income is taxed at the corporation income tax rate (maximum 34 percent) and income distributed to shareholders is also taxable.

There are two methods of taxing the income of farm corporations. The standard method, alluded to above, taxes income to the corporation. An alternate method permits shareholders to choose to have corporate income taxed to them individually (Subchapter S). There are several potential benefits that cause some farmers to incorporate.[8]

First, the total tax cost on corporate income will sometimes be lower than would be the case if the income were earned by an individual. It may be possible to accumulate profits of a corporation that are not paid out as dividends at lower tax cost than if the profits had been earned by individuals because corporate tax rates under the TRA are lower than individual rates at lower income levels. Second, by incorporating and then transferring shares of stock each year, farm transfers can be more easily made without physically dividing a farm. Third, the cost of fringe benefits such as meals, health insurance, and group life insurance can be deducted by the corporation but their value need not be included in the gross income of shareholders (or other employees).[9] In addition corporate ownership has the advantages of limited liability and it provides a means of pooling capital. Aside from tax considerations, the disadvantages of incorporation are the initial cost and the time and expense of maintaining records.

Farming as a Tax Shelter

A tax shelter is an investment that allows taxpayers to reduce or eliminate tax liabilities on income by utilizing preferential provisions of income tax laws. Tax liabilities are lowered to the extent that deductions are claimed against income earned from other sources while income from the tax shelter is delayed or reported in a way that subjects it to a relatively low tax rate.

Prior to the TRA of 1986, U.S. tax laws favored agricultural investments in four ways. Investors in agriculture were provided: (1) the option of using cash rather than accrual accounting, (2) the opportunity to expense certain capital investments, (3) a lower tax rate on capital gains than on ordinary income, and (4) investment tax credits. Of these provisions, all were significantly changed by the 1986 legislation.

The TRA of 1986 also prevents an investor from using a loss from a "passive activity" to shelter "active income" from other sources (including salary and portfolio income). For example, tax losses from farming cannot be written off against income from other sources received by nonfarm investors. This crackdown on tax shelters takes effect gradually over a five-year period. The limitation on passive losses was aimed at preserving tax advantages for bona fide farmers. Farmers who qualify as "material participants" in production are not affected by the new passive-loss rules.

Implications for Agriculture

Tax laws have had a significant effect on U.S. agriculture.[10] First, investments in agriculture as a tax-sheltered industry have tended to find their way into the hands of the highest-bracket taxpayers. That is, since tax preferences in agriculture are more valuable the higher the marginal tax rate, tax laws have tended to concentrate farmland ownership in the hands of high-income farmers and nonfarmers. Moreover, the increased demand for farms as tax shelters exerted upward pressure on prices of farm real estate. Changes in the late 1986 TRA reduced marginal tax rates and significantly weakened other tax provisions that made agriculture a widely used tax shelter.

Second, the federal tax system affects the resource mix within agriculture. Tax policies tend to encourage the use of capital and to discourage the use of labor. The cost of investments in capital facilities is encouraged through expensing and accelerated depreciation of depreciable property. Some capital inputs are depreciated much faster than other capital inputs relative to their expected economic lives. Thus tax policies both encourage the use of capital relative to labor and alter the capital mix in farming.

Third, tax policies attract additional resources into agriculture, bringing about an increase in farm output, particularly of the most tax-favored commodities. The result is lower prices for farm products in general. Again, the 1986 tax changes significantly reduced the effects of tax considerations in the production and marketing of agricultural products.

Summary

Federal tax laws historically have extended favorable treatment to individuals engaged in agricultural operations. In the case of income taxes, farmers are permitted to use the cash rather than accrual method of accounting. Accelerated depreciation rules effectively reduce the cost of investment in capital assets. Farms (and other businesses) can expense up to $10,000 of newly acquired depreciable property. The depreciation schedule for a capital asset is also frequently shorter than the economic life of the asset. The result is a reduction in near-term taxable income. In addition, some capital expenditures, such as fertilizer, lime and USDA-approved soil and water conservation expenditures can be expensed. In the case of estate taxes, it is often possible to have farmland valued on the basis of its "agricultural use value" instead of its market value. Farmers are also allowed a longer time to pay the tax.

The federal income tax is progressive, taxing higher incomes at higher rates. Consequently, the tax preferences in agriculture are more valuable to the individual taxpayer, the higher the marginal tax rate. Thus large farms, which generate higher incomes, are likely to gain proportionately more from tax policies favorable to agriculture than smaller farms.[11] Marginal tax rates and tax preferences in agriculture were significantly reduced under the 1986 TRA. In addition, tax shelters were curtailed. Capital gains no longer receive preferential taxation relative to ordinary income. Moreover, only those involved in farming on a "regular, continuous, and substantial basis" can now use farm losses to offset wage and salary income.[12] The long-run result will likely be a higher proportion of owner-operators, lower land prices, reduced production, and higher prices for farm products.

Taxation in agriculture is but another example of the phenomenon described throughout the preceding chapters. There are always unintended and indirect effects of government policies. Moreover, quite often the effects are antithetical to other goals. For example, the tax preferences in farming result in higher land prices and encourage the substitution of capital for labor, both of which make it more difficult for beginning farmers. Competition causes prices of farm land and other specialized resources to increase as long as expected returns in agriculture are higher than those of alternative investments. Capital will tend to flow between sectors until rates of return, net of taxes, are equaled at the margin. Thus, as in the case of other farm programs, tax preferences in agriculture have only a transitory effect on farm incomes.

Notes

1. James D. Gwartney and Richard Stroup, *Economics: Private and Public Choice*, 4th ed. (New York: Academic Press, 1987), p. 106.

2. Edgar L. Feige, "How Big Is the Irregular Economy?" *Challenge*, Nov.–Dec. 1979, 5–13.

3. Charles Davenport, Michael B. Boehlje, and David B. H. Martin, *The Effects of Tax Policy on American Agriculture*, ERS Agricultural Economic Report No. 480 (Washington, D.C.: U.S. Government Printing Office, 1982).

4. Carol D. Peterson, William Shear, and Charles L. Vehorn, "Cash Accounting Rules for Farmers: Differential Benefits and Federal Costs," *Journal of Economic Issues* 21 (June 1987): 642.

5. Ibid.

6. Ibid., pp. 641–42.

7. *The RIA Complete Analysis of the Revenue Act and Pension Protection Act of 1987* (New York: Research Institute of America, 1988), p. 35.

8. Davenport, Boehlje, and Martin, *Effects of Tax Policy*, p. 11.

9. Ibid., p. 12.

10. Joint Economic Committee Print, *The Effects of Federal Income Tax Policy on U.S. Agriculture*, S. Prt. 98-273, 98th Congress, 2nd session (Washington, D.C.: U. S. Government Printing Office, 1985), pp. 25–29.

11. *Economic Report of the President* (Washington, D.C.: U.S. Government Printing Office, 1984), p. 130.

12. *Economic Report of the President* (Washington, D.C.: U.S. Government Printing Office, 1987), p. 160.

20

The Effects of Government Farm Programs

The economic evaluation of U.S. farm programs is not simple or easy. Quite often, the impacts of different programs are offsetting. In this chapter, farm programs and the related expenditures are classified into several broad categories and the major gainers and losers from these programs identified. Most of the effects of specific programs described in this chapter have already been discussed in connection with the analysis of particular programs. The objective of this chapter is to describe the major effects of government programs in agriculture as a whole.

Programs that Increase Product Prices to Farmers

The data in table 20.1 represent an attempt to separate budget outlays for various programs on the basis of their impact on the demand, supply, and price of farm products.[1] The second and third columns include outlays that tend to increase producer prices of U.S. farm products. Product prices are increased in some cases by decreasing supply and in others by increasing demand. Production controls for sugar, tobacco, peanuts, cotton, wheat, rice, and feed grains reduce the supply of farm products, thereby increasing prices to farmers (figure 20.1). Programs reduce supply in a number of ways, depending upon the specific nature of the particular program. In the case of tobacco and peanuts, production is controlled directly through tobacco acreage allotments and marketing quotas and through peanut marketing quotas. Production is controlled indirectly in the case of price supports for cotton, wheat, rice, and feed grain programs through acreage reduction including set-aside programs. The supply of farm products is also reduced by import restrictions of price supported products imposed to prevent consumers from consuming lower-priced imported products. Regardless of how production is reduced, however, the result is to reduce supply and to increase product prices to farmers.[2]

Domestic and foreign food assistance and nutrition programs increase the demand for farm products through government purchases, food subsidies, and export subsidies, thereby increasing product prices (figure 20.2). Price supports for milk are implemented through government pur-

Table 20.1.   U.S. Department of Agriculture Expenditures (millions of dollars).

CL6

DATE	(1) TOTAL[a]	(2) STABILIZATION OF FARM PRICES AND INCOME[b]	(3) FOOD AND NUTRITION PROGRAMS	(4) FINANCING FARMERS AND RURAL DEVELOPMENT	(5) FINANCING RURAL ELECTRIFICATION AND TELEPHONES[c]	(6) CONSERVATION OF LAND AND WATER RESOURCES	(7) RESEARCH EXTENSION, AND OTHER SERVICES[d]
1929	172	—	—	6	—	—	166
1935	1,218	749	—	81	10	—	378
1940	1,416	1,013	—	241	38	29	95
1945	2,265	1,470	—	340	16	325	114
1950	2,956	1,844	—	146	293	337	336
1955	4,636	3,506	84	180	204	286	376
1960	5,419	3,693	234	292	330	368	302
1965	7,298	5,084	300	285	392	425	812
1970	8,307	5,090	960	142	338	459	1,318
1975	14,977	1,855	6,174	3,252	274	652	2,770
1980	34,823	4,022	13,555	9,918	3,413	915	3,000
1985	55,530	19,488	17,994	11,093	1,555	984	4,456
1986	58,666	26,986	18,153	8,001	431	825	4,270
1987	49,593	23,424	18,435	3,748	-238	844	3,380

SOURCE: Data from 1929 to 1980 were taken from Clifton B. Luttrell, *Down on the Farm with Uncle Sam* (Los Angeles: International Institute for Economic Research, 1983), p. 17. Data for 1985, 1986, and 1987 from Department of the Treasury, *Final Monthly Treasury Statement*; Office of Management and Budget, *Budget of the U.S. Government*, and *Historical Tables: Budget of the U.S. Government*.

[a] Includes off-budget outlays of $5,000 million for Farmers Home Administration and $255 million for electrification and telephones in 1975; and $6,881 million and $3,387 million for these purposes, respectively, in 1980. REA and FmHA outlays through the Federal Financing Bank are no longer off-budget and are included in spending totals for 1985, 1986, and 1987.

[b] Includes outlays for ASCS (excluding ACP cost-sharing and environmental programs), CCC, and special sugar and foreign assistance programs such as PL 480.

[c] Net expenditures may be negative because of prepayments of outstanding REA guaranteed loans.

[d] Includes outlays for forest service; plant, animal, and food protection; crop insurance, and administrative expenses.

237

Agriculture and the State

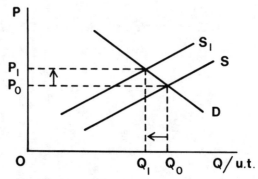

Figure 20.1. Production controls reduce supply and increase product prices.

chases of manufactured milk products. Food-stamp, school-lunch, and other assistance programs increase the demand for farm products by subsidizing food purchases. Indeed, in the original New Deal food-stamp and school-lunch programs, the emphasis was much more on the disposal of surpluses than on adequate and suitable diets for the undernourished.[3] Similarly, much of the political support for PL 480 ("Food for Peace") as a program of foreign food aid over the years has arisen from its role in increasing the demand for farm products.[4] A wide range of domestic and foreign food aid programs continue to be important in maintaining the demand for U.S. agricultural products.

International grain agreements (with Russia in 1975 and China in 1980 for five- and four-year periods, respectively) were designed to stabilize prices and increase overall demand for U.S. grain. The agreements specified a range of grain exports to these nations each year at market prices. However, such agreements have relatively little impact on world demand and prices since any increase in U.S. exports is likely to be largely offset by reductions in trade with other nations. But the agreements may, at least to some extent, increase the demand for U.S. farm products. In general, government programs that increase demand thus increase the prices of farm products and food prices to those who are not the direct beneficiaries of the programs.

Programs that Reduce Prices

USDA Programs

The remaining columns in table 20.1, columns 4 through 7, include expenditures for programs that increase the supply of farm products and reduce farm product prices. Government subsidies for agricultural credit and electric power, conservation of land and water resources (including flood control, irrigation and land reclamation), and research and extension services reduce farm production costs, increase output, and decrease product prices (figure 20.3). Subsidized credit by the FmHA, for example, adds to total resources in agriculture by providing more credit than would be available at competitive market rates and terms. Farmers are able to acquire equipment, livestock, fertilizer, seed, and other farm inputs at reduced costs and improve the productivity of land through subsidized drainage, irrigation, flood control, and rural electric power. Research and extension activities reduce per-unit costs and increase total farm output. The ASCS, in conjunction with the SCS, provides cost-sharing to farmers to carry out conservation and environmental practices along with the development of soil and water conservation programs. Subsidized soil conservation and research activities tend to increase production in the long run, whereas irrigation and floodwater control provide immediate gains in output. Other government programs affecting agriculture, such as export controls on farm products, embargoes, tax preferences, and domestic wage and price controls may have sizable impacts on farm product prices but have relatively little effect on direct budget outlays.

Department of Interior Water and Power Subsidies in the West

Irrigation is highly important to agricultural production in the West and water is frequently priced to farmers below its value in nonagricultural uses.[5] Substantial subsidies for surface water to agriculture in the west have been provided through water projects of the Bureau of Reclamation. Irrigation districts also use artificially low-priced electricity produced by federally funded dams to pump groundwater for irrigation.[6] Although only about 150,000 farms benefit from federal water projects, the per-farm stakes may be quite large. The capitalized value of the irrigation subsidies for a 160-acre California farm, for example, may be in excess of $100,000.[7]

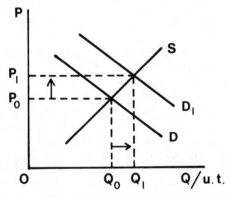

Figure 20.2. Government purchases of farm products increase demand and product price.

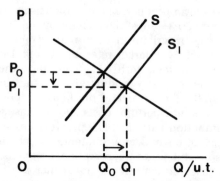

Figure 20.3. Subsidized credit, conservation practices, and research and extension services increase supply and decrease product prices.

Although it is difficult or impossible to determine the magnitude of these water and power subsidies over time, "certainly it is in the billions" of dollars.[8] These subsidies arise through programs of the Department of Interior rather than the Department of Agriculture and are not included in the government outlays shown in table 20.1.

Agricultural production in the West has been significantly increased through Department of Interior water and power subsidies. There is a basic inconsistency, however, between these subsidies which increase agricultural output and USDA programs designed to decrease farm output. Without irrigation water, California would be relatively unimportant in agricultural production.[9] With the subsidized irrigation water, California is the leading agricultural state in the United States. The water and power subsidies in the West not only distort the geographical pattern of agricultural production within the U.S. They also increase the scarcity of water for recreation and urban uses in the West.

Net Effects: Who Wins? Who Loses?

Since some programs increase product prices received by farmers at the same time other programs decrease prices, some of the expenditures are offsetting. Omitting the subsidized food programs, USDA expenditures that increase prices received by farmers totalled about $27 billion in 1986 (column 1, table 20.1). These expenditures were ostensibly designed to "stabilize farm prices and income." At the same time, expenditures that increase supply and decrease farm product prices including outlays on credit, irrigation, research and extension subsidies totalled about $13.5 billion (columns 4 through 7, table 20.1). Thus while $27 billion was spent on farm programs to *increase* farm product prices received by farmers, about half as much was spent on programs that *decreased* farm product prices. If the dollars spent on programs were equally efficient in achieving their conflicting objectives, expenditures that decrease prices would offset an equal amount of expenditures that increase product prices to farmers. This suggests that $27 billion in 1986 may have been spent on activities having little (or no) net impact on food costs, farm prices, or total farm incomes. However, this does not suggest that the programs were neutral in impact. There are important gainers and losers from farm programs, even if the expenditures, on average, are self-defeating. The identification of winners and losers is important in understanding the political support for farm programs.

Consumers and Taxpayers

The treasury outlays on government programs that increase supply and place downward pressure on product prices are quite large, as shown above. However, the potential beneficial effects of reduced prices to consumers are often negated by other programs that raise domestic product prices above world market levels. Prices of sugar, tobacco, peanuts, milk, fresh oranges, and a number of other products are higher than they would otherwise be, owing to the network of farm programs, most of which are quite similar to their New Deal predecessors. In the absence of domestic price support programs and the accompanying import restrictions, U.S. consumers would be able to purchase many food products at prices lower, in some cases much lower, than those now paid. Consumers also pay for farm programs through higher taxes that are required to operate and administer the programs.

USDA budget outlays were $49.6 billion in 1987 (table 20.1). This figure includes only federal outlays. "Outlays" are cash disbursements from the Treasury. However, treasury outlays do not clearly reflect the total magnitude of federal activities in U.S. agriculture because interest subsidies and costs generally of guaranteed and direct loan programs are either excluded or presented in net terms after repayments and sales of assets are considered. The USDA also develops a "program level" budget which is designed to represent the total financial value of benefits provided to the public including direct or guaranteed loans (including interest subsidies), and in-kind benefits such as commodities. The program level budget for 1987 totalled $69.3 billion—almost $20 billion higher than the official "budget outlay." Even this figure does not represent the full impact of government influence since it does not include loans by the Farm Credit System, a government-sponsored enterprise.

Owners of Specialized Resources

Within the agricultural sector, owners of land, allotments, and other specialized resources are the biggest gainers from farm programs. Owners of specialized resources receive windfall gains when price support programs are initiated. In the case of the tobacco price support program, for example, the market value of the right to produce often exceeds $1,000 per acre per year. In addition, some farmers have received major gains in the form of subsidized credit and conservation subsidies. Although owners of land and other specialized factors receive windfall gains either when a price support program is initiated or when a price support level is increased, the gains to later entrants into production are largely negated by higher production costs as expected benefits are capitalized into higher prices of land, allotments, and other specialized factors. Moreover, once a price support program is in operation, its elimination imposes windfall losses on owners of affected specialized resources, regardless of whether they benefited from the original windfall. In reality, owners of land and production rights at any given time quite often are not the same people who received the windfalls when the programs were initiated (or benefit levels increased).

Farmers as Producers versus Farmers as Asset Owners

The distribution of gains between producers and asset owners depends on how quickly the expected benefits or costs of program changes are incorporated into asset values. However, the preceding discussion suggests that it is resource owners rather than farmers as producers who are the major gainers when prices of farm assets increase. And many owners of land and other farm assets are not farmers. As shown in the previous chapter, however, tax shelters in agriculture were considerably reduced under the 1986 Tax Reform Act.

Labor versus Other Specialized Resources

Farmers as owners of specialized skills benefit from programs to assist agriculture. However, the effect of government programs on specialized labor is different in one respect from that of programs affecting specialized land or capital resources. The gains from government programs that reduce input prices or increase product prices are incorporated into higher market prices of land and other assets if property rights are well defined and assets can be bought and sold. In such cases, the farmer's wealth increases as a result of the increases in asset values, but following this increase the asset-owner can then expect to receive a normal rate of return.

The situation is different in the case of specialized labor or entrepreneurship where the service provided is hired for a period of time but cannot be bought or sold (see chapter 12). In this case, asset value is based on the expected contribution during the contracted time period. Moreover, the asset owner receives an increased return each year as long as product price remains higher. Thus, the gain from an increase in product price in the case of labor is not transitory in the way that it is for private property that can be bought and sold.

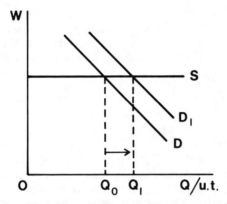

Figure 20.4. The effects of price support programs on farm labor.

Farm Operators and Farm Labor

Price supports and subsidized inputs provide incentives for increased agricultural production, but competition for labor and entrepreneurial skills in other sectors tends to equate returns throughout the labor market. D. Gale Johnson, on the basis of a number of empirical studies, concludes that the supply of labor in agriculture is highly responsive to changes in wage rates.[10] If this is correct it indicates that specialization of labor is not very important in analyzing the effects of farm programs. It also suggests that changes in product prices and the demand for labor result mainly in changes in farm employment rather than changes in returns to farm labor (figure 20.4). Johnson concludes that the return to labor in the rest of the economy is the main determinant of incomes to farm people.[11] Any tendency for agricultural wages to increase as farm output increases due to farm programs provides an incentive for workers to move into the agricultural sector. The highly elastic supply of labor implies that non-farm labor readily moves into agriculture if farm wage rates increase.

Some farm programs increase the demand for labor while others decrease the demand for labor. An increase in product price, other things constant, will increase the demand for labor. On the other hand, subsidized credit and tax preferences in agriculture reduce the cost of capital relative to labor and increase the rate of substitution of capital for labor, thereby reducing the demand for farm labor. Since the supply of labor is quite elastic, however, the effect of farm programs on farm wage rates is likely to be quite small. Consequently, farm product prices, whether high or low, have little effect on the return to farm labor.[12]

The effects of subsidized credit, conservation, research, and education programs that reduce cost and increase supply vary widely between farm operators. In the case of programs that increase technology, innovators gain, while those adopting later benefit little because of the increases in output and reductions in product prices. While some farm operators gain from subsidized credit and conservation programs, which reduce their costs of production, programs that increase output and decrease product prices have a harmful effect on those producers not receiving the subsidies.

Government Employees

Government employees also gain from farm programs. The number of USDA employees increased more than fourfold from 1929 to 1985 even as the number of farms and farmers was decreasing at a dramatic rate. As the number of commercial farms and farmers has decreased, there has been an expansion of USDA activities into rural development, rural recreation, nutrition, and other areas as predicted by the theory of public choice. Consequently, there is now a huge number of employees in the various agencies of the USDA who have a vested interest in maintaining and expanding the scope of agricultural programs.

Resource Allocation

In a market system, resources are allocated to various uses on the basis of market prices. When resources are allocated on the basis of political priorities, the pattern of resource use will change. Consider the example of agricultural credit. In the market, lenders lend money at different rates to various borrowers depending upon the credit risk. Competition equalizes the rates charged in agriculture with those in other sectors for loans of similar risk. Subsidizing agricultural credit leads to increased credit in agriculture and less credit extended to other sectors. Credit (and other inputs) will be used by producers as long as the value of the marginal product exceeds the interest rate. If the use of credit is subsidized, the rate of return on investment will be lower in agriculture than in other sectors.

It is important to recognize that a program that subsidizes credit is similar to other programs that arbitrarily change market prices. When the market price of credit is subsidized to a particular group, there is no objective procedure for determining how large the subsidy should be and no objective basis for allocating credit between agriculture and other sectors. For example, there is no standard measure of performance, such as profit, for assessing the success of federal loans or loan guarantees.

Similarly, land use, when allocated by market forces, is based on the expected return. Thus land having the highest expected use in agriculture is used for agricultural production, land having the highest use for housing is used for housing, and so on. Production control programs in agriculture divert some of the world's most productive farmland into nonproductive uses through the target price and land set-aside program. More generally, there has been a movement in recent years to consciously ignore land market price signals and to determine the pattern of land use through the political process. However, in the absence of market prices, there is no realistic way to determine which land to use for agriculture, for recreation, for housing, or for other uses. That is, there is no known way by which a public planner can obtain the necessary information on consumer preferences, resource supplies, and production opportunities to determine the pattern of land use that will best accommodate the competing demands for land. Indeed, there is a strong a priori case for decentralized competitive markets as the most effective means of coping with changing economic conditions in land use and other areas.

Policy Implications

It was pointed out earlier that there are two explanations for farm programs—income redistribution and the public interest. In the latter view, it is held that programs designed to increase and stabilize farm income benefit the public at large. Regardless of the rationale for the initiation of the programs, the continued existence of most farm programs such as price supports and credit subsidies appears to be better explained by income redistribution. These programs mainly benefit large farmers whose incomes, on average, already exceed incomes of the nonfarm population. It has been estimated, for example, that the largest 10 percent of the farms receive more than half of the net benefits of farm programs.[13] Thus it is likely that farm programs, commonly rationalized as measures to assist small family farmers, actually make incomes within agriculture more unequal.

The argument that farm programs are necessary to stabilize agricultural markets ostensibly appears to be stronger than the justification based on income redistribution. The stabilization rationale for farm programs, however, is also weak. Indeed, much of the recent instability in U.S. agriculture has been caused or exacerbated by government policies, including inflationary monetary and fiscal policies, subsidized credit, and trade restrictions. Government attempts to stabilize agricultural markets are limited by the same incentive and information problems that thwart attempts by government to stabilize the overall level of economic activity. Moreover, as the dependence of U.S. agriculture on international trade increases, domestic price support policies that reduce the competitiveness of U.S. farm products are increasingly counterproductive. There is an important lesson for U.S. agriculture—government might make its greatest contribution to economic stability by attempting to do less.[14] Specifically, noninflationary monetary and fiscal policies and a more open economy are likely to be more beneficial to agriculture in the long run than government action programs designed specifically for the farm sector.

Protectionism and the Deregulation of U.S. Agriculture[15]

Increased recognition of the shortcomings of government "action programs" in agriculture along with political pressure to reduce federal spending on farm programs have created the most favorable opportunity since the 1930s to move away from protectionist farm policies—both domestically and in the global agricultural trading system. Huge outlays on farm programs and domestic budget pressures, especially in the United States and the European Community, are important factors in developing the climate necessary to bring about serious consideration of changes in GATT rules affecting trade in farm products. It is estimated that some $150 to $100 billion are spent each year on farm programs around the world.

The Uruguay Round of GATT negotiations has significant implications for upcoming U.S. farm legislation to replace the Food Security Act of 1985 which expires in 1990. The GATT objective of liberalizing trade is no less appropriate in agriculture than in other sectors of the economy. It is ironic that the United States, the world's leading exporter of farm products, has been a perennial problem in GATT attempts to reduce trade barriers in agriculture.

The United States has the opportunity to push within GATT for the elimination of agricultural subsidies and trade barriers on a multilateral basis. There is the potential to open up agricultural markets, prevent worldwide stockpiles of food, and reduce taxpayer outlays on food subsidies by tens of billions of dollars. It would be most beneficial if all countries acted together in eliminating price supports and other trade barriers for farm products. The United States stands to gain from the deregulation of U.S. agriculture, however, regardless of whether agriculture is deregulated on a multilateral basis. Dismantling farm programs could lead toward freer world trade which would contribute to economic development throughout the world. It would also ease tensions among Western nations over agricultural subsidies.[16]

"Decoupling" versus Strict Supply Controls

The United States proposed a sweeping GATT initiative in July 1987 to phase out all trade-distorting agricultural subsidies in all countries by the year 2000. The objective of the proposal is to eliminate price supports and other farm programs that distort production, prices, and trade. However, implications of this proposal for government spending on the agricultural sector are not as drastic as they may initially appear to be. The United States and other countries would be free to provide income transfers to farmers as long as such aid did not subsidize the output of farm products.

The separation of government payments to farmers from the production of farm commodities has been called "decoupling." In this approach to making farm policy more compatible with free trade, any governmental assistance to the farm sector would take the form of lump-sum transfers to farmers rather than government payments based on units of output of wheat, corn, and other products produced, as is currently done. That is, farm income support would not be directly related to production of farm products. Farmers would be free to produce whatever crops they wished and actual production would be based on market signals rather than on government policy. Moreover, if rights to transfer payments were granted to individuals and were not transferable with land, the payments to farmers would have little effect on values of land and other assets—or on cost of producing farm commodities.

Government payments of any kind will have some affect on economic behavior of producers and consumers. However, payments that are unrelated to production would alter consumer and producer behavior much less than current farm policies, including price supports, subsidized credit, export subsidies, import quotas, and so on.

The Reagan Administration's "decoupling" proposal that government payments to farmers be separated from the production of farm commodities envisaged that farmers would continue to receive income support over a transition period following the end of product price supports and trade restrictions before being phased out. However, income redistribution is determined by political considerations rather than by economics. No system of transferring income from taxpayers to farmers can be justified as increasing social utility where one group is benefited at the expense of the taxpaying public.[17] Thus, the desirability of welfare payments to farmers is a separate issue from the deregulation of agriculture. Elimination of the current system of farm programs that distort output, product prices, and international trade would be beneficial, regardless of whether income transfers are made to farmers.

Proposals less far-reaching than decoupling have been made as a way of reducing current trade-distorting farm subsidies. In one proposal, payments to farmers would not be tied to production but the quantity of output eligible for support at the individual farm level would be limited and all other agricultural trade barriers and domestic support measures would be eliminated so that domestic market prices would equal world prices.[18] There are an infinite number of half-way measures of this kind to deregulate agriculture. However, all distort econommic activity when compared with the decentralized competitive norm.

All-out protectionism is touted by some as a preferred alternative to decoupling. Senator Harkin and Representative Gephardt have proposed that the tobacco program model of strict supply controls be extended to other farm commodities. In this approach, product prices would be raised by limiting the amount of individual farm products that could be produced and sold. The secretary of agriculture would establish a national marketing quota for each commodity that would attempt to balance supply and demand at the price support level determined by the parity-price approach.[19] Acreage allotments based on the national marketing quota then would be allocated to farmers. Marketing certificates, required to sell farm products, would be issued to producers based on their acreage allotment and established yield for each product.

Strict supply controls represent a throwback to the cartelization initiatives of the New Deal era. Moreover, the Harkin-Gephardt proposal would extend government planning of agriculture to a global basis by having the President negotiate a multilateral agreement to set up international cartels for farm products. This "Fortress America" type protectionism ignores the gains from trade and is not an enlightened (or a realistic) alternative in an increasingly interdependent world.

Summary

U.S. agricultural policies have increased prices of milk, sugar, tobacco, wheat, and other products above market clearing levels since the New Deal era. Agricultural surpluses can be attributed directly to price support programs. Attempts to solve these problems through payments to producers, land retirement, and other means bring about a misallocation of resources and require restrictions on imports to prevent consumers from purchasing cheaper imported products.

There are incentives to overproduce because the subsidies are tied to production. The overproduction incentive and the adverse side effects of farm programs will be eliminated only when the incentive to produce for the government is replaced by the incentive to produce for the market.[20]

Most of the benefits of farm programs are received by large farmers whose incomes already exceed, on average, incomes in the nonfarm sector. Farm programs mainly provide short-run gains to owners of land, allotments, and other specialized resources, as the higher product prices received by farmers are quickly offset by higher production costs. Price supports, income tax preferences for farmers, and subsidized credit programs also encourage farmers to invest in land and capital facilities when there is already widespread concern about farm size and debt. Finally, marketing orders, import controls, price supports, and other restrictions on competition not only distort the allocation of resources but also restrict the freedom of individuals to engage in mutually beneficial exchange and are inconsistent with achieving a more open economy. Thus, there is a great deal of evidence that farm programs are better explained by income redistribution than by the public interest.

The GATT objective of liberalizing trade is no less appropriate in agriculture than in other sectors. It is ironic that U.S. agriculture, the world's leading exporter of agricultural products, has been a perennial problem in GATT attempts to reduce trade barriers. There is no persuasive evidence that the competitive market process is incapable of coordinating economic activity in agriculture. Indeed, with some 25 percent of U.S. agricultural production being exported, the paradox of protectionist domestic farm programs is increasingly apparent. Regardless of whether the

United States can muster the will to reduce trade barriers on the basis of enlightened self-interest, however, increases in agricultural productivity throughout the world and domestic budget pressures are likely to bring about significant changes in domestic farm policies.

How should the nation move to increase the role of market forces in agriculture? An abrupt dismantling would involve sharp declines in returns to farm resources for a year or two until sizable adjustments are made. Dealing with these transition problems, however, is not as difficult as achieving the political consensus that will be required to base agricultural production and marketing decisions on market signals. Luttrell's assessment of the failure to dismantle protectionist farm policies may well be correct: a continuation of farm programs "at ever-increasing costs to taxpayers and consumers, resulting in further regulation and more highly inefficient, centralized decision making."[21]

Finally, the notion of individual rights, including the rights of individuals to make voluntary economic transactions is central to questions concerning the appropriate role of government in agriculture and in other sectors. The objective of public policy affecting agriculture should be the development of an institutional framework that provides the maximum scope for individual choice. Only in this way can the nation's agricultural resources be used most effectively and the interests of farmers, consumers, and taxpayers best be served.

Notes

1. The classification of expenditures and method of analysis in the ensuing discussion was adapted from Clifton B. Luttrell, *Down on the Farm with Uncle Sam* (Los Angeles: International Institute for Economic Research, 1983), p. 17.

2. The effects of price supports and accompanying production controls may decrease prices paid by consumers while increasing prices received by farmers. Target prices on wheat, feed grains, cotton and rice, for example, increase prices to farmers. However, if production is increased under these programs the increased output will reduce prices to consumers since market prices are freely established, given the program constraints.

3. M. R. Benedict, *Farm Policies of the United States, 1790–1950* (New York: Twentieth Century Fund, 1953), p. 385.

4. Bruce L. Gardner, *The Governing of Agriculture* (Lawrence, Kan.: Regents Press of Kansas, 1981), p. 20.

5. B. Delworth Gardner, "Water Pricing and Rent Seeking in California Agriculture," in *Water Rights,* ed. Terry L. Anderson (San Francisco: Pacific Institute for Public Policy Research, 1983), p. 84.

6. Vincent Carroll, "How the West is Watered," *Reason* 18, no. 3 (July 1986): 38–40.

7. Alfred G. Cuzan, "Appropriators versus Expropriators: The Political Economy of Water in the West," in Anderson, *Water Rights,* p. 36.

8. David Seckler and Robert A. Young, "Economic and Policy Implications of

the 160-Acre Limitation in Federal Reclamation Law," *American Journal of Agricultural Economics* 60, no. 4 (November 1978): 575.

9. Gardner, "Water Pricing," p. 83.

10. D. Gale Johnson, "The Performance of Past Policies: A Critique," in *Alternative Agricultural and Food Policies and the 1985 Farm Bill*, ed. Gordon C. Rausser and K. R. Farrell (Berkeley, Calif.: Giannini Foundation, 1985), pp. 11–36.

11. Ibid., p. 28.

12. Ibid., p. 34.

13. Ibid., p. 32.

14. Paul Heyne, *The Economic Way of Thinking*, 4th ed. (Chicago: Science Research Associates, 1983), p. 448.

15. Much of this section is adapted from E. C. Pasour, Jr., *Price Support Programs for U.S. Farm Products: A Deregulation Opportunity*, Madison Paper Number 2 (Tallahassee, Fla.: The Madison Institute, 1988), pp. 27–31.

16. Clifton B. Luttrell, *The High Cost of Farm Welfare* (Washington, D.C.: The Cato Institute, 1989), p. 130.

17. David Osterfeld, "Social Utility and Government Transfers of Wealth: An Austrian Perspective," *The Review of Austrian Economics* (Lexington, Mass.: D.C. Heath and Co., 1988), p. 83.

18. David Blandford, Harry de Gorter, Bruce Gardner, and David Harvey, "There Is a Way To Support Farm Income with Minimal Trade Distortions," *Choices* 4 (1989/1):21.

19. Robert G. Chambers, *How To Wean the Family Farmer from Washington*, The Heritage Foundation, *Backgrounder*, no. 657 (June 1988), p. 6.

20. Thomas Gale Moore, "Farm Policy: Justifications, Failures and the Need for Reform," *Federal Reserve Bank of St. Louis Review* 69, no. 8 (October 1987): 7.

21. Luttrell, *The High Cost of Farm Welfare*, p. 128.

Index